"excellent"–*Parents* Magazine, October 1990

"perfect prelude to a telecommuting job search . . . [a] comprehensive classic"–*Home Office Computing*, Sept. 1990

"one of the best books on the market on this subject"–*Small Press Reviews*

"an excellent reference to getting a job that lets you work at home"–*The Secretary* Magazine

"eye-opening, I'd even say inspiring"–*Whole Earth Review*

"a wealth of information . . . very practical advice . . . Besides being a tremendous financial resource, this book is just plain fun to read"–*Welcome Home*

" a neat package" –*The Salt Lake Tribune*

"an invaluable source of information to anyone who wants to find a job working at home" –*Northwest Arkansas Times*

" I recommend it most enthusiastically; compliments to author Lynie Arden for a job well done" –R.H. Hoffman, WNWK TV

"Packed with solid information on how to make home-working work for you . . . " –*Looks at Books*

THE
WORK
-AT-
HOME
SOURCEBOOK

Fourth Edition

LIVE OAK

Lynie Arden

Live Oak Publications
Boulder, Colorado

Note: If you are in a position to hire home-based workers and you want your company to be listed in future editions, please send your name, address and phone number to Lynie Arden, c/o Live Oak Publications, at the address below:

Live Oak Publications
P.O. Box 2193
Boulder, CO 80306

© 1992, 1990, 1988, 1987 by Lynie Arden

Library of Congress Cataloging-in-Publication Data
Arden, Lynie, 1949-
    The work-at-home sourcebook/ Lynie Arden. --4th ed.
    p. cm.
    Includes indexes.
    ISBN 0-911781-09-9 : $14.95

    1. Home labor--United States--Directories. 2. Home-based businesses--United States--Directories. 3. Business enterprises--United States--Directories. I. Title.
HD2336.U5A73   1992
338.7'4'02573--dc20   91-30758
                                        CIP

Disclaimer

Every attempt has been made to make this book as accurate and complete as possible. There may be mistakes of content or typography, however, and the author and publisher make no guarantees, warranties, or representations of any kind. This book is designed as a general guide to the subject. The reader is urged to investigate and verify information and its applicability under any particular situation or circumstances.

The author and publisher shall have no liability or responsibility to anyone with respect to contacts, negotiations, or agreements that may result from information in this book, or for any loss or damage caused or alleged to have been caused directly or indirectly by such information. If legal advice or other expert assistance is required, the services of a competent professional person should be sought.

Table of Contents

WORKING AT HOME

How To Go To Work From Your Home

"This is our lifestyle; it's called freedom."
—Janice Katz, Sacramento Professional Typists Network

Personnel manager Pat Mahy wasn't looking for a job at home, but when Escrow Overload asked her to give it a try a couple of years ago, she said okay.

"Starting out I had my doubts. I couldn't imagine being without the stimulation of other people at work. It had some appeal, though. I figured my time might be better spent if I wasn't wasting it commuting. Well, I was thrilled within a week!

Pat is one of the 40 million Americans who currently work at home, a number that is currently growing at a rate of almost 20% a year. Some government studies have indicated that as much as 75% of the work done in this country could eventually be moved home.

Not everyone would be happy working at home, of course, and many people are simply not interested in moving their work home. Still, more and more people are having the same experience as Pat Mahy, who says "I'm still finding more hidden benefits to working at home the longer I do it."

Using This Book

If you want to give working at home at try, this book can be a good place to start. It won't teach you how to start a home business from scratch and it won't duplicate certain other work-at-home topics that are well covered in other books.* As far as we know, though, nowhere else can you find as many specific opportunities for working at home—involving so many diverse options—already assembled for you into one neat package.

For an unusually good selection of home-business books see the catalog available from The New Careers Center, listed in the Resource Guide at the back of this book.

A Wide Range of Possibilities

You'll quickly notice that there are a variety of work styles represented in this book. Once you leave the confines of the traditional nine-to-five centralized work mode, a colorful rainbow of employment options appear. There is freelancing, independent contracting, working on commission, salaried positions, co-oping, and various combinations of these and other ways of working. You can get paid by the hour, by the piece, by the sale, by the project, or by the year.

You'll want to consider your needs carefully. Do you need the security of a salary? If so, freelancing is not for you. Have you always wished you could get paid for what you produce because you do it faster and better than almost everybody else? Then you may be able to boost your income by opting for piece rates. Alternately, you might want to be able to depend on a set salary, yet have lots of opportunities for earning more than the base rate by earning commissions, bonuses or other incentives. Telemarketing and market research positions, for example, often offer this type of compensation package.

One other point needs to be made about salaries. In comparing the salaries (and other forms of compensation) offered for working at home to those of conventional employment, be sure to take into consideration the many savings you'll enjoy by working at home. The money you'll save on clothing, commuting, parking, lunches and other items may make it worthwhile for you to take a home-based job that, on the surface at least, offers less money than you would make going into an office every day.

Opportunities Everywhere

You'll find over 1,000 companies in this book which have work-at-home arrangements, but it's important to keep in mind that these listings represent only a small sample of the work-at-home opportunities actually available today. This book will be most valuable to you if you use it as an idea generator.

Suppose, for example, that in skimming through the company listings you notice there are a number of typesetting jobs at home. You had a job setting type for a publishing company for several years and feel confident you could do the work, but for one reason or another none of the specific jobs in the listings are exactly right for your situation.

By all means don't be discouraged. Study the job listings carefully, noting the names of the companies, their pay structure, how many home workers they employ and other pertinent information. Then go talk to each publishing company in your town. They may never have considered hiring home workers before but if you can explain how other publishing companies have organized their home work programs—and the benefits they are getting from their programs—you'll have a good chance at getting exactly the work you want.

Some of the benefits you'll want to mention are the following (and they're not limited to publishing companies):

Increased Productivity
A 20% increase in productivity is average, with some employers reporting substantially more than that. Some dedicated telecommuters have reported up to an 80% increase over their office-bound counterparts.

Lower Turnover
Once settled into a home-based job, would you give it up? Turnover among home-working employees is so low, some companies have waiting lists up to a year long for new applicants.

Near Zero Absenteeism
Flexiplace usually means flexitime, too. Work schedules can be manipulated to accomodate child-care needs, fevers and sniffles, and yes, an occasional case of playing hookey on a beautiful spring day. As long as the work gets done within the overall time limits of the job, everyone's happy.

Improved Recruiting
In areas with low unemployment, flexiplace is often used as an added inducement to potential employees. This is especially true for fields like computer programming where demand for highly qualified workers often exceeds supply. Several years ago, Continental Illinois Bank had a problem finding qualified secretaries in the Chicago area. They reasoned that many competent women were at home with children and were therefore unable to participate in the job market. The bank started Project HomeWork to solve the problem.

Lower Costs
Many companies start home work programs when they run out of room for expansion and don't want to tie up additional capital in office space. Insurance, utilities, training, maintenance and other costs often go down when workers go home.

The important thing to remember is that home work programs benefit businesses as well as employees. In asking for a job at home, you're not asking for any favors; you're asking for an arrangement that will be beneficial to all .

HOME WORK AND THE LAW

There are two areas of the law that directly affect home workers; labor laws and zoning ordinances.

Labor Laws

Only a handful of states have labor laws specifically regarding working at home. In each case, their purpose is to govern "industrial home work" (work which would normally be done in a factory such as product assembly). Industrial home work is usually low skilled, low pay work in which there has been a history of worker exploitation. The purpose of the state labor laws is to insure worker safety and insure that minimum wage requirements are met.

States without labor laws specifically relating to home work fall under the jurisdiction of the U.S. Dept. of Labor and its Fair Labor Standards Act of 1938 (FLSA).

The FLSA initially prohibited seven industries from using home workers. In 1938, this was a good idea since sweatshop conditions were the established norm. In December, 1984, after years of see-sawing through the courts, the ban on knitted outerwear was lifted. The remaining prohibited industries were: gloves and mittens, belts and buckles, jewelry, women's apparel, embroidery, and handkerchiefs.

Senator Orrin Hatch introduced the Freedom of the Workplace bill (S.665) soon after the ban on knitted outerwear was lifted. It calls for the complete reversal of the FLSA restrictions on home work. As written, workers' rights would be protected by the same certification process that is required for home knitters.

Congresswoman Olympia Snowe of Maine introduced a similar bill, the Home Employment Enterprise Act (HR2815) in the House of Representatives. It was virtually the House twin of Hatch's bill. Congresswoman Snowe told the House, "Cottage industries play a vital role in the economy of the state of Maine, large parts of New England, and other areas of the nation. The independent nature of home work and the unavailability of alternative employment opportunities make working at home ideal. It is time to safeguard the freedom to choose to work at home."

Before either bill came up for a vote, prohibitions on industrial home work in five of the six industries were lifted by the U.S. Dept. of Labor, effective January 9, 1989. New, tougher enforcement requirements went into effect at the same time.

Ann McLaughlin, Secretary of Labor, said "Workforce flexibility is a critical element of our effort to create jobs, enhance the quality of worklife for American workers and improve our competitive edge in world markets. The changing workforce demographics demand that we provide employment opportunities that allow workers the freedom to choose flexible alternatives including the ability to work in one's own home. Women, for example, have entered the workforce by the millions; home work adds a measure of worker flexibility and economic freedom.

"At a time when flexibility is an operatonal imperative to our competitive advantage, government should enhance, not impede, workers' choices," McLaughlin added.

There is only one industry the FLSA still prohibits from using home workers — women's apparel. This omission was apparently an attempt on behalf of the DOL to avoid direct confrontation with its most active opponent in this action, The International Ladies Garment Workers Union. Aside from the prohibition mentioned here, there are no other occupations covered by labor laws. Furthermore, these laws only pertain to employees, not independent contractors, independent business people, or otherwise self-employed workers.

Zoning

Before working at home in any capacity, you should find out what your local zoning ordinance has to say about it. If you live in a rural area, chances are good that you have nothing to worry about. In populated areas, however, there are often specific provisions in the zoning laws pertaining to home occupations.

Zoning laws tend to focus on the impact of a given activity. Sometimes called "nuisance laws," they are designed to protect neighborhoods from disruptive noise, traffic, odors, etc.

Chicago is an extreme example. Within the city limits, it is illegal to use electrical equipment in a home occupation. That means no calculators, no typewriters, no computers. The laws are outdated in Chicago and are too often outdated elsewhere around the country. The city council in Chicago is working on a new ordinance that will be more accomodating to home work, and it's possible for you to initiate zoning changes in your city, too.

Zoning boards are made up of your neighbors and local business people, and it is likely they are unaware of problems caused by outdated zoning ordinances. If you are frustrated by your city's zoning code, get to know these people, attend some meetings, and propose that the laws be changed.

Independent Contractor Status and Tax Savings

More often than not, home workers are paid as independent contractors. In essence, this means you are totally responsible for your own work. While different government agencies don't necessarily agree on the definition of independent contractor, generally speaking, there are two major factors affecting how home workers are classified. They are the "degree of control which the employer exercises over the manner in which the work is performed," and "opportunities for profit and loss."

It should be noted that no government agency will take you on your word that you are an independent contractor. Even if you have a written contract with a company declaring that you both agree to an employer/independent contractor relationship, the legitimacy of that relationship must be proven.

The issue here is not whether being an employee is better or worse than being an independent contractor. There are advantages and disadvantages in every situation. Rather, the issue is whether the term "independent contractor" is being applied consistantly and correctly. If you meet all I.R.S. criteria for independent contractor status, you'll be responsible for your own taxes, most notably Social Security tax, which is renamed "Self-Employment Tax" for this purpose.

The present rate of self-employment tax hovers close to 14% percent for any income over $600 or under $48,000 annually. To a new independent contractor, this may sound totally outrageous. After all, wasn't it bad enough when the boss deducted half of that? Acutally, the independent contractor is at a real advantage because the tax is based on net income—that is, your profit after all your business deductions have been taken.

Notice the word "profit." This may be new to you, but being an independent contractor means being self-employed—and that means being in business. If you're in business, that means you're making a profit (hopefully) after paying your business expenses.

Business expenses will help you at tax time, so you need to keep records right from the start of any and all expenditures. Business expenses generally fall into two categories: direct and indirect.

Direct expenses are those which occur in the day-to-day operation of your business. Costs for office supplies, phone service, advertising, bookkeeping, equipment, books, trade publications and seminars related to your work, and insurance are all examples of direct, fully deductible expenses.

You shouldn't forget the more subtle types of deductions, either. Entertainment in the course of your work, whether in your own home or not, is ordinarily deductible if you discuss or conduct business while you're entertaining and keep a record of what went on and with whom.

The same thing is true for vacations. You can generally write off a portion of your vacation expenses if you spend some time along the way looking for new business. Remember, the government expects you to try to expand your business.

Indirect expenses are those that are a part of your usual domestic bills—utilities, rent or mortgage payments, maintenance and housecleaning, property insurance, etc. Indirect expenses come under the heading of the Home Office Deduction.

The Home Office Deduction is the most common and significant way for home workers to reduce their federal tax. In order to claim the deduction, you must show that your home work space is used regularly and exclusively as your principal place of business and meeting place. (If you are a salaried employee, you may also be eligible if you can prove that your employer requires you to keep a home office as a condition of employment. In this case, you should consult an expert to determine if you meet the requirements.)

Home office expenses are deductible at the rate of whatever percentage of square footage your work space takes up. If your home is 1,000 square feet and you use 200 square feet exclusively for work space, you can normally deduct 20% of those receipts. A word of caution: if you use your work space for any other purpose than work, you can not deduct any of these expenses. Therefore, working on the kitchen table is a bad idea unless you really don't have any choice.

At last count, there were some 23 possible deductions for a home office. To make sure you don't miss any, get a copy of I.R.S. Publication 587, "Business Use of the Home." It is available free from any I.R.S. office and is updated annually.

Making the Most of Working at Home

If you perservere in your efforts to land a home job, in time you're likely to succeed. Your home work space is where you will be spending a large portion of your life—in fact, you will most likely spend more time there than any other place. The consideration you give to its design could have a tremendous impact on the success of your home work experience.

Wouldn't it be wonderful to have a work place all your own, some private space free from distractions? A beautiful office maybe, with a separate entrance, big windows facing out onto a garden, with elegant furniture and the latest equipment modern technology has to offer. Fortunately, dreaming is free.

You may have to start out on the kitchen table or in a corner of the living room. Millions have started the same way and that's okay—for a while. To make the most out of working at home, though, you'll need to begin planning ways to make your working space more comfortable, efficient and permanent.

Five elements directly affect mental attitude and productivity in every work space: light, sound, furniture, air quality, and color.

Proper lighting is essential to the good health of any worker. It has been conclusively demonstrated that improper or inadequate light has varying degrees of negative effects on people. At the very least, it can cause significant decreases in productivity. Some people have more serious reactions, including long term bouts with depression.

Adequate overall lighting is not necessarily optimal lighting. Care should be taken to reduce glare from both direct and indirect sources. Whether light is reflected from a bright window or from a video display terminal (VDT), glare can cause eyestrain and headaches. You can usually solve glare problems by moving your furniture around, changing the type and strength of your lightbulbs, or installing screens over windows and VDTs.

Sound doesn't usually have the same impact on the work place as light, but it is an important factor to consider. Noise can come from traffic, children and lawnmowers outside and appliances, children, pets and your own work equipment inside, causing distraction and lower productivity. You can install sound absorbing material to reduce noise or you can attempt to mask the noise with neutral sounds (white noise) or with music. Most electronics stores sell white noise generators.

The right furniture can also make a difference in your work performance and satisfaction. The type of work surface you need depends on the type of work you're doing, but in any case it doesn't have to be fancy or expensive. What is important is that the surface be large enough to suit the task, that the height is right for you, and that it is sturdy enough to hold your equipment without wobbling.

A good chair is definitely worth the investment. It should provide ample back support, thereby reducing fatigue and backaches. Features such as adjustable back tension, an easily-adjusted height mechanism and rollers will make your life easier, too. If you work with a keyboard, even for short periods of time, don't get a chair with armrests. Armrests can prevent you from getting close enough to the edge, with resulting aches and pains in your back, neck and shoulders.

Air quality and temperature can also have a major impact on your physical comfort. Ideally, you want fresh, clean air no warmer than 75 degrees or cooler than 68 degrees. Indoor pollution can be caused by lack of ventilation, especially with highly weatherized homes. Pollution sources include carpets, upholstery, stoves, aerosols and cleaning fluids, to name only a few. In addition, there are few jobs that don't involve their own polluting substances. Correction fluid, hobby and craft supplies, paint, glue and lint are examples.

The best way to clean up your indoor air is with ventilation. Plants help, too. Certain common houseplants, such as Spider Plants, gobble up indoor toxins. Electric air filters can help, too. They cost more than plants, but require less care. Negative ion generators are especially helpful in the presence of electronic equipment such as computers.

Color is the final factor which you should consider. It can set the overall tone of your work space and make it a place you want to be—or a place you'd rather avoid.

White and very light colors aren't stimulating, but do reflect the most light, making a space appear larger than it is. Blacks, browns, and greys make a space appear smaller than it is, absorbing light and creating feelings of fatigue. Blues and greens are relaxing, feel cool, and reduce blood pressure. Reds, oranges, and yellows are bright, stimulating, cheerful and warm. In too strong a contrast, however, they can cause irritability and increased blood pressure.

Carefully choosing the color scheme and other aspects of your work space can make a big difference in your productivity as well as how you feel about your work. It's usually not necessary to spend a lot of money to make your work place pleasant; just use some imagination and take the time to think through how you can make the most of the space that's available to you.

IN ANSWER TO YOUR QUESTIONS....

1. How are the listings in the book obtained?

Compiling a list of opportunities as diverse as those in this book requires constant searching. The listings actually come from many different sources including government agencies, industry associations, trade directories, advertisements, and telephone surveys of certain types of businesses. Of course, some companies write in asking to be listed, but most of the time it's not that easy.

2. How do I know these listings are legitimate opportunities?

This question stems from the frustration many of you have experienced over being ripped off by so-called home employment directories that turned out to be worthless. There are thousands more real work-at-home opportunities than are listed in this book, and yet, *The Work-at-Home Sourcebook* is still the only guide to real work-at-home jobs and business opportunities. After five years in publication, there have been no reports of any deceptive practices among the employers listed. Each listing has been verified—and those firms which write in asking to be listed are screened with special care. If there is any question as to the legitimacy of the offer, an interview with at least one worker is required.

3. What if I don't find what I'm looking for in my area?

There are over 350 listings in the job bank that can be done either in a large region or anywhere in the country. And, most of the business opportunities can likewise be operated from where ever you are. But if you still want to pursue a particular job type in a town where there is none listed in this book, you need only follow the instructions found at the beginning of The Work-at-Home Job Bank. Do not contact an employer that can only hire local residents if you don't live in the same area. You will only be wasting your time and theirs.

4. Is it okay to call a prospective employer?

Unless there is a telephone number published with the listing, the answer is definitely no. Most employers simply don't have the manpower available to talk to anyone who might have questions or be somewhat interested in their company. If you call before you are invited to, you will only alienate a potential employer.

5. Is it better to send a letter of interest or a resume?

That depends. If an employer has a preference, it will be stated in the listing. Most of the time, a letter of interest is more welcome. A resume is best in the case of professions requiring a high level of education and experience.

6. What should I do when I don't get a reply to my letter of interest or resume?

If you don't get a response within a few weeks, you have to assume that there is no interest or no openings. In either case, you shouldn't sit around waiting for that to change. Look for opportunities elsewhere. Finding the work-at-home job you want takes time and diligence.

7. Will I have to pay money to work for any of these companies?

Just as a general rule, you should always be wary of any employer that requires money to work for them. (This does not pertain to business opportunities, which almost always involve an investment.) There are exceptions, however. Positions in sales often require a deposit for a sales kit to get started. And there are a handful of crafts and assembly jobs listed in this book that likewise require a fee for a start-up kit. All of the listings in this book that require money upfront will refund your money if you change your mind and return the kit in reusable condition. Never pay money to a company if you don't know exactly what the job is and what you are getting for your money.

8. How do you handle complaints about listings?

Fortunately, this is a rare problem. Readers' complaints are usually about a company that has moved, changed its policy towards working-at-home, or simply hasn't responded. Sometimes, an employer will become swamped with applications and ask to be removed from the listings. These requests are always complied with at the first available opportunity.

9. Can I work for more than one company?

Since most work-at-home job opportunities are for independent contractors, it is your right (and obligation according to the I.R.S.) to seek out multiple sources of income. Most employers know that you will need to do this and understand if there is an occasional conflict. If the position or business will require full time participation, the company will tell you before you begin.

10. Are there any shortcuts to find the listings I want in the book?

Much thought has gone into the organization of this book. It is not always easy to categorize an opportunity. The lines between job opportunities and business opportunities, for instance, are not always clear. Likewise, it is not always easy to decide in what grouping a particular type of opportunity should be placed. For these reasons, and so that you will not miss out on anything, you should take the time to browse through the entire book. You would do yourself a disservice to go to the location index and, seeing that there are not many listings in your particular area, give up before you even get started. If you know exactly what you're looking for, though, you can save a lot of time by looking first at the Table of Contents. There you will see the layout of the book and find the general categories broken down into major sections. There are also several indexes in the back of the book to help you zero in on specific companies and their locations.

THE WORK-AT-HOME JOB BANK

Getting a Home-Based Job, Step-by-Step

The first step in getting the home-based job of your choice is to define exactly what it is you want. You should ask yourself what kind of a commitment you are willing to make. Are you looking for a long-term career or just a short-term job? Do you need to support yourself or do you just need some extra income? Do you want to work in the same industry where you've always worked or try something new?

A wide range of occupations are covered in this book. Do you see something you like? If not, back up and give some thought to the type of jobs that can be done at home. While opportunities for home work span a wide spectrum of employment possibilities, not all work can effectively be moved home.

First of all, home work is work which can be easily measured. Why? Because you and your employer need to know what to expect, such as when the work will begin and when it will be completed. If you are paid a piece rate, which is very common, this factor is crucial. Besides that, your employer wants to know that he's getting his money's worth. Along these same lines, the work should require minimal supervision after initial training.

It is also important to know whether there are physical barriers to doing a particular type of work at home. Work which requires minimal space and no large and/or expensive equipment is ideal. In some cases, the type of equipment and the amount of space used for home work is restricted by local zoning ordinances.

Where The Work Is

In general, home work tends to be available at very large corporations and at very small companies. Mid-sized firms often lack the management expertise available at large companies and may be less willing to take risks than small companies. There are many exceptions to this, however, especially among companies originally started using home workers.

Information-intensive industries such as the banking industry, the insurance industry and the computer software industry are prime candidates for home work because so much of their work is done via computer and telephone.

All types of sales organizations have traditionally been open to working at home. Real estate, publishing, insurance, pharmaceuticals, apparel, cosmetics, and printing are just a few of the businesses that typically use home-based representatives.

Home businesses are often forced by zoning ordinances to use home workers or else move out of their original home base. Such businesses may need secretaries, sales reps, bookkeepers, assemblers, shipping clerks, artists, copy writers, public relations consultants, programmers, lawyers, and accountants.

Any rapidly growing company may also be a good bet. Whenever a company suddenly outgrows its available space, the option of having additional workers provide their own space can be very appealing. Besides, if the growth is temporary, the money spent on additional facilities would be wasted. It is normally far cheaper for a company to pay for extra phone lines, computer terminals, or other equipment for employee's homes than to build new office space.

Starting From Scratch

If you're presently not working and need to find a job you can do at home right from the start, there is a good chance the type of work you're looking for is secondary to your need to be at home. (This has proven to be true about 75% of the time.)

The first thing you should do is examine your skills and match them up with possible job types. If you don't see anything here that you're already trained in, consider what you would like to learn. Many jobs offer training at a central location or right in your home.

Preparing a Resume

It's time to prepare a resume that stresses skills needed to work at home. In other words, you should emphasize anything that demonstrates your ability to work well without supervision. Because your employer won't see you very often (or ever, in some cases), your reliability is extremely important. For every job you apply for, you should write a cover letter openly stressing your desire and ability to work efficiently and effectively at home.

There are basically two kinds of resumes—chronological and functional. Both include identifying information, work history, and educational background. Neither is necessarily better than the other, but generally speaking, employers prefer the chronological style because its format is quick and easy to read.

The chronological resume simply lists your work history according to datges, starting with the most recent and working backwards. Educational background is handled in the same way.

The functional resume presents essentially the same information, but in a different order. The purpose of this type of resume is to emphasize your skills. Instead of starting with dates, you head each descriptive paragraph with a job title.

Regardless of the style of resume you choose, the following rules apply:
• Include only information that is directly relevant to the job for which you are applying. While it is great to have many skills and accomplishments, employers are only interested in what you can offer them in particular.

• Limit your resume to two pages. A ten page resume may look impressive, but what employer has time to read it? It will be easier to keep your resume brief if you carefully follow the rule above.

• Present a professional image. Your resume should be typed or typeset in a neat and orderly fashion. Leave sufficient margins and double space between paragraphs. Proofread carefully. Grammatical errors and typos could cost you a highly desirable job.

The Cover Letter

A cover letter is a personalized letter stating your interest in a job in clear, concise terms. You should indicate which job you are applying for and point out a few good reasons why you should be considered. There is no need to repeat any of the information included in the resume.

Letter of Interest

In some cases an employer is more interested in your aptitude and enthusiasm than in your background. This is often the situation when a training course will be provided, or for "people jobs" such as sales, customer service, and market research positions. The basic requirement here is an ability to relate to people and communicate effectively. How do you prove that ability with a resume? You can't, really, so you use a letter of interest.

A letter of interest is similar to a cover letter except that you (briefly) describe any background or personality traits that are applicable to the position and then request an application or an interview, or both.

Phone Interviews

Prospective home workers are often interviewed over the phone; many are hired without ever meeting their new employers.

After sending in an application, you can normally expect to be called within a week or two if you are going to be considered for an opening in the near future. Of course, you won't know exactly when to expect the call, but you should be prepared right from the start.

• Find out as much as you can about the company ahead of time. Then, make a list of questions you want to ask about the job. Keep the list and a copy of your application near the phone. Don't forget to keep a pen or pencil and paper handy, too.

• Try to use a phone in a quiet part of the house where you will not be interrupted.

• Listen carefully, take your time and answer all questions in a clear, steady voice. Don't mumble. Speak with confidence and honesty.

• Be polite and friendly, but not "chummy."

• Be enthusiastic even if you're not sure you want the job. You can always change your mind later.

• Be prepared to give references if asked.

Most important, you want to present yourself as the right candidate for the job. Ask yourself one question: "Why should this company hire me?" This is, after all, what they are calling to find out.

Don't Expect Too Much

Looking for a job that you can do from home is essentially no different, and definitely no easier, than looking for a job in a "traditional" work place. You cannot assume that because an employer uses home workers, that somehow means the employer is desperate for help and getting the job is going to be easy. On the contrary, employers often offer the work-at-home option as an incentive in order to have a larger pool of applicants to choose from. A single small ad in a local newspaper mentioning a job that can be done at home typically elicits hundreds of responses. That means competition, and lots of it, for you. It's up to you, and you alone, to convince any prospective employer that you're a cut above the rest and that you will handle the job professionally with a minimal amount of supervision.

Most home worker employers never advertise at all (like most of the ones in this book). They don't need to because the jobs are so sought after, word-of-mouth alone often creates a waiting list of eager applicants. If you should apply to any of these firms and don't receive a reply, understand that they don't have the manpower or the time to do so and your name has been placed on file for possible future openings. Rather than sit around waiting for a response that may not come for quite a while, your time would be better spent seeking out new opportunities in your field that nobody else knows about yet.

Opportunities in Arts

Artists of all kinds have been working at home since the beginning. An artist is a special breed of worker, with a need for freedom that may be stronger than the need for security. To be able to work when the flash of inspiration strikes is important to the artist; not being forced to work when there is no inspiration is equally important.

Included in the following pages are freelance opportunities for graphic artists, illustrators, designers, calligraphers, photographers, writers, and editors. To get work in any artistic field, the primary requirement is proof of talent, skill, and dependability. Some prospective employers may require evidence of previous publication; others are on the lookout for new talent and will take a look at samples.

Graphic art is a growing field that has traditionally accepted the work-at-home option. Currently, about 75% of all graphic artists work in their own studios as independent contractors. They design, by hand or computer, the visuals for commercials, brochures, corporate reports, books, record covers, posters, logos, packaging, and more. Their major clients are ad agencies, publishers, broadcast companies, textile manufacturers, and printers.

Illustrators and calligraphers may find that work is more sporadic. Illustrators often work for publishers, but both illustrators and calligraphers will find the most opportunities among ad agencies and greeting card publishers. Both of these are huge industries. The greeting card industry has grown rapidly over the past five years, and it is now worth $3.8 billion a year. Photographers, writers, and poets will also find this to be fertile ground for home work.

The biggest field for photographers is still advertising. Agencies large and small are in constant need of professional photographers who can deliver high quality work according to the concept developed by the agency. Rarely will an agency use an inexperienced photographer; the business is too fast-paced to risk losing time on a photographer who may not work out. A freelance photographer looking for any kind of work should be prepared with a professional portfolio of his/her best work, tearsheets of previously published photos if possible, a resume, business cards, and samples that can be left on file.

AARDVARK PRESS, 562 Boston Ave., Bridgeport, CT 06610.
Positions: Aardvark Press is very unusual in that it hires full-time novelists to write multi-generational sagas according to company-provided outlines.
Requirements: Writers need personal computers with modems. Must be previously published. Inquiries are welcome, but local people are preferred.

LESLIE AARON ASSOCIATES, 520 Westfield Ave., Elizabeth, NJ 07208.
Positions: Freelance photographers work on assignment basis only for this advertising agency. Agency's clients are in heavy industry.
Requirements: Must be local and experienced in the advertising business.
Submit resume, samples, and business card.
Provisions: Pay methods vary.

ABBEY PRESS, Hill Dr., St. Meinrad, IN 47577.
Positions: Freelance artists, poets, and photographers. Abbey Press produces greeting cards, gift wrap, and stationery. Greeting cards are all occasions; gift wrap is for Christmas only.
Requirements: Prefers long poetic verses; poets send samples. Artists should submit several sketches. Photographers submit tear sheets.

ADELE'S II, INC., 2832 Angelo Dr., Los Angeles, CA 90077.
Positions: This producer of high quality personalized giftware uses freelance artists for product design.
Requirements: Submit resume along with photographs of work samples.

ALBION CARDS, Box 102, Albion, MI 49224.
Positions: Artists are used in the production of greeting cards and related products. Albion uses a very special style of high contrast line art accented with calligraphy. Interested artists should send for guidelines first; include SASE with request. If you send no SASE, your request will be ignored.
Requirements: Only serious artists that can produce very high quality work should inquire. After studying the guidelines, send a letter of interest with samples.
Provisions: Pays a royalty.

ALLIED ADVERTISING AGENCY, INC., 800 Statler Building, Boston, MA 02116.
Positions: Photographers are assigned to all sorts of work connected with advertising: direct mail, magazines, packaging, etc. All subject matter is covered.
Requirements: Works only with experienced local photographers. Submit several sample transparancies that represent your best work. Include resume and request interview.

AMBERLY GREETING CARD COMPANY, 11510 Goldcoast Dr., Cincinnati, OH 45249.
Positions: Freelance writers and illustrators for studio style cards.
Requirements: Writers can live anywhere, but artists work on assignment and must be local. Both writers and artists can send for market guidelines before submitting work samples.

AMERICAN CRAFTS, 13010 Woodland, Cleveland, OH 44120.
Positions: Contemporary fiber arts are accepted on consignment.

Requirements: Submit slides (only) and prices you want. Include SASE.
Provisions: Pays 50/50 split.

AMERICAN GREETING CORPORATION, 10500 American Rd., Cleveland, OH 44102.
Positions: Artists, writers, and photographers. Company makes cards, wrapping paper, posters, calendars, stationary, and post cards. Work is on a freelance basis; some is assigned, some is bought.
Requirements: Must send for submission forms first, then send samples of work with letter of interest. If appropriate, ask to arranged for a personal interview to show portfolio.

ARDREY INC., Suite 314, 100 Menlo Pk., Edison, NJ 08837.
Positions: Photographers on assignment basis only. This is a public relations firm that works exclusively with industrial clients.
Requirements: Submit resume, business card, and tear sheets to be kept on file. Work will be conducted on industrial locations so be sure to indicate how far you can travel.
Provisions: Pays day rates.

ARGONAUT PRESS, 1706 Vilas Ave., Madison, WI 53711.
Positions: Photographers. Company produces postcards with contemporary themes.
Requirements: Submit transparencies along with resume. A guideline sheet is available upon request.
Provisions: Pays for photos outright or in royalties.

ARGUS COMMUNICATIONS, One DLM Park, Allen, TX 75002.
Positions: Argus publishes humorous, quality greeting cards. Freelance assignments are available for artists, photographers, and writers.
Requirements: To be considered, send six samples of your work in any form (originals, copies, slides, etc.) along with SASE for their safe return. Resume is also required; include a list of credits and a business card to be kept on file.

ARTFORMS CARD CORPORATION, 725 County Line Rd., Dearfield, IL 60015.
Positions: Artists and writers.
Requirements: Artists, send sketches only for consideration. Writers, send batches of 10 samples. All work must have a Jewish theme suitable for the greeting card market. Send for market list and include SASE.
Provisions: Artists' rates vary according to assignment. Writers are paid per verse. 50% of work is freelance.

CAROLYN BEAN PUBLISHING, 2230 W. Winton Ave., Hayward, CA 94545.
Positions: Writers, artists, and photographers for contemporary greeting card company.
Requirements: To be considered, writers should send SASE with 25c postage for guidelines. Artists send samples of work (any medium okay) along with SASE. Do not send originals. Photographers shold arrange personal interview to show portfolio. Bring slides only, tear sheets and business card; the two latter items will be kept on file. "About 90% of our work is done by freelancers."

BEAUTYWAY, Box 340, Flagstaff, AZ 86002.
Positions: Photographers. Company produces postcards, calendars, and posters.

Interested mostly in scenics and animals.

Requirements: Submit any size transparencies. Guidelines are available; include SASE with request. Prefers to work with previously published photographers.

Provisions: Pays one-time fee for each photo used.

BENTLEY HOUSE, P.O. Box 5551, Art Sources Department, Walnut Creek, CA 94596.

Positions: Bentley House has been a major national publisher of art for over eight years. They sell to major accounts, print shops, and distributors at the rate of 100,000 per month. For the first time, new artists are being sought. Preferred subject matter includes anything of interest to "Middle America"; nostalgia, country, scapes, local folk arts, people, animals, etc. Can be any medium; oils, water color, acrylics... Original art will be reproduced for mass sale.

Requirements: No prior publishing is required. Bentley House is most interested in long term working relationships. To be considered, send slides (only) of your work plus a cover letter to introduce yourself. Be sure to number your slides and keep a file of them at home for later reference. Bentley House requires no investment of any kind and suggests strongly that any artist who is approached by a buyer of any kind asking for money up front <u>Beware.</u>

Provisions: Reproduced prints sell in the $15 to $60 range. Different arrangements are worked out with different artists; buys outright, on commission, and other. A new line is introduced every four to five months.

B.M. ENTERPRISES, Box 421, Farrell, PA 16121.

Positions: Freelance artists. Company is a clip art service bureau. Assigns line drawings and cartoons to previously published artists only.

Requirements: Write first for market guide. Then submit letter of interest with tear sheets.

Provisions: Payment is a 50/50 split.

BRADFORD EXCHANGE, 9333 Milwaukee, Chicago, IL 60648.

Positions: Bradford is a manufacturer of collectible plates. Freelance professional artists are used to design landscapes and portraits that will be reproduced on the plates.

Requirements: Submit resume, samples that can be kept on file, and references or tear sheets.

BRETT-FORER GREETINGS, INC., 790 Madison Ave., Suite 201, New York, NY 10021.

Positions: Freelance artists and writers. Brett-Forer cards are whimsical; mostly Christmas and everyday with a few other occasions. Writers can submit verse for consideration. Artists are usually assigned.

Requirements: Writers should send batches of 10 verses. Artists submit samples and business card.

Provisions: Pays flat fee.

BUCKBOARD ANTIQUES, 1411 N. May, Oklahoma City, OK 73107.

Positions: Folk art and other traditional country crafts like rag dolls and quilted items will be considered.

Requirements: Send photos and prices you want along with an SASE.

BURGOYNE, INC., 2030 E. Byberry Rd., Philadelphia, PA 19116.
Positions: Company produces greeting cards and calendars with Christmas theme only. Uses freelance artists for design, illustration, and calligraphy.
Requirements: Experienced artists only. Submit letter of interest with work samples and business card.

"We're always looking for responsible people,
especially full-timers."

--Gallup Poll

CALIFORNIA DREAMERS, 445 W. Erie, Chicago, IL 60610.
Positions: Photographers and writers. California Dreamers is a greeting card company with a very unique style. They have replaced illustrative cartoons with photo "cartoons". **Requirements:** Study the company's line very carefully first; then send for guidelines. All ideas must be innovative, contemporary, and above all, have a sense of humor about what's happening socially. "You should be on the mark for today; if it hits home or makes you laugh, let us see it. We're looking for what people are really talking about today. The number one rule is clarity of concept." This advice is mostly for writers who should send sample copy and concepts with SASE. Photographers are also encouraged to send transparencies as samples of style and skill.
Provisions: All work is done on a freelance basis. Photographers are paid $400 and up per assignment. Writers are paid $100 to $150 per line. If a writer is "hot," company will offer a royalty deal tied to sales goals.

CANTERBURY DESIGNS, INC., Box 4060, Martinez, GA 30907.
Positions: Freelance artists are used to produce new designs for needlework design books.
Requirements: Send photographs of your work samples. Include letters of interest that indicates professional background.
Provisions: Pay methods vary.

CAPE SHORE PAPER PRODUCTS, INC., 42A N. Elm Street, Box 537, Yarmouth, ME 04096.
Positions: Freelance artists for design and illustrations of giftwrap and stationery products. Company uses primarily nautical theme with some Americana, Christmas, and other traditional themes such as floral, birds, and animals.
Requirements: Send for guidelines first. Then submit letter of interest with samples.
Provisions: Pays flat fee.

CARLTON CARDS, 10500 American Rd., Cleveland, OH 44144.
Positions: Artists, writers, and photographers design cards and calendars.
Requirements: Artists should submit sketches; photographers submit color transparencies. Send sample portfolio with return postage included. Writers should submit ideas on 3x5 index cards. Be sure name and address is on the back of each card submitted.
Provisions: Payment depends on individual situation. Sometimes ideas are purchased

outright, sometimes work is assigned and paid for by the project. New talent is actively solicited.

CHESAPEAKE BAY MAGAZINE, 1819 Bay Ridge Ave., Suite 200, Annapolis, MD 21403.
Positions: Freelance writers and photographers.
Requirements: Any material about the Chesapeake region will be considered. Photographers submit color photos only. Writers can submit either proposal or complete manuscript.
Provisions: Pays on acceptance.

CMP PUBLICATIONS, 600 Community Dr., Manhasset, NY 11030.
Positions: Editors, associate editors, reporters, and writers are all outfitted with computers and modems in order to transmit material from the field. Freelance stringers are hired to cover business news from all over the country.
Requirements: Hard news reporting experience a must. Must feel comfortable going to top industrial companies looking for stories and information. Apply with resume and previously published clips.
Provisions: Payment varies. Some reporters are salaried, some are paid by individual contract. Phone charges are reimbursed.

COMMUNICATIONS DYNAMICS CORPORATION, Box 3060, Glen Ellyn, IL 60137.
Positions: Freelance copy writers and technical writers.
Requirements: Must be reliable and experienced. Send resume and work sample. Must be local resident.
Provisions: Pays by the job.

COMMUNICATIONS ELECTRONICS, Box 1045, Ann Arbor, MI 48106.
Positions: Freelance artists for advertising work.
Requirements: Send resume and samples or tear sheets to be kept on file.
Request an appointment to show portfolio. Only local artists will be considered.
Provisions: Pays by the project.

CRYSTAL GREETINGS INC., 53 Noll St., Waukegan, IL 60085.
Positions: Writers and artists. Company produces humorous everyday cards as well as Christmas cards and gift wrap.
Requirements: Send work samples with letter of interest.

CUSTOM STUDIOS, 1337 W. Devon Ave., Chicago, IL 60660.
Positions: Freelance photographers on assignment basis only for Christmas card department. Offer over 100 assignments annually.
Requirements: To be considered, send letter of interest with SASE requesting "Photo Guideines". Include business card.
Provisions: Pays by the job, $50 minimum.

DEADY ADVERTISING, 17 E. Cary St., Richmond, VA 23236.
Positions: Freelance illustrators.
Requirements: Must be very experienced in the advertising field. Local artists only. Submit resume and work samples.
Provisions: Pay methods vary from project to project.

Jim Lienhart, Tom White and Herb Murrie (from left to right), founders of California Dreamers

It was only five years ago that California Dreamers started by offering 81 card designs at the West Coast Gift and Stationery Show. Only 16 of the cards drew any interest at the time, but that was enough to grow on. Today, they have over 1,200 items in their line and *Forbes Magazine* called them the number one company in the alternative card market. Founders Jim Lienhart, Tom White, and Herb Murrie will introduce gift wrap, calendars, new greeting card lines, post cards, and invitations this year. The Chicago-based company is recognized for its attention grabbing non-occasion photographs and illustrative cards.

"We replaced illustrative cartoons with photo cartoons," says president Herb Murrie. "They stuck out like a sore thumb. What we've got going for us is creativity."

If you're a copy writer or photographer with a contemporary vision, you might want to send some samples of your work to California Dreamers. "We only want to see work that is on the mark for today. You've got to be up-to-date and professional. It's a war out there!"

DIGITAL NEWS, 33 West Street, Boston, MA 02111
Positions: This is an in-house publication that covers equipment made by Digital. Writers and reporters routinely work at home.
Requirements: Resumes are accepted from experienced computer industry writers.
Provisions: Some home workers receive benefits; others do not.

DISPLAYCO, 2055 McCarter Highway, Newark, NJ 07104.
Positions: Freelance artists. Company manufacturers advertising display fixtures.
Requirements: Must have experience working in the advertising field and, in particular, with display fixtures. Submit work samples or photos of work and resumes. Prefers local artists.
Provisions: Pays by the project.

EMBOSOGRAPH DISPLAY MANUFACTURING COMPANY, 1430 W. Wrightwood, Chicago, IL 60614.
Positions: Freelance artists design and illustrate custom advertising display fixtures.
Requirements: Local artists preferred. Must be previously published in this field. Submit resume with samples of published work only.
Provisions: Pays by the hour.

ENESCO IMPORTS CORPORATION, 1 Enesco Plaza, Elk Grove Village, IL 60007.
Positions: Artists, designers, and sample makers for giftware line.
Requirements: Artists and designers must have exceptional creativity and the work samples to prove it. Sample makers must have all necessary tools to produce samples from artists' renderings. Must be local resident.
Provisions: Artwork is often bought outright. Others are paid by the project or by the hour.

THE EVERGREEN PRESS, INC., 3380 Vincent Rd., Pleasant Hill, CA 94523.
Positions: Artists for design and illustrations of cards, gift wrap, children's picture books, and bookmarks. Cards are generally produced in a series with a common theme. Especially in need of Christmas card designs. Gift wrap is also for Christmas; prefers country or folk art theme.
Requirements: Send for guidelines first. To be considered for assignment, send a group of samples and resume.
Provisions: Generally pays royalty.

FELLERS LACY GADDIS, 5th Floor, 5918 W. Courtyard Dr., Austin, TX 78730.
Positions: Freelance photographers are used by this advertising agency. Photos are used in consumer publications.
Requirements: Prefers to work only with local photographers. Must be experienced and have professional portfolio. Write letter of interest requesting appointment to show portfolio.
Provisions: Pays photographers regular rates.

FILLMAN ADVERTISING, INC., 304 W. Hill St., Champaign, IL 61820.
Positions: Freelance illustrators for the production of direct mail packages and brochures.
Requirements: Must be local and experienced. Send resume and sample line drawings.

Include business card to be kept on file.
Provisions: Pay methods vary with different projects.

FREEDOM GREETING CARD COMPANY, P.O. Box 715, Bristol, PA 19007.
Positions: Writers and artists. Writers sell verses outright. Artists work on assignment only.
Requirements: Samples of work, letter of interest, and SASE required for either type of work.

G.A.I., INC., Box 30309, Indianapolis, IN 46203.
Positions: G.A.I. is a licensing agent in the collectibles industry. Freelance artists that seek representation are encouraged to submit samples of people-type art in any medium. There is no fee; G.A.I. takes a commission for successfully completed projects.
Requirements: Send resume and color photographs of work samples. Include SASE for reply.
Provisions: Artists are generally paid a royalty.

GERBIG, SNELL, WEISHEIMER & ASSOCIATES, Suite 600, 425 Metro Pl. North, Dublin, OH 43017
Positions: Freelance illustrators and photographers used for the production of advertising materials.
Requirements: Works only with local experienced people. Submit resume, tear sheets, and business card.

C.R. GIBSON, COMPANY, 32 Knight Street, Norwalk, CT 06856.
Positions: Freelance artists. Company produces stationery products and buys new designs.
Requirements: Only previously established artists are considered. Submit samples and resume.
Provisions: Pays flat rate for each design accepted.

GLENCOE PUBLISHING COMPANY, 15319 Chatsworth St., Mission Hills, CA 91345.
Positions: Freelance artists illustrate textbooks.
Requirements: Work must be top notch. Submit resume and tear sheets. Will consider only previously published illustrators.
Provisions: Pays by the project.

GREETING CARD MASTERS, INC., 2990 Griffin Road, Ft. Lauderdale, FL 33312.
Positions: Freelance artists and photographers for the design of seasonal and everyday greeting cards.
Requirements: Artists send actual samples with letter of interest. Photographers send transparencies and business card.

HALLMARK GREETING CARDS, P.O. Box 419580, Kansas City, MO 64108.
Positions: Hallmark, the largest greeting card company in the country, is also the biggest employer of artists. Writers and artists of all kinds design greeting cards, other paper products, and gift items, and do public relations and advertising work. Currently has hundreds in home work pool.
"We have so many, the total number is uncertain at any given moment."

Requirements: Start by sending for guidelines. Follow up with samples of work and letter of interest. Although Hallmark is constantly on the lookout for new talent, only the most outstanding creative people can expect to get in.
Provisions: Positions include all types of situations from freelance to full-time, regular employees (at home). Workers are found through submissions, word-of-mouth, referrals, and in-house employees.

HARCOURT BRACE JOVANOVICH PUBLICATIONS, 1250 6th Ave., San Diego, CA 92101.
Positions: Freelance writing assignments are available from this major business publisher. Artists also work on assignment.
Requirements: Only very experienced writers will be considered. Apply with resume and writing samples along with letter of interest. Artists should send samples of work along with letter of interest and bio describing in detail background experience.

HERFF JONES, Box 6500, Providence RI, 02940.
Positions: Freelance illustrators and designers. Company makes medals, trophies, and class rings.
Requirements: Several years of experience is required. Submit resume and samples.
Provisions: Pays by the project.

HIAWATHA, INC., 6100 N Keystone Ave., Suite 627, Indianapolis, IN 46220.
Positions: Lyrical style poetry is used by this greeting card company.
Requirements: Submit ideas and/or samples of your work on 3x5 cards; include SASE.
Provisions: Pays on acceptance.

IN TOUCH, The International Tours Travel Magazine, 192 Newbury St., Boston, MA 02116.
Positions: Freelance writers and photographers. All material is travel related.
Requirements: Both writers and photographers should send for guidelines first; include SASE.

THE INQUISITIVE TRAVELER, Travel Quest, 20103 La Roda Ct., Cupertino, CA 95014.
Positions: Freelance writers and photographers for quarterly travel magazine.
Requirements: Writers should send for guidelines first; include SASE with request. Photographers send samples of travel photos.

INTERCONTINENTAL GREETINGS, LTD., 176 Madison Ave., New York, NY 10016.
Positions: Freelance artists for greeting cards, gift wrap, calendars, posters, and stationery. Prefers very graphic designs with some cartoon style illustrations.
Requirements: Works only with professionals. Send resume, work samples, and include SASE.
Provisions: Generally pays royalties.

KERSTEN BROTHERS, P.O. Box 1765, Scottsdale, AZ 85252.
Positions: Writers and artists for greeting cards. All cards are humorous and seasonal; Christmas, Thanksgiving, Halloween, Mother's Day, Father's Day, Graduation, Easter,

Dana Cassell, President
Writer Data Bank

"To make it as a writer, you've got to be competitive. Start by making your manuscript look better. The look of it has a lot to do with whether you get the assignment. It's just like you look and talk, it's the image that sticks.

"If you have no specific field, try a little bit of everything until you find your niche. Look for the field where you are getting the highest ratio of return from query letters, then sales, and so on. A full-time writer can work into $20,000 and more. One writer I know makes $50,000 a year in the medical field.

Valentine's Day, and St. Patrick's Day.
Requirements: Writers submit batches of short verses for consideration. Artists send sketches or photocopies of finished originals.

KLITZNER INDUSTRIES, 44 Warren St., Providence, RI 02901.
Positions: Freelance designers and illustrators for advertising specialty products.
Requirements: Must have experience in the advertising field and the proven ability to follow through on assignments. Submit resume and tear sheets. Prefers local artists.
Provisions: Pays by the project.

LAFF MASTERS, INC., 557 Oak St., Copiague, NY 11726.
Positions: Illustrators work on assignment only for this greeting card publisher. Style is very contemporary and sophisticated.
Requirements: Only previously published artists experienced in the greeting card industry are considered for assignments. Must be local artist. Submit resume and tear sheets.
Provisions: Pays by the project.

LASER CRAFT, 3300 Coffey Lane, Santa Rosa, CA 95401.
Positions: Established greeting card company always on the lookout for artists with new ideas for greeting card designs. Company prefers humorous themes, but anything innovative (and good) will be considered.
Requirements: Submit ideas/designs in card format and send with SASE.
Provisions: Pays for each design.

LIFE BEAT MAGAZINE, R.R. 2, Box 64a, Blanchardville, WI 53516.
Positions: Freelance writers work on assignment for this monthly magazine about dynamic lifestyles.
Requirements: Send for guidelines; include SASE.

LIGHT IMAGES, 207 Miller Ave., Mill Valley, CA 94941.
Positions: Light Images is a stock photo agency that occasionally takes on new freelance photographers.
Requirements: Must be highly professional photographer; only top-notch work will be considered. Must have experience shooting for advertising. Send resume and request interview in order to show portfolio. Prefers Bay area photographers only.

LILLIAN VERNON CORPORATION, 510 South Fulton Ave., Mount Vernon, NY 10550.
Positions: Lillian Vernon is one of those rare "kitchen table" success stories. The company is one of the most successful of all direct mail catalog marketers. Products include all kinds of paper products, textiles, housewares, etc. Freelance artists design and illustrate on assignment only.
Requirements: Only regional artists are used. Prefers artists with experience, but is willing to look at someone with exceptional talent. Send letter of interest with tear sheets or samples that can be kept on file.
Provisions: Pays flat fee.

LINTAS, NEW YORK, 1 Dag Hammarskjold Plza, New York, NY 10017.
Positions: Freelance graphic artists, photographers, and illustrators work on a variety of assignments in the advertising field.
Requirements: Submit letter of interest, business card, and tear sheets.

LOS ANGELES REVIEW OF BOOKS, 7536 Circuit Dr., Citrus Heights, CA 95610.
Positions: Stringers and staff writers for reviews, features, and interviews with writers and others in the publishing industry.
Requirements: At least one sample of previous (published) work. Knowledge of the publishing industry is preferred.
Provisions: Staff members are salaried employees. Stringers are paid per assignment.

ROB MACINTOSH COMMUNICATIONS, INC., 43 Brucewood St., Boston, MA 02132.
Positions: Graphic artists work on assignment for this ad agency.
Requirements: Submit resume and work samples or tear sheets. Submissions should indicate the particular skills of the artist and the level of experience.

THE MAIN EVENT, 1717 State Rt 208, Fair Lawn, NJ 07410.
Positions: Freelance sports writers work as stringers from several major cities.
Requirements: Solid knowledge of sports in general is necessary with additional knowledge of medicine preferred. Resume and published clips required.

MAINE LINE COMPANY, PO Box 947, Rockport, ME 04841.
Positions: Writers, artists, and photographers. Company produces greeting cards, postcards, plaques, books, T-shirts, buttons, mugs, and stickers with a humorous theme.
Requirements: Start by sending a #10 envelope with three stamps for a current market list and creative guidelines. Format instructions will be included. Photographers send sample slides, no snaps, with SASE. Artists design cartoons, graphics, and illustrations. Send sketches of work. Writers, send ideas/samples with SASE. Company prefers multi-talented people.

MANGAN, RAINS, GINNAVEN, HOLCOMB, 911 Savers Federal Building, Little Rock, AR 72201.
Positions: Freelance artists work on a variety of advertising materials.
Requirements: Prefers experienced local artists. Submit letter of interest and business card. Request appointment to show portfolio.
Provisions: Pays hourly rates.

MARTIN-WILLIAMS ADVERTISING, INC., 10 South Fifth St., Minneapolis, MN 55402.
Positions: Freelance photographers work on assignment.
Requirements: Works with experienced local photographers only. Submit resume and tear sheets. Request appointment to show portfolio.

MASTERPIECE STUDIOS, 5400 West 35th St., Chicago, IL 60650.
Positions: Freelance artists for seasonal greeting cards. Especially needs highly stylized designs for Christmas cards.
Requirements: Send for guidelines first. Submit full color sketches or finished art. Samples will not be returned.
Provisions: Pays flat fee for each design. Pays higher fees for assigned illustration.

MCGRAW-HILL, School Division, 1200 N.W. 63rd St., Oklahoma City, OK 73116.
Positions: Freelance illustrators work on educational books.
Requirements: Only highly experienced, previously published artists are considered. Submit letter of interest with tear sheets.

MECKLER PUBLISHING CORPORATION, 11 Ferry Lane West, Westport, CT 06880
Positions: Meckler publishs books and journals about computer databases and other electronic information storage products. There are about 40 home-based writers, editors, and even some local keyboarders.
Requirements: Resumes are accepted from qualified writers and editors with experience in this field.

MEDIA REVIEW, Box 146717, San Francisco, CA 94114.
Positions: Freelance writers and editors. Media Review is a humorous new magazine that parodies mainstream media.
Requirements: Submit resume with copies of articles, sample ideas, and include SASE.

MERION PUBLICATIONS, INC., 636 School Line Dr., King of Prussia, PA 19406.
Positions: Freelance staff writers for newspaper read by health professionals.
Requirements: Must live in the area. Need experience and resume with samples.
Provisions: Story leads are provided for features.

METRO CREATIVE GRAPHICS, 33 West 34th St., 4th Floor, New York, NY 10005.
Positions: Freelance illustrators. Metro is a clip art dealer that works with dozens of artists.
Requirements: Must apply with resume and request personal interview to show portfolio of professional work samples. Prefers New York artists, but will consider anyone with real talent.

Provisions: Pay worked out on an individual basis.

MIDWEST LIVING, 1912 Grand Avenue, Des Moines, IA 50336.
Positions: Freelance writers work on assignment for this monthly travel and leisure magazine.
Requirements: Send proposal along with clips of previously published material.
Provisions: Pays excellent rates upon acceptance.

MORNING STAR, INC., 6680 Shady Oak Rd., Eden Prairie, MN 55344.
Positions: Freelance artists for the design and illustration of greeting cards, giftware, stationery, and associated products. All products have a Christian theme. Also assigns artists for bordering and calligraphy.
Requirements: Send letter of interest with work samples.
Provisions: Pays flat fee.

NATIONAL HARDWOOD MAGAZINE, P.O. Box 34808, Memphis, TN 38184.
Positions: Freelance writers work on assignment basis in various metropolitan areas around the country. Publication is a wood industry trade journal.
Requirements: Send resume and writing samples.

THOMAS NELSON PUBLISHERS, Box 141000, Elm Hill Pike, Nashville, TN 37284.
Positions: Freelance artists illustrate religious publications and design advertising materials.
Requirements: Only local experienced artists are considered. Submit letter of interest and tear sheets.

NEW DOMINION, P.O. Box 19714, Alexandria, VA 22320.
Positions: Freelance writers write most of this quarterly magazine for northern Virginia.
Requirements: Must be regional writer. Send for guidelines and sample issue first.
Provisions: Pays by the word.

NEWSBYTES NEWS SERVICE, 822 Arkansas Street, San Francisco, CA 94107
Positions: Newsbytes is similar to AP and UPI in that it is a news service. The difference is that it specializes in news about the computer industry. The entire staff is comprised of a dozen writers scattered throughout the world, each running his or her own bureau from home. Each is a permanent, though part-time employee of the company.
Requirements: Resumes are accepted from experienced computer industry reporters.

NU-ART, INC., Box 2002, Bedford, IL 60499.
Positions: Writers and artists for greeting cards, wedding invitations and accessories, and boxed stationery. Cards are for Christmas only.
Requirements: Writers submit verse along with design ideas for total concept. Artists submit color roughs or finished art.

OATMEAL STUDIOS, Box 138, Rochester, VT 05767.
Positions: Writers and illustrators for greeting card design.
Requirements: The first step for both positions is to send for Oatmeal's guidelines and current market list. Include SASE with your request. Then send several samples with a letter of interest.
Provisions: Writers are paid for each idea that is accepted. Pay for artists depends on the situation. 90% of Oatmeal's work is done by freelancers.

PAMCO SECURITIES AND INSURANCE SERVICES, 16030 Ventura Blvd. #500, Encino, CA 91436.
Positions: Freelance writer for composing banking training manuals.
Requirements: Must be local resident. Minimum five years experience in this type of writing is required. Must have thorough knowledge of banking industry. Must own IBM compatible word processor. Submit resume and references.

PAPEL, Box 9879, North Holywood, CA 91609.
Positions: Freelance illustrators, designers, and calligraphers work on greeting cards and ceramic souvenir items.
Requirements: Several years experience is required. Submit resume and tear sheets.
Provisions: Pays by the project.

PARAMOUNT CARDS INC., Box 6546, Providence, RI 02940.
Positions: Writers, artists, and photographers for greeting card production and promotional work. Cards are seasonal and everyday with a humorous theme (studio style).
Requirements: First send for instruction sheet, including SASE with request. Then send samples with letter of interest. Be sure to include SASE with any samples.
Provisions: Specific art assignments and purchase agreements are given to freelance artists/designers. Pay methods vary.

PC WEEK, 800 Boylston Street, Boston, MA 02199.
Positions: Technical analysts review computer software and hardware.
Requirements: Only the best technical reviewers will be considered. Send resume.

PENDLETON HAND WEAVERS, P.O. Box 233, Sedona, AZ 86336.
Positions: Will consider hand woven and other fabric art pieces for inclusion in regular retail line.

Requirements: Send either slides or photos along with written description and prices of your offerings. Include SASE.

PHILLIPS PUBLISHING, INC., 7811 Montrose Road, Potomac, MD 20854.
Positions: This newsletter publisher uses up to ten freelance writers.
Requirements: Must have the necessary expertise to write on high technology topics. Prefers local residents.
Provisions: Equipment such as personal computers and fax machines are provided as needed.

PORTAL PUBLICATIONS, 21 Tamal Vista Blvd., Corte Madera, CA 94925,
Positions: Freelance writers. Company produces greeting cards especially for young adult working women.
Requirements: Study the line first and send for market guidelines. Then submit verses on index cards in small batches with SASE.

PROFESSIONAL MARINER, 55 John Street, New York, NY 10038.
Positions: Freelance writers/stringers produce most of the articles on marine subjects for this magazine.
Requirements: Send sample ideas along with clips of previously published work. Must have some particular knowledge of marine subjects.

PSYCH IT, 6507 Bimini Court, Apollo Beach, FL 33570.
Positions: Freelance writers, poets, artists, and cartoonists produce all of the material in this quarterly publication.
Requirements: Need not be previously published to be considered. Must first send for sample issue; $1.50 plus SASE.

RAINBOW WORLD CARDS, 5400 W. 35th St., Chicago, IL 60650.
Positions: Freelance designers and illustrators for contemporary greeting cards.
Requirements: Send for market guidelines first. Then send samples along with resume.

RAINFALL GREETINGS, INC., 90 Market S.W., P.O. Box 7321, Grand Rapids, MI 49510.
Positions: Writers, artists, and photographers for greeting cards, stationery, and stickers.
Requirements: Writers should submit poetry or humorous, whimsical, or inspirational verse. Artists should submit samples of cartoons or graphics.

READER SEARCH COMMITTEE, 12224 Victory Blvd., North Hollywood, CA 91606.
Positions: Freelance writers work as stringers for this weekly arts publication.
Requirements: Must be local resident. Resume and three previously published clips with byline required.

RECYCLED PAPER PRODUCTS, INC., 3636 N. Broadway, Chicago, IL 60613.
Positions: Freelance artists and calligraphers. Company produces greeting cards and other stationery items.
Requirements: Submit samples and letter of interest. Guidelines are available for SASE.

RED FARM STUDIO, P.O. Box 347, 334 Pleasant St., Pawtucket, RI 02862.
Positions: Writers and artists. Company produces greeting cards, gift wrap, and note papers.
Requirements: Send for a current market list; include a business size SASE. Then send letter of interest with work samples.
Provisions: Writers are paid by the line. Artists' pay varies depending on the situation.

REED STARLINE CARD COMPANY, P.O. Box 2368, Lake Arrowhead, CA 92352.
Positions: Artists and writers for work involved in the production and promotion of greeting cards. 100% of all work is done by freelancers on assignment basis only.
Requirements: To be considered for any of the hundreds of project assignments each year, start by sending for company guidelines and market list; include SASE with request. Then send samples of your style with SASE. Include business card which will be kept on file for future assignments.

> "The beauty of our company is we have no quotas, set territories, or anyone looking over our shoulders."   --The Creative Circle

RENAISSANCE GREETING CARDS, P.O. Box 845, Springvale, ME 04083.
Positions: Writers and artists for all occasion and Christmas cards.
Requirements: Writers send verse ideas; especially likes humorous verse. Include ideas for design. Artists send samples of full color work in batches of a dozen; include resume. Prefers bright cartoons.

ROUSANA CARDS, 145 Lehigh Ave., Lakewood, NJ 08701.
Positions: Writers and artists for everyday and seasonal cards.
Requirements: Works only with established greeting card designers. Submit work samples with resume and/or tear sheets.

SAN FRANCISCO BAY GUARDIAN, 2700 19th St., San Francisco, CA 94110.
Positions: Freelance writers produce over half of the contents of this alternative newsweekly.
Requirements: Only previously published Bay Area writers will be considered. Especially interested in investigative reporters. Send query with clips of previously published work.

SANGAMON COMPANY, Route 48 West, Taylorville, IL 62558.
Positions: Writers and artists for greeting card and gift wrap design.
Requirements: Writers should submit verses with SASE included. Artists submit finished art or color sketches.

SAWYER CAMERA & INSTRUMENT COMPANY, 1208 Isabel St., Burbank, CA 91506.
Positions: Freelance photographers work on assignment for this multimedia ad agency.
Requirements: Local photographers only. Must have experience in multimedia production. Submit resume, business card, and tear sheets.
Provisions: Pays by the project..

SEYBOLD CONSULTING GROUP, INC., 148 State Street, Suite 612, Boston, MA 02109.
Positions: Independent writers are contracted by the year to write stories from evaluation reports of automated office systems and software. Company publishes 35 to 40 reports each month on UNIX and Office systems.
Requirements: Experience and references are required. Send letter of interest with work samples. Prefers to work with writers in Boston.
Provisions: Pay is worked out on an individual contract basis.

SHEEHY & KOPF, INC., 10400 Linn Station Rd., Louisville, KY 40223.
Positions: Freelance artists handle illustrations and lettering for advertisments.
Requirements: Submit resume and work samples.
Provisions: Pay methods vary.

SHOSS & ASSOCIATES, INC., 1750 S. Brentwood Blvd., Suite 259, St Louis, MO 63144.
Positions: Freelance local photographers work on assignment for this ad agency.
Requirements: Submit work samples that include product shots. Include resume and request appointment to show portfolio.

SHULSINGER SALES, INC., 50 Washington St., Brooklyn, NY 11201.
Positions: Freelance artists design greeting cards and gift wrap with Jewish themes.
Requirements: Submit work samples and resume.

SINGER COMMUNICATIONS, INC., 3164 Tyler Avenue, Anaheim, CA 92801.
Positions: Freelance cartoonists. Singer is a large syndicate that buys thousands of cartoons for distribution worldwide each year.
Requirements: Must be previously published. Submit copies of published work.
Provisions: Pays a percentage split.

BETH SMITH & ASSOCIATES, 1151 NE Todd George Rd., Lees Summit, MO 64137.
Positions: Positions are open to writers, typesetters, and graphic artists. Company publishes a newsletter, Business Line, for home-based and small businesses primarily in the Southern California area. Especially looking for other home-based business people who have tips, suggestions, and success stories that will motivate people. For this, there is no pay offered, but free publicity and byline is given in the newsletter and in classes on "How to Start a Home-based Business" in local colleges.
Requirements: Experience with writing and all areas of publishing is required.

SOUTHWEST FREELANCER, P.O. Box 160, Morrow, AR 72749.
Positions: This is a newsletter and market update for writers, photographers, artists, and poets living in Arkansas, Louisiana, Missouri, Oklahoma, and Texas. Freelance

submissions of articles are sought.
Requirements: Send for a copy of writer's guidelines.

ST. MARTIN'S PRESS, 175 Fifth Ave., New York, NY 10010
Positions: Freelance copy editors.
Requirements: Must be computer literate and experienced. New York residents only.
Provisions: Apply by sending resume to the managing editor, trade division.

SUNRISE PUBLICATIONS, INC., P.O. Box 2699, Bloomington, IN 47402.
Positions: Writers and artists for production of greeting cards.
Requirements: First, send for Sunrise's Creative Guidelines and current market list. Then send letter of interest with work samples. Include SASE.
Provisions: Payment varies..

SUPERMARKET BUSINESS MAGAZINE, 25 West 43rd St., New York, NY 10036.
Positions: Freelance correspondents write about the food and grocery industry within their assigned areas.
Requirements: Send letter of interest with writing samples. Must be familiar with the industry.

SUPPORT OUR SYSTEMS (SOS), 10 Mechanic Street, Red Bank, NJ 07701.
Positions: SOS has a pool of over 60 home-based technical writers that produce user guides for computer systems at large companies.
Requirements: Experience and top skills are a must. You will be tested before starting work for your writing ability and study habits. You must own a computer and a modem and have the ability to communicate electronically by several means. Although your schedule is your own, you will be required to check in with the compnay several times a day.

SYNDICATION ASSOCIATES, INC., P.O. Box 1000, Bixby, OK 74008.
Positions: This company sells patterns and plans for fabric, craft, and woodworking projects through newspaper syndication which amounts to a potential readership base of a whopping 34 million. Submissions of new, original, and unpublished designs are accepted.
Requirements: Send for submission instructions.
Provisions: Payment for accepted material is worked out on an individual basis for either lump sum payment in advance and/or royalties.

TAVERNON PHOTO ENGRAVING COMPANY, 27 First Ave., Paterson, NJ 07514.
Positions: Campany makes silk screens for wallpaper and fabric. Hand work consists of color separation of textile designs. Freelance artists do all the design work.
Requirements: Must live in Paterson in order to pick up and deliver supplies and finished work. Experience is required.
Provisions: Pay depends on the colors and intricacy of the design.

TURNROTH SIGN COMPANY, 1207 East Rock Falls Road, Rock Falls, IL 61071.
Positions: Freelance artists design billboards and other kinds of signs on assignment.

Requirements: Submit letter of interest with sketches or finished work samples. Include SASE with all correspondence.
Provisions: Pays flat rates for each project.

UNIVERSITY OF NEW HAVEN, 300 Orange Ave., Public Relations Department, West Haven, CT 06516.
Positions: Freelance photographers take shots of campus life, working on assignment basis only. Work is used in all sorts of PR presentations.
Requirements: Send letter of interest along with resume and at least one sample shot to be kept on file. Include SASE and business card. You will be contacted for an interview. Be ready with a portfolio. Local photographers only.
Provisions: Pays by the hour at a minmum of $20.

UNIX, MULTIUSER, MULTITASKING SYSTEM, Tech Valley Publishing, 444 Castro St., Mountain View, CA 94041.
Positions: Freelance writers work on assignment for this monthly magazine.
Requirements: Must have thorough knowledge of this end of the computer industry. Send query along with clips of previously published work.
Provisions: Pays for articles on acceptance. Sometimes pays expenses

WARNER PRESS, INC., Box 2499, Anderson, IN 46018.
Positions: Writers and artists for work on greeting cards, calendars, posters, postcards, and plaques. Artists work on assignment. Writers are freelance.
Requirements: Before applying, write for current market list and guidelines. Include SASE. Be sure to study company's style before sending samples. Talented new artists are especially sought.
Provisions: Pay varies.

WILDER LIMITED, P.O. Box 8367, Universal City, CA 91608.
Positions: Silkscreen artists, calligraphers, and translators. Company produces children's wallhangings.
Requirements: Experience is required. Send letter of interest; state fee desired.
Provisions: Pays by the job.

WILLIAMHOUSE-REGENCY, INC., 28 West 23rd St., New York, NY 10010.
Positions: Freelance artists design wedding invitations and related stationery pieces.
Requirements: Submit sketches or finished samples.

WILLITTS DESIGNS, 1327 Clegg Street, Box 178, Petaluma, CA 94953.
Positions: Designers and illustrators for porcelain and earthware giftware. Some calligraphy. All designs are three-dimensional and range from the light and whimsical to the detailed and serious.
Requirements: Submit full color design samples with resume.
Provisions: Pay methods vary from outright purchase to royalties.

WOMEN'S CIRCLE HOME COOKING, Box 198, Henniker, NY 03242.
Positions: Freelance writers and photographers produce all of the material in this monthly magazine.

Requirements: Send for guidelines first; include SASE.

WORLDLING DESIGNS/NYC CARD COMPANY, INC., P.O. Box 1935, Madison Square Station, New York, NY 10159.
Positions: Writers and artists for contemporary style greeting cards and related paper products. All products have a strong New York City look. Also assigns some calligraphy work.
Requirements: Send resume or letter of interest with work samples showing highest quality work. Writers send only short verses that are upbeat. Writers guidelines are available upon request. Be sure to include SASE with all correspondence. Artists send resume and samples of bold, stylistic work in any medium. Artists guidelines are also available. Request appointment to show portfolio.
Provisions: Pays flat rate.

WRITER DATA BANK, Cassell Communicaitons, Inc., P.O. Box 9844, Fort Lauderdale, FL 33310.
Positions: The Writer Data Bank is a national computerized listing of freelance writers categorized according to experience, areas of expertise, subject specialties, and geographic locations. Editors, PR firms or departments, and other clients who need the services of a writer call the Data Bank toll free (and without a search fee) and a writer with the appropriate expertise will be referred to them.
Requirements: Writers can be listed for an annual processing/update fee of $25. Then, when the writer receives payment from any assignment resulting from the Data Bank listing, he or she remits 5% of that fee back to Cassell Communications, Inc. Send for the "Writer Data Bank Info Form."
Provisions: Contracts are worked out by the writers and clients.

Opportunities in Crafts

A craft is any occupation that requires manual dexterity or artistic skill. In this section, you'll find quite a few crafts represented—jewelry making, macrame, knitting, embroidery and merrowing, sewing, and silkscreen among others.

Knitting is one of the original seven industries that was banned from using home workers in 1938 under the Fair Labor Standards Act. The ban was lifted on knitting alone in December of 1985, after many years of struggling in the courts. Now there are dozens of companies that are certified by the U.S. Dept. of Labor to hire home workers. Most of these companies are based in New England, where home knitting has been a traditional occupation for generations.

Most knitting is still done by hand, but knitting machines are being used in increasing numbers. As you can imagine, using a knitting machine speeds up the process and allows the knitter to make more clothing and therefore more money.

Sewing is among the remaining six industries that are still banned from using home workers. Actually, only certain types of sewing are banned and most have to do with women's and children's apparel. That doesn't mean there isn't any home sewing going on. There are tens of thousands of home sewers across the country, but most are working "underground." The companies listed here are all located in states with labor laws that allow home sewing under specific certification procedures. (State labor laws supercede federal laws.) Unfortunately, in March of 1991, New Jersey reversed its longstanding tolerance of home work in ladies apparel. Now any home work involved in the manufacture of ladies apparel is outlawed. That meant dropping over 40 employers from this edition!

Sewing is a skill that most women learn to some extent, but that doesn't mean that every woman is qualified to be a professional home sewer. Most home sewing is specialized so that each sewer works on a particular type of garment or, in many cases, a particular piece of garment. Employers have indicated that it isn't easy finding workers who are capable of doing quality work.

No matter what kind of craft you want to do, in order to get a job you will have to show samples of your work in order to prove that you have the necessary skills. There are a few situations mentioned in the following pages that offer training to inexperienced people, but these are the exceptions to the rule.

ADLER & YORK, 3400 Industrial Lane 10-B, Broomfield, CO 80020.
Positions: Embroidery.
Requirements: Must be local resident and be skilled.

ALERT EMBROIDERY, INC., 757 Main Ave. Floor 2, Passaic, NJ 07055.
Positions: Trimming threads, merrowing, and pressing of place mats.
Hand work only, no machinery is used. Mostly rush work and overflow.
Requirements: No experience is required. Must live in Passaic.
Provisions: Company will pick up and deliver supplies and finished
work, usually in the evening, every day. Pays piece rates.

C. M. ALMY & SONS, INC., Ruth Road, Pittsfield, ME 04967.
Positions: Embroidery.
Requirements: Must be local resident and be skilled.

AMERICAN GLOVE CO. INC., P.O. Box 51, Lyerly, GA 30730
Positions: Home manufacture of gloves and mittens.
Requirements: Must be local resident and be skilled.

AMERICAN HOME CRAFTS, P.O. Box 326, Suisun, CA 94585-0326.
Positions: Sewing of baby items such as appliqued burping pads.
Requirements: A good sewing machine is necessary. Must purchase a beginners
package for $30. The package includes a pattern, fabrics, and complete instructions for
product assembly.
Provisions: American Home Crafts will pay $50.97 for production and $36.92 for supply
cost on each unit of three dozen baby burp pads completed. Producers are limited to four
units per week for a possible income of $351.56 total. Can live anywhere in U.S.

AMSTER NOVELTY COMPANY, INC., 75-13 - 71St Ave., Middle Village, NY
11375.
Positions: Sewing, trimming, stringing, and other hand work involved in
the manufacture of soft tote bags, pouches for cosmetics , and decorations
(bows and appliques) for little girls' dresses. Currently has about 100 home workers.
Requirements: No experience is necessary. Must be local resident.
Provisions: Pays piece rates.

ANDREA STRONGWATER DESIGNS, 465 West End Ave., Manhattan, NY 10024.
Postions: Home-based knitting of outerwear.
Requirements: Must be local resident and be skilled.

APPLE TREE DESIGNS, P.O. Box 2355, West Scarboro, ME 04074.
Positions: Home knitters produce outerwear.
Requirements: Must be local resident.

ATLAS MFG. CO., INC., Rt. 1 Box 662, Rest Home Rd., Claremont, NC 28610.
Positions: Home-based stitchers produce gloves.
Requirements: Must be local resident.

BABBIDGE PATCH, 31 Babbidge Rd., Falmouth, ME 04105.
Positions: Sewing of sweater sleeves. Currently has 20 home workers.
Requirements: Sewing machine is required. Must be local resident.

Provisions: Some training is provided. Pays piece rates.

BARRY MANUFACTURING COMPANY, INC., Bubier St., Lynn, MA 01901.
Positions: Stitching and hand assembly of infant and children's shoe parts.
Requirements: Experience is required.. Must be local resident.
Provisions: Some of the work requires machinery, which is supplied by the employer. Pays piece rates equal to minimum wage, which is the same in-house workers are paid for the same work.

> "The best thing about working at home is the 30 second commute down the hall--it can also be the worst."
> --John Everett, home worker

BERLIN GLOVES CO., 150 W. Franklin, PO Box 230, Berlin, WI 54923-0230.
Positions: Home stitchers manufacture gloves.
Requirements: Must be local resident and be skilled.

BLUEBERRY WOOLENS, P.O. Box 318 Randall St., Anson, ME 04911.
Positions: Machine knitting of whole sweaters for wholesaler. This is an established and growing company with close to $1 million in annual sales. Currently has a pool of 60 knitters.
Requirements: Enrollment in company's training classes and submission of acceptable samples is required. Must own a knitting machine or purchase one from the company. Must be local in order to pick up and deliver supplies and finished sweaters.
Provisions: Pays per finished sweater. Hours can be full time or part time. Workers are independent contractors. Inquiries are welcome as company continues to grow.

BORDEAUX, INC., 102 East Washington Street, Clarinda, IA 51632
Bordeaux has over 150 home workers sewing appliques onto ladies' sportswear, mostly sweatsuits. The company was started by Bertha Turner and her two partners six years ago. Since then, the company has grown to a $3.5 million a year business. Clarinda is in an economically depressed farm community. All of the home workers are farm wives (or ex-farm wives). Each day, a van delivers work to farmhouses up to 50 miles away from headquarters.
Each seamstress is considered by Bordeaux to be an independent contractor and is paid piece rates. Unfortunately, this independent contractor status is being challenged in court by the U.S. Department of Labor at the insistence of the Ladies' Garment Workers Union. Unfortunate, because if Bordeaux loses, all work will have to be conducted in a factory. Not only is the idea of working in a factory dismal, but most of the workers will not be able to commute and will simply lose their jobs. Bertha Turner says all applications for home work are on hold until the matter is resolved.

BRC INTERNATIONAL, INC., 7760 W. 20th Av., Bay #5, Miami, FL 33016.
Positions: Embroidery.
Requirements: Must be local resident and be skilled.

Janet Nagel sews at her home for Boston-based Rocking Horse clothing store for children. Photo courtesy of The Salt Lake Tribune.

BRUDER NECKWEAR COMPANY, INC., 1 East 33rd St., New York, NY 10016.
Positions: Sewing, cutting and folding of men's neckties.
Requirements: Must be local and have a minimum five years experience making men's neckties.
Provisions: Pays piece rates.

BRYSTIE, INC., P.O. Box 1106, Mountain Rd., Stowe, VT 05672.
Positions: Home-based knitters produce outerwear.
Requirements: Must be local resident.

BUTTERFLIES & RAINBOWS, INC., 1177 E. Lazy Lake Road, Dunedin, FL 34697-1231.
Positions: Home manufacture of jewelry.
Requirements: Must be local resident and be skilled.

CARBAREE, 4904 Briar Grove, Dallas, TX 75287.
Positions: This company uses home-based knitters to produce outerwear.
Requirements: Must be local resident.

CEAU MAR, 14868 Deveau Place, Minnetonka, MN 55345.
Positions: Home-based knitting of outerwear.
Requirements: Must be local resident and be skilled.

CENTURY KNITS, 2409 Century Loop, Union, OR 99850.
Positions: Home knitters produce outerwear.
Requirements: Must be local resident. Experience is necessary.

CHICAGO KNITTING MILLS, 3344 West Montrose Ave., Chicago, IL 60618.
Positions: Home-based knitting of outerwear.
Requirements: Must be local resident and be skilled. Must obtain a home workers certificate from Illinois Department of Labor.

CHIPITA ACCESSORIES, P.O. Box 1250, Walthenburg, CO 81089.
Positions: Between 75 and 250 home workers handcraft jewelry using beads, stones, semi-precious stones, silver, crystal, and gold. The number of home workers fluctuates with the time of year, number of orders, and number of available workers in this rural area in southern Colorado. Walthenburg is, like most rural areas, economically depressed, but has a history of handcrafts of all kinds created by local artisans. Chipita started by producing and selling one kind of beaded earrings and grew from there. Home workers here are completely independent, having total control over their hours, how often and when they work, etc. The company will sell kits to workers, will show and attempt to sell from new sample designs for workers, or will buy outright as much jewelry as a worker can produce as long as it meets quality standards. A worker can work part -time or full-time, with the opportunity to earn a "regular income".
Requirements: Must be a local resident. Contact the company with letter of interest.

COMET INDUSTRIES CORPORATION, 3630 South Iron St., Chicago, IL 60609.
Positions: Comet manufactures model airplane kits and crafts. Part-time home workers paint craft samples for buyers.
Requirements: Must be local resident. Only referrals are considered. Must obtain home worker certificate from Illinois State Department of Labor.
Provisions: Pays piece rates.

COUNTRY CURTAINS, INC., Main St., Stockbridge, MA 01262.
Positions: Sewing trim on basic curtains. Currently has about 25 home workers.
Requirements: Need sewing machine. Must be local resident.
Provisions: Pick up and delivery provided. Pays piece rates equal to minimum wage.

COUNTRY KNITS, P.O. Box 186, St. Albans Bay, VT 05481.
Positions: Home knitters produce outerwear.
Requirements: Must be local resident and be skilled.

THE CREATIVE CIRCLE, 9243 Cody St., Overland Park, KS 66214.
Positions: Party plan sales of needlework kits. Work involves conducting classes in needlework.
Requirements: $40 investment buys $90 worth of merchandise and paperwork supplies for three classes.
Provisions: Pays 25% commission plus incentives. Also provides thank you gifts for hostesses and premiums used during parties. Managerial opportunities available. "The beauty of our company is we have no quotas, set territories, or anyone looking over our shoulders."

CREATIVE TREASURES, 6836 Duckling Way, Sacramento, CA 95842.
Positions: Creative Treasures is a home party business that markets quality handcrafts of all kinds. Crafter can submit any item for approval. If an item is approved, it is included in the company's regular line and sold one of three ways. Consignment orders: Company receives 40% of retail price. Party orders: Items are ordered from a sample that is provided by the crafter. Company receives 45% of retail price. Delivery for these items

is 15 days from order date. Wholesale orders: These items will be stocked and paid for by Creative Treasures for wholesaling. Company receives 50% of retail price. Send good photo of item, or a sample, with letter of interest including suggested retail price for consideration. Home party demonstrators and their supervisors also used. Write letter of interest.

DAINTY MAID MANUFACTURING CO., 12 North St., Fitchburg,MA 10420.
Positions: Sewing aprons.
Requirements: Must be local resident and own sewing machine. Experience is required.
Provisions: Material is supplied. Pays piece rates equal to approximately $4 an hour.

DESIGN SOURCE, Box 158, Greenleaf, ID 83626.
Positions: Crafting of soft sculptured wall hangings, holiday table ornaments, patterns, kits and "craft packs". Company sells these products through hospital gift shops, catalogs, and other wholesale outlets. Workers are independent contractors. Design Source contracts by the week, determining how many items will be produced and when they are due. Currently has 30 regulars, with number increasing in the fall to about 60.
Requirements: Must have sewing machine and must live nearby. Some kind of sewing experience is necessary.
Provisions: Specific training, such as tricks for working with felt and other difficult fabrics, is provided. Pays piece rates.

DEVA CLOTHING COMPANY, a Cottage Industry, Box C, 303 East Main Street, Burkittsville, MD 21718.
Positions: DEVA has been using the cottage industry method for producing unisex, natural fiber apparel for 10 years. About two dozen local stitchers work as true independent contractors; they work on their own equipment, set their own prices, set their own production schedules, etc. Since the company's philosophy is based upon quality, only quality workers remain. "More of our stitchers wash out for not being businesslike. It is hard for them to get organized working at home. They need discipline and they have to find it for themselves without the structure of the factory." Must be local, skilled stitcher, with a commercial or industrial grade serger/overlock machine.

DOMACO INDUSTRIAL SEWING, 2838 Camp Jackson Rd., Cahokia, IL 62206.
Positions: Sewing.
Requirements: Must have own machinery. Local residents only. Must obtain a home worker certificate from Illinois State Department of Labor.
Provisions: Pays piece rates.

DUKE SPORTS, 40250 County Road 129, Steamboat Springs, CO 80477.
Positions: Knitting of outerwear.
Requirements: Must be local resident and be experienced.

LEE ENGLAND, 27 Alta St., San Francisco, CA 94133.
Positions: Sewing, bead stringers and hand knotters for jewelry designer. All positions are on an independent contractor basis. Number of worker depends upon orders, season, etc. Averages more than 10. Company was much larger in the past, but it has been reduced to "a more manageable size with creativity the primary empahsis."
Requirements: Sewing requires experience with fine and antique fabrics and trims for

high-fashion evening jackets. Sewing machine required. Stringers need no experience. Knotters do need experience. Must be local resident.

Provisions: Limited training available. Pick up and delivery provided only if necessary. Pay rates per producation based upon difficulty of project.

ET PUIS, INC., 101-3 Church St., Matawan, NJ 07747.
Positions: Sewing and finished fabric promotions and decorative items such as pillows. Company was originally started as a home business.
Requirements: Must be experienced and own sewing machine. Must live in Matawan.
Provisions: Pays piece rates.

EVERREADY EMBROIDERY, INC., 235 Orient Ave., Jersey City, NJ 07305.
Positions: Taping and hand cutting of emblems.
Requirements: Must be local resident.

EWE FIRST, 2081 Meeting Street, Hennepin, MN 55391.
Positions: Home knitters produce outerwear.
Requirements: Must be local resident and be skilled.

FIT-RITE HEADWEAR, INC., 92 South Empire Street, Wilkes-Barre, PA 18702
Positions: About a dozen home workers sew industrial headwear.
Requirements: Must be local resident. Must qualify as Pennsylvania industrial home worker (be either disabled or need to care for invalid family member).
Provisions: Pays piece rates.

FRENCH CREEK SHEEP AND WOOL COMPANY, INC., Route 345, R.D. #1, Elverson, PA 19520.
Positions: Knitting sweaters on hand operated machines. Currently has about 40 workers.
Requirements: Must be local resident in order to pick up and deliver supplies and finished sweaters.
Provisions: Some training, specific to the work here, is provided. Pays production rate, which is "well above minimum wage."

FUNCRAFT, P.O. Box 6090, Fairfield, CA 94533.
Positions: Sewing of baby bibs. Company is in its fifth year.
Requirements: All workers are independent contractors and must own their own sewing machines and buy their own supplies. The initial kit which includes instructions costs $29.95 plus $4.95 for postage (refundable).
Provisions: Workers can earn up to $365 per week. Can live anywhere in U.S. Currently not accepting new workers in California.

GATER SPORTS, 3565 SW Temple, Suite 5, Salt Lake City, UT 84115
Positions: Sewing cold weather sports accessories, socks, face protectors, eyeglass cases, etc. Currently uses 25 to 50 home workers.
Requirements: Need some sewing experience and own sewing machine. Must be local resident in order to pick up and deliver supplies and finished work.
Provisions: Will train for specifics of the job. Pays piece rates. Workers are independent contractors. At this time, most of the available work fluctuates seasonally, but the company is growing and hopes to be able to offer full-time, year-round work in the near future.

GEIER GLOVE CO., 810 W. Main, Centralia, WA 98531
Positions: Hand manufacturing of gloves and mittens.
Requirements: Must be local resident and be skilled.

GOLDEN ENTERPRISES, HACAP, Skywalk Level, 308 3rd St., S.E. , Cedar Rapids, IA 52401.
Positions: Handcrafting of gifts and keepsake type items: baby things, dolls, wall signs, hangings, quilts, and comforters. Program is designed to provide income for home-based senior citizens by marketing handcrafts through retail and catalog orders. Currently has over 100 active participants, but the organization is expanding rapidly. Inquiries are welcome from senior citizens in Cedar Rapids **only**.
Provisions: Buys some items outright; others are accepted on consignment.

ESTELLE GRACER, INC., 950 West Hatcher Rd., Phoenix, AZ 85021.
Positions: Knitting and crocheting jackets and sweaters. Work has previously been done by hand only, but company is now going into machine knitting. Currently has over 50 home workers; that number fluctuates up to 200. "Inquiries are always welcome."
Requirements: Must be experienced. Phoenix residents only.
Provisions: Specific training is provided. Home workers are full employees. Pays for production.

GRANDE RONDE KNITS, INC., Route 1, Box 1727, LaGrande, OR 97850.
Positions: Knitting of outerwear.
Requirements: Must be local resident and be skilled.

HAIR BOWS, P.O. Box 5800, Dept. WC, Danville, CA 94526.
Positions: Assembly of fancy ladies' hair bows.
Requirements: This is work that requires medium skills. There is no sewing per se, but you will need a needle and thread and glue. The materials which include ribbons, netting, clips, and beads will be obtained by you. To get started, send a self-addressed, stamped envelope for details. If you decide you want to do this, you will need to purchase a start-up kit for $29.95 which will include instructions and materials for a sample product. Opportunities exist nationwide.

Provisions: Pay is approximately $142 (there is a $42 supply allowance so your profit would be $100) for each unit of 48 hair bows. The company will buy up to three units per week.

HAIRITAGE, INC., 16909 Parthenia St., Suite 202, Sepulveda, CA 91343.
Positions: Sewing hairpieces.
Requirements: Specific experience is necessary. "This is very intricate work. Our home workers were Max Factor employees before they came to us." Must be local residents.
Provisions: Pick up and delivery of supplies and finished work is provided. Pays piece rates.

HEADLINER HAIRPIECES, INC., 1448 N. Sierra Bonita, Los Angeles, CA 90046.
Positions: Hand sewing and assembly of hairpieces.
Requirements: Must live nearby and have specific experience with this kind of work.
Provisions: Pays piece rates equal to about $5 an hour.

HI LINE KNITS, 1707 Second, La Grande, OR 97850.
Positions: Hand knitting of outerwear.
Requirements: Must be local resident.

H.O.M.E, INC., Route 1, Orland, ME 04472.
Positions: H.O.M.E. stands for Homeworkers Organized for More Employment. It is a non-profit co-operative founded in 1970 for the purpose of marketing handcrafted products from this economically depressed area. H.O.M.E. operates a country store, many types of craft and trade workshhops, a child-care center. The Learning Center for adult education, a sawmill, a shingle mill, a woodlot and two hospitality houses. It also publishes a quarterly newspaper ("This Time") and a crafts catalog, and builds homes for otherwise homeless neighbors. Currently has 3,500 members. Anyone living in the area is encouraged to participate.

HOME GROWN WOODS OF PIGEON FORGE, P.O. Box 5350, Severville, TN 37864.
Positions: The major product of this company is called the Original Appalachian Door Harp. It is a stringed musical instrument that hangs on a door and when the door opens, hanging wooden balls strike the metal strings to create music much like chimes. Over a dozen artists hand-paint designs on the harps working out of their own home studios.
Requirements: Must be local resident and have the talent and skill required to do quality work.

HOME SPUN, P.O. BOX 3338, Fairfield, CA 94533.
Positions: Sewing of dining room chair pad pillows. The pillows are made from light weight cotton fabric and can be sewn on a ordinary home sewing machine.
Requirements: Send a self-addressed stamped envelope for information.
Provisions: Pays piece rates. Can live anywhere in U.S.

HOMESTEAD HANDCRAFTS, North 1301 Pines Rd., Spokane, WA 92206.
Positions: Company markets quality handcrafts with a country theme such as tole painting. Different situations are worked out on an individual basis.
Requirements: Must live in Spokane.

PAT HUBBARD CO., 4938 Driftwood, Milford, MI 48042.
Positions: Home-based knitters produce outerwear.
Requirements: Must be local resident.

JAZEE DESIGNS, 8760 W. 64th Place, Arvada, Co 80004.
Positions: Embroidery.
Requirements: Must be local resident and be skilled.

K-C PRODUCTS, 1600 East 6th Steet, Los Angeles, CA 90023.
Positions: Sewing vinyl travel bags, garment bags, mattress covers, and appliance covers. Up to 16 home workers are employed.
Requirements: Need ordinary sewing machine. Must live nearby.
Provisions: Pays piece rates.

KALEIDESKOP, 4799 Meadow Dr. #1, Vail, CO 81657.
Positions: Knitting of outerwear.
Requirements: Must be local resident. Experience is required.

KAREN KOVERS, 25 Old Dover Road, Rochester, NH 03867.
Positions: Home knitters produce outerwear.
Requirements: Must be local resident and be skilled.

KAREN'S, 15620 Herriman Blvd., Noblesville, IN 46060.
Positions: Hand embroidery.
Requirements: Must be local resident.

KAY COMPANY, 17731 Merridy St., Northridge, CA 91325.
Positions: Kay Company is a jewelry "manufacturer" that retails both from a storefront and through craft shows in Los Angeles. Uses bead workers.
Requirements: Prefers someone who is dependable and willing to make a minimum committment of six months. About $50 worth of small tools will be required. Prefers someone with some kind of handcraft experience. Must live in the West Valley in order to pick up and deliver inventory and supplies.
Provisions: Training will be provided and owner Kim Bovino says the training is very valuable and can be transferred to other companies upon leaving Kay Company. The work is part-time, on-call as orders come in. Pays piece rates.

KIPI OF MAINE, P.O. Box 311, Bingham, ME 04920.
Positions: Knitting, sewing, and blocking sweaters, pants, and other sportswear. Handcrafting of gift items for retail store and wholesale orders for catalog companies. Currently has around 50 home workers. "We have several knitters we have never seen." Number fluctuates seasonally.
Inquiries are welcome.
Requirements: Must live within 200 miles radius of company. Must submit a sample of work.
Provisions: Training is provided, particularly on Singer and Studio knitting machines for which the patterns are made. Pick up and delivery is provided. UPS is used for workers outside local area, but for these people only repetitive, larger orders are available so the work may not be steady. All workers are regular employees with full benefits provided by law. Quotas and tests are conducted to insure income meets D.O.L. requirements. Pays piece rates.

KIRSTEN SCARCELLI, 9 Union St., Hallowell, ME 04347.
Positions: Knitting of outerwear.
Requirements: Must be local resident. Must be skilled.

KNIT PICKEN, RFD #1, Box 1517, Rt. 11, Casco, ME 04015.
Positions: Hand knitting outerwear.
Requirements: Must be local resident.

KNITS BY CLAUDIA, 9 Main Street, Chittenden, VT 05648.
Positions: Knitting of outerwear.
Requirements: Must be local resident. Must be experienced.

LACE -TRENDS, INC., 324 -61st St., West New York, NJ 07093.
Positions: Hand cutting, trimming and merrowing of embroidery, appliques, and fabric pieces.
Requirements: Must be local resident.
Provisions: Specific training is provided, mostly to show time-saving techniques. Pick up and delivery of supplies and finished work is provided daily. Workers are independent contractors and are paid piece rates bi-weekly. "We treat our home workers with respect. We invite them to our Christmas parties, for instance, to keep them involved with the rest of the company. We don't cheat them, either. If someone makes a mistake, the company absorbs the loss."

THE LANCE CORPORATION, 321 Central St., Hudson, MA 01749.
Positions: Lance is a manufacturer of pewter ceramic-like figurines. About a dozen home workers paint the unfinished figurines.
Requirements: Must be local residents.
Provisions: Pick up and delivery is provided. Pays piece rates.

LEHUA HAWAII, INC., 1001 Dillingham, Suite 319, Honolulu, HI 96817.
Positions: Productions sewing of mu-mus, dresses, bras, and shirts.
Requirements: Must be experienced and own sewing interlocking sewing machine. Must be an in-house employee prior to moving work home. Local residents only.
Provisions: Pays hourly wages.

LENOX KITES, 98 Main St., Lenox, MA 01240.
Positions: Sewing of appliques, designs, and pockets onto kites.
Requirements: Must own sewing machine and have experience working with fine fabics. Must be local resident in order to pick up and deliver supplies and finished work. Currently has only 3 home workers.
Provisions: Pays piece rates equal to a minimum of $4 an hour.

LISE'S SWEATERS, Box 318, New Castle, UT 81647.
Positions: Hand knitting of sweaters.
Requirements: Must be local resident.

LITTLE LAMBS, 4742 Herrin Rd., N.E., Salem, OR 97305.
Positions: Hand knitting of sweaters.
Requirements: Must be local resident.

A Closer Look: H.O.M.E.

No one ever said it is easy to live in Maine. The weather is harsh, the land rocky and hard to till, and jobs are not easy to come by.

Nonetheless, Mainers have always stuck together, not just for survival, but to defend their way of life in their staunch New England style.

It was in 1970 when the first Bangor shoe factory stopped providing work for home stitchers. In this mostly rural area, employees, almost all of them women, were faced with little hope beyond welfare and poverty.   Oe of those women was Sister Lucy Poulin, a Carmelite nun living in a convent in nearby Orland. Sister Lucy was determined not to let unemployment destroy her or her neighbors. She set about organizing a cooperative of crafts people and called it H.O.M.E., or Homeworkers Organized for More Employment. The original purpose was to provide a marketing outlet for homemade products.

H.O.M.E. may well go down in history as the classic community effort. Since those fragile beginnings, it has grown into a comprehensive organization "engaged in rural economic development and social reconstruction." Today it boasts 3,500 members.

Local handcrafts are sold at the H.O.M.E. crafts store and through a mail-order catalog that is published annually.

The facilities include much more than that, though. The Learning Center has child-care, an accredicted high school and adult education courses. Farming skills are taught and four craft workshops teach woodworking, pottery, weaving, leatherwork and more. There are two hospitality houses for those in extreme need. Seven 1,200 sq. ft. homes have been built for what would otherwise have been homeless families. Each is located on 10 acres, complete with a greenhouse.

H.O.M.E. set out early to build a stable economy based on the area's only natural resources, wood and land. It owns an extensive wood lot which provides firewood to the elderly and poor. There is also a sawmill which provides lumber for the building projects and, in the process, a number of jobs too.

There are 65 families involved in the Down Home Farms Project, which helps members improve their farming skills and supplies animals to poor farm families. Since 1983, the Project has operated a year-around market to sell local produce, dried fruit and nuts, and grains and seeds both to the co-op members and the general public.

It took 13 years but H.O.M.E. now operates in the black. 1983 was the year when the co-op began breaking even in all departments. Considering the recession of 1981 and 1982, when the remaining shoe factories either closed their doors or sent their work to cheap labor markets abroad, becoming self-supporting was a major victory.

Hard work and persistance have paid off for thousands of Mainers in a community literally made up of home workers.

LIVING EARTH CRAFTS, 600 E. Todd Rd., Santa Rosa, CA 95407.
Positions: Production of several types of crafts. Most work consists of sewing bags, vinyl pieces, sheets, blankets and pad covers.
Requirements: Must own sewing machine. Must live in Santa Rosa. Experience is required.
Provisions: Materials are supplied. Workers are considered regular employees with medical and dental insurance, paid holidays and sick leave. Pays piece rates equal to an average of $8 an hour. Applications are kept on file indefinitely.

LUCINDA YATES, 402 Forest Ave., Portland, ME 04103.
Positions: Jewelry production.
Requirements: Must be local resident.

MAINE BRAND MFG., INC., P.O. Box 860, Houton, ME 04730
Positions: Stitching of gloves.
Requirements: Must be local resident and be skilled.

MAINE MAD HATTER, RFD # 1, Box 790, Augusta, ME 04330.
Positions: Knitting of ski hats.
Requirements: Must be local resident and be skilled.

MANDALA DESIGNS, RFD #1, Box 480, Starks, ME 04911.
Positions: Machine knitting of woolen outerwear including sweaters, jackets, socks, scarves, and hats.
Requirements: Prefers local knitters. Must be experienced and own knitting machine.
Provisions: Provides supplies and patterns. Pays piece rates.

MARCEAU SPORTS, 6600 France Ave. S., Ste 245, Minneapolis, MN 55435.
Positions: Knitting of outerwear.
Requirements: Must be local resident.

MC DESIGNS, 115 Altura Way, Greenbrae, CA 94904.
Positions: Hand knitters are used by sweater designer.
Requirements: Must be local resident. Professional level experience required. Apply with resume only.
Provisions: Pays piece rates.

MECA SPORTSWEAR, INC., 2363 University Ave., St. Paul MN 55114.
Positions: Embroidery.
Requirements: Must be local resident with experience.

MIDWEST SWISS EMBROIDERIES CO., INC., 5590 Northwest Highway, Chicago, IL 60630.
Positions: Embroidery.
Requirements: Must be local resident with skills and experience.

MORIARTIE'S HATS AND SWEATERS, Mountain Rd., Stowe, VT 05672.
Positions: Mrs. Moriartie started this company in the late '50's when she handknitted a hat for her son and almost single-handedly launched the New England home knitting industry as it is today. Moriartie's has a reputation for being the best hat and sweater store in the world. Home knitters make hats, Christmas stockings, ornaments, and sweaters.

Work is done on hand-operated machines. Company sells products wholesale as well as retail. Currently has 30 permanent home workers.

Requirements: Must be local resident in order to come in once a week to get supplies. Must own machine.

Provisions: Knitters can select designs, patterns and yarns from stock and make as many or as few items as they like. Can accept custom orders, too. "Each knitter has something they like to do especially and they usually stick to it. Some prefer to knit hats that only take 25 minutes to complete. Others prefer sweaters that take much longer. It's up to them." Pays piece rates.

"We treat our home workers with respect. We invite them to our Christmas parties, for instance, to keep them involved with the rest of the company. We don't cheat them either. If someone makes a mistake, the company absorbs the loss." --Lace-Trends, Inc.

MOUNTAINSIDE INDUSTRIES, INC., 838 Cliff St., P.O. Box 181, Shamokin, PA 17872.

Positions: Sewing of double drawstring pouches.

Requirements: Must be local resident. Must qualify as Pennsylvania industrial home worker (be either disabled or need to care for invalid family member).

Provisions: Pays piece rates.

MOUNTAIN LADIES & EWE, INC., Box 391 Route 7, Manchester Village, VT 05254.

Positions: Knitters make ski hats and sweaters. Products are sold both retail and wholesale. Currently has 25 permanent home workers.

Requirements: Prefers workers that live within a 60-mile radius of Manchester Village. Must own knitting machine. Pick up and delivery of supplies and finished work is required of each knitter.

Provisions: Specific training is provided. All supplies are provided.

Pays production rates, but workers are considered regular employees and receive basic benefits provided by law. Inquiries are welcome from qualified applicants.

NEUMA AGINS DESIGN, INC., Main St., Southfield, MA 01105.

Positions: Embroidery of sweaters according to custom orders. Decorations may also be applied. Currently has over 200 home workers.

Requirements: Must have experience and do quality work. Local residents only.

Provisions: Pays about $3.65 an hour.

NEW JERSEY CASKET COMPANY, INC., 1350 Clinton St., Hoboken, NJ 07030.

Positions: Hand sewing of velvet material for caskets.

Requirements: Must have experience doing quality work. Must be local resident.

Provisions: Pays piece rates.

NORTH OF BOSTON, P.O. Box 1308, Stowe, VT 05672.
Positions: Knitting sweaters for wholesale orders. Currently has 30 home workers.
Requirements: Must own knitting machine and live in the area. Workers are required to pick up and deliver supplies and finished work or use the mail for that purpose.
Provisions: Some training is provided. Pays piece rates.

NOVELTY NITWEAR, Route 100, Box 115, South Londonderry, VT 05155.
Positions: Knitting of outerwear.
Requirements: Must be local resident with experience.

PANHANDLE KNITS, 2101 Pine St., Sandpoint, ID 83864.
Positions: Knitting of outerwear.
Requirements: Must be local resident and experienced.

PARK SCHIFFLI, INC., 9221 Kennedy Blvd., North Bergen, NJ 07047.
Positions: Hand cutters trim embroidery products.
Requirements: Must be local residents.

PATTY ANNE, 1212 Crespi Dr., Pacifica, CA 94044.
Positions: This well-established retailer/wholesaler of children's apparel and gifts uses home-bases seamstresses. There are different jobs for different types of machines; appliques, blind hems, etc.
Requirements: Industrial overlock machine is necessary. Experience is required. Must live within reasonable proximity to Pacifica.
Provisions: Pick up and delivery provided. Pays piece rates equal to about $7.50 an hour for an average part-time income of $75 to $100 a week. Work tends to be seasonal.

PAX KNITS, 316 E. Louisiana, Denver, CO 80210.
Positions: Knitting of outerwear.
Requirements: Must be local resident with experience.

PENELOPE'S WEB, P.O. Box 326, North Anson, ME 04958.
Positions: Knitting of outerwear.
Requirements: Must be local resident with good skills.

PERIWINKLE, 555 De Haro #380, San Francisco, CA 94107.
Positions: Hand knitting of high fashion sweaters that match dresses, jackets, and coats. No finishing involved.
Requirements: Must be experienced, especially with all types of special yarns. Only local residents will be considered.
Provisions: Supplies and patterns are provided. For knitters that live too far away to come in regularly, supplies will be sent UPS. Pays by the piece, ranging from $30 to $55 each.

P.R.W. DESIGNS, P.O. Box 684, Union Town, OH 46685.
Positions: Knitting and sewing of outerwear.
Requirements: Must be experienced and local resident.
Provisions: Pays piece rates.

PRINTEX LABELS, INC., 55 Wanaque Avenue, Pompton Lakes, NJ 07442.
Positions: Inspection of woven and printed labels and hand pinking/cutting.

Requirements: Must be local resident in order to pick up and deliver supplies and finished work. Experience is necessary.
Provisions: Pays hourly wage.

QUIK CUT, INC., 2101 Kerrigan Ave., Union City, NJ 07087.
Positions: Machine and hand cutting of embroidery products.
Requirements: Must be local resident.

ROCKY MOUNTAIN WOOLENS, 1605 31st Avenue, Seattle, WA 98122.
Positions: Knitting of outerwear.
Requirements: Must be local resident with experience.

SAN FRANCISCO JEWELRY CO., P.O. Box 10267, San Rafael, CA 94912.
Positions: Hand assembly of beaded earrings. This company has been in business since July of 1987 and now has over 80 wholesale and retail accounts around the U.S. All workers are independent contractors and must purchase their own supplies and take care of their own taxes. Glass beads and findings will be supplied by the company if there is no source available where the worker lives. Postage costs are shared by the company.
Requirements: Ability to follow instructions, work with small pieces, and complete at least one unit (25 pairs) of earrings every 70 days.
Provisions: Pays piece rates up to $245..65 per week. Can live anywhere in U.S.

SANDCASTLE CREATIONS, P.O. Box 563, Newport, OR 97365.
Positions: Processing mohair for doll hair. This consists of washing and combing.
Requirements: This is a simple hand cleaning procedure that requires no special skills or equipment. Must purchase beginners practice package for $29.95 (fully refundable).
Provisions: Complete instructions are provided as is telephone consultation. Pay piece rates amounting to a maximum of $450 per week. Send self-addressed envelope for information. Can live anywhere.

SHE SHELLS, 2996 Koapaka St., Honolulu, HI 96819.
Positions: Hand assembly of shell jewelry.
Requirements: Must be local resident.

SHUBE'S MFG., INC., 2010 Ridgecrest SE, Bernatlilo, NM 87108.
Positions: Jewelry production.
Requirements: Must be local resident.

JANE SMITH LIMITED, 533 E. Hopkins, Aspen, CO 81611.
Positions: Hand knitting of outerwear.
Requirements: Must be local resident.

SNO KNITS BY DETHA, Box 713, Basalt, CO 81621.
Positions: Hand knitting of outerwear.
Requirements: Must be local resident.

SNOWSHOE CREATIONS, 764 Cedar Ct., Rifle, CO 81650.
Positions: Hand kniting of outerwear.
Requirements: Must be local resident.

SNOWY RIVER WOOLENS, Round Mountain Loop Rd., Box 215, Clackamas, OR 97028.
Positions: Hand knitting of outerwear.
Requirements: Must be local resident.

SOHO CREATIONS, a Division of Aldegrino, Inc., 1133 Broadway, Room 430, New York, NY 10010.
Positions: Part-time sewing of sweat bands.
Requirements: Professional experience required. Must live nearby.
Provisions: Pays piece rates. Currently has a waiting list.

SOUTHERN GLOVE MFG. CO., INC., Highway 321 South, Conover, NC 28613.
Positions: Stitching of gloves.
Requirements: Must be local resident.

ST. MARYS WOOLENS, Bruce Mountain, St. Marys, IA 50241.
Positions: Knitting and hand stitching of outerwear; sweaters, hats, and scarves. Company is described as "vertically integrated" since it does everything from raising special sheep for the color and texture of their wool to marketing the finished products through retail outlets and catalogs. Currently has 10 home knitters.
Requirements: Must live nearby and provide samples of quality work.
Provisions: Training and supplies are provided. Knitting machine will be rented to worker if necessary. Knitters are independent contractors so there are no benefits. Pays piece rates. Work is part-time: average annual income is $7,000. "Inquiries are okay, but we have a very low turnover rate and a waiting list."

STONE KNITTING MILLS, P.O. Box 2110, 925 Red Sandstone Rd., Vail, CO 81657.
Positions: Home-based knitting of outerwear.
Requirements: Must be local resident.

STOWE HAT COMPANY, RR #2, Box 3825, Shaw Hill, VT 05672.
Positions: Hand knitting of outerwear.
Requirements: Must be local resident.

STOWE WOOLENS, RR 1, Box 1420, Stowe, VT 05672.
Positions: Knitting of outerwear; sweaters, hats, and scarves. Currently has 40 to 50 home knitters.
Requirements: Must be experienced and have own knitting machine. Must live within an hour's drive from Stowe.
Provisions: Pays piece rates.

STREAMLINE INDUSTRIES, 845 Stuart Avenue, Garden City, NY 11530.
Positions: Hand sewing cloth onto buttons and buckles.
Requirements: Must live nearby.
Provisions: Pays piece rates.

SUITCASE BOUTIQUE, 12228 Spring Place Court, Maryland Heights, MO 63043.
Positions: Suitcase Boutique is a home party business. Company buys many types of handcrafted items included stuffed animals, wood crafts, toys, soft sculpture, framed

pictures, and cross-stitch.
Requirements: Crafters should send photo of product and description.

SUMMIT MARKETING, INC., 15260 Herriman Blvd., Noblesville, IN 46060.
Positions: Embroidery.
Requirements: Must be local resident with skills and experience.

> ## "Talented new writers are especially sought."
> ### --Warner Press, Inc.

SWISS MAID EMBLEMS, INC., 26 Industrial Ave., Fairview, NJ 07022.
Positions: Manual trimming and merrowing of embroidered appliques and emblems. Also bagging and counting of emblems. Currently has about a dozen home workers.
Requirements: Must be local resident.
Provisions: Training is provided. Pick up and delivery of supplies and finished work will be provided if necessary. Workers are considered regular employees and are paid hourly wages plus benefits. Inquiries are welcome.

TAVERNON PHOTO ENGRAVING COMPANY, 27 First Avenue, Paterson, NJ 07514.
Positions: Company makes silk screen for wallpaper and fabric. Hand work consists of color separation of textile designs. Freelance artists do all the design work.
Requirements: Must be local in order to pick up and deliver supplies and finished work. Experience is required.
Provisions: Pay depends on the colors and intricacy of the design.

THEATRICAL ACCESSORIES, INC., 2102 Harrison St., Findlay, OH 45840.
Positions: Embroideries, button and buckle manufacturing, gloves and mittens industries, and jewely manufacturing.
Requirements: Must be local resident and be skilled.

JOSEPH TITONE & SONS, INC., Jacksonville Rd., Burlington, NJ 08016.
Positions: Cutting, tying, and packing of hair nets. Currently has 10 home workers.
Requirements: Must be local residents.
Provisions: Training and appropriate equipment is provided. Pick up and delivery of supplies and finished work is provided weekly. Home workers are considered regular employees and are given basic benefits in addition to being paid piece rates equal to about $3.40 an hour.

TOMORROW TODAY CORPORATION, P.O. Box 6125, Westfield, MA 01085.
Positions: Hand work consists of tying bows and working with flowers to make decorations. Currently has 23 home workers.
Requirements: Must live in Westfield.
Provisions: Pays minimum wage.

TOP NOTCH KNITS, 12840 N.E. 88th, Kirkland, WA 98033.
Positions: Knitting and sewing of complete garments. Currently has 50 home workers.
Requirements: Must own knitting machine (any type is okay). Will only accept applications from experienced local residents.
Provisions: Pick up and delivery of supplies and finished work is provided. Pays production rates.

TOTSY MANUFACTURING COMPANY, INC., Cabot & Bigelow Streets, Holyoke, MA 10140.
Positions: Sewing of doll clothes and accessories. Currently has about 20 home workers, a number which has decreased over the last few years.
Requirements: Must be local resident. Experience and sewing machine are required.
Provisions: Pick up and delivery is provided. Pays minimum wage.

TRI-STATE GLOVE COMPANY, 429 South Fifth St., Cushocton, OH 43812.
Positions: Home manufacturing of gloves and mittens.
Requirements: Must be local resident and be skilled.

TWIN ASPEN AND COMPANY, P.O. Box 1758, Glenwood Springs, CO 81602.
Positions: Home-based knitting of outerwear.
Requirements: Must be local resident and be skilled.

TWIN CITY BRIDAL SHOP, P.O. Box 118, Mount Zion, IL 62549.
Positions: Sewing of specialty orders.
Requirements: Experience working with fine fabrics is required. Must be local resident. Must obtain home worker certificate from Illinois Department of Labor.
Provisions: Pays piece rates.

UBG'S IDEA FACTORY, P.O. Box 906, Kalispell, MT 59903.
Positions: This is a store that carries only handmade crafted items, preferably by homebased artisans.
Requirements: Send samples or photos of products along with pricing information and quantities available.
Provisions: Buys outright in small quantities.

UNCOMMON TOUCH EMBROIDERIES, INC., 429 - 62nd St., West New York, NJ 07093.
Positions: Hand mending of embroidery samples. Currently has up to 30 home workers.
Requirements: Must be local resident.
Provisions: Pays piece rates.

UNDERWOOD'S FURNITURE GALLERIES, 2417 N. University St., Peoria, IL 61605.
Positions: ABout half a dozen home workers sew draperies and accessories for this retail interior design and furniture store.
Requirements: Must have machinery and experience. Local residents only. Must obtain home worker certificate from Illinois Department of Labor.
Provisions: Pays piece rates.

UNIQUE 1, P.O. Box 744, 2 Bayview Street, Camden, ME 04843.
Positions: Knitting of sweaters using both wool and cotton yarn for retail shop.

Currently has 14 home workers.
Requirements: Must be experienced and be a local resident.
Provisions: Training is provided. If home worker doesn't own a knitting machine, Unique 1 will lease one. Pays piece rates. "Camden is a tourist town, so the summer is the best time for us, especially for custom orders."

VERMONT COZIES, RR 2, Box 1610, Stowe, VT 05672.
Positions: Hand knitting.
Requirements: Must be resident of Stowe.

VERMONT ORIGINALS, INC., RR1, Box 370, East Harkwick, VT 05836.
Positions: Knitting of outerwear.
Requirements: Must be local resident with skills and experience.

THE VILLAGE OF THE SMOKY HILLS, Osage, MN 56570.
Positions: Crafts of all kinds made by local home-based craftspeople are sold at the Village. Currently has over 350 home workers.

WAGON WHEEL WESTERN WEAR, 2765 W. Jefferson, Springfield, IL.
Positions: This is a custom shop that has home workers sew together pre-cut pieces.
Requirements: Machinery and experience required. Must be local resident. Must obtain home worker certificte from Illinois Department of Labor.
Provisions: Pays piece rates.

WAIN MANUFACTURING CORPORATION, 589 Essex St., Lynn, MA 01901.
Positions: Stitching and thread trimming of eye glass cases.
Requirements: Must be local resident with experience.
Provisions: Training and machinery are provided. Pays $4 an hour.

WASHINGTON GARTER CORP., 195 Front St., Brooklyn, NY 11201.
Positions: Sewing and hand assembly of ladies garters and mens suspenders. Up to 35 home workers are employed.
Requirements: Must live nearby and be experienced.
Provisions: Pays piece rates.

WEEKS, INC., P.O. Box 302, Noxapater, MS 39346.
Positions: Home-based knitting of outerwear.
Requirements: Must be local resident and be skilled.

WEST HILL WEAVERS, Box 108, Stowe, VT 05672.
Positions: Knitting and sewing of outerwear. Also some handwoven clothing and crafts. Currently has about 30 home workers located all over the state.
Requirements: Must own and have full knowledge of proper machinery. Pick up and delivery of supplies and finished work is the responsibility of the home worker; therefore must be local.
Provisions: Training for particular designs is provided. Pays piece rates. Inquiries are welcome. "When we're hiring, we're hiring. Otherwise we will keep your name on file for future work."

WIRTH MANUFACTURING CO., INC., 335 Hamilton St., Allentown, PA 18101.
Positions: Sewing of children's tops.

Requirements: Must be local resident. Must qualify as Pennsylvania industrial home worker (be either disabled or need to care for invalid family member.)
Provisions: Sewing machines are provided. Pays piece rates.

ZAUDER BROTHERS, INC., 10 Henry St., Freeport, NY 11520.
Positions: Hand work involved in the manufacture of wigs, toupes, and theatrical makeup. Up to eight home workers are employed here.
Requirements: Must have specific experience with this kind of work. Must be local resident.

Computer-Based Opportunities

This section includes any situation that requires a computer to get the job done. This doesn't necessarily mean that you must own your own equipment. In the case of typesetting input, for example, many companies provide computer terminals to their home keyers. On the other hand, a contract programmer not only needs to own a computer, but often several different computers.

By its nature, computerized work generally pays more than office work that is done on conventional typewriters. Therefore, if you are a very good typist, you may find it to your advantage to transfer your typing skills to the computer keyboard. Word processors are in great demand to handle assignments from small businesses and huge corporations alike. It'll take a few months to get the hang of it all; the computer itself, the software, and the printer. There are classes available at most community colleges and vocational schools. If you're sharp, you can get paid while you learn by signing on with a temporary help agency. Kelly Services and Manpower, to name just two, have excellent training programs–including cross-training on different systems–available to anyone who is on the roster and available for work.

Experienced typists with exceptional accuracy can make money by becoming a typesetting input operator. Typesetting is a job that was done on very expensive equipment in composition shops before the personal computer came along. Now it is common for home-based operators to do the job at home by typing material into the computer and embedding code into the text that will instruct the shop's specialized printer to use certain fonts, type size or style, and special characters. Most shops have their own special code and train typists in how to use it. It is most common for typesetters that handle books (rather than advertising or brochures) to use home keyers. Typesetting input operators are paid for each character typed and average earnings run from $10 to $25 an hour.

Contract programmers will find the field a little crowded these days. There is still a lot of work in converting programs to run on different computers than they were written for, but that work will soon disappear. Computers are being programmed to do the conversions automatically. Writing programs to specifications pays better, but only very experienced programmers get this work. The key to getting work as a programmer is to continue learning about languages, compilers, and systems design. Employers like programmers who are enthusiastic about what the company is doing, pay attention to deadlines, document their work properly, and submit bug-free programs.

ABILITY GROUP, 1700 K St., NW, Washington, D.C. 20006.
Positions: Word processing specializing in transcription of medical, legal and verbatim tapes. Occasional assignments are mostly overflow.
Requirements: Must be local resident. Word processing equipment is required. Any major word processing software is okay as long as it is IBM compatible so that it can be converted. Experienced professionals only.

ACADEMY SOFTWARE, Box 6277, San Rafael, CA 94903.
Positions: Contract programmers and technical writers. Contract programmers are used for conversions from Commodore software to Apple, Atari, and IBM. Also buys unique educational software from freelancers. Some original programming to company specifications available. Technical writers work on user manuals.
Requirements: Must be local resident. Extensive experience required.
Provisions: Payment for both positions can be by the job, by the hour, or on a royalty basis. Credit is given to both in most cases.

ADDISON-WESLEY PUBLISHING CO., Jacob Way, Reading, MA 01867.
Positions: Contract programmers. Company publishes over 100 programs for the Apple, IBM, and Macintosh. Freelance programmers can submit educational programs for consideration or seek assignments in conversions or original programming to company guidelines.
Requirements: Send resume indicating particular expertise and equipment availability and knowledge.
Provisions: Assignments pay by the project.

ADVANCED AUTOMATION ASSOC., 21 Alpha Rd., Chelmsford, MA 01824.
Positions: About 25 home-based keyboarders input data for this data management service.

ALPHA MICROSYSTEMS, 3501 Sunflower, Box 25059, Santa Ana, CA 92799.
Positions: Contract programmers for Alpha Micro computers only. Contracts include vertical appilcations in specific business areas.
Requirements: Resume and references required.

ALTERNATE SOURCE, 704 North Pennsylvania, Lansing, MI 48906.
Positions: Contract programmers. Company seeks submissions of vertical applications software for any MS-DOS or CP/M computer. Submissions must include complete documentation and be bug-free.
Requirements: Send letter of interest that describes finished software. Guidelines are available for SASE.
Provisions: Pays 20% royalties.

AMERICAN EXPRESS BANK, LTD., American Express Plaza, New York, NY 10004.
Positions: Word processors.
Requirements: Must be local, physically handicapped and disabled. Job requires transcription skills.
Provisions: Complete training is provided. Equipment provided includes Wang word processing terminals, Lanier central dictation system, and Exxon telecopier. Telephone lines link the home work station to company headquarters on Wall Street. A company supervisor can dictate into the system from anywhere; likewise a home worker is able to

access the system any time 24 hours a day to transcribe the dictation. The finished product in hard copy form is then sent back to headquarters via the telecopier. All activity is identified and monitored through the Control Center. "Project Homebound" currently has 10 full-time regular employees of American Express.

AMERICAN STRATFORD, Putney, Box 810, Brattleboro, VT 05301.
Positions: Typesetting input operators. Currently has 14 home keyers.
Requirements: Must be local resident. Must own computer and be competent word processor.

ANDENT, INC., 1000 North Avenue, Waukegan, IL 60085.
Positions: Contract programmers. Company publishes business software for the Apple II series. Submissions of original programs are accepted for consideration. Some contract programming, mostly conversions, is also available from time to time.
Requirements: Send proposal before submitting program. Work samples and references required for contract work.
Provisions: Contracts pay by the project. Original programs accepted for publication are either bought outright or royalties are paid.

APPALACHIAN COMPUTER SERVICES, Highway 25 South, P.O. Box 140, London, KY 40741.
Positions: Appalachian Computer Services is among a growing number of service bureaus that has solved the problem of stabilizing workflow with a home work program. The initial pool of cottage keyers was formed out of former in-house employees. Most of them had left their jobs because they needed to be at home with their families. The program accomplished what it was supposed to. The workflow went smoothly, the keyers were happy with the arrangement (no one dropped out), and the company overhead fell. Now that Appalachian Computer Services is sure the home work program is the solution they've been looking for, plans are underway to expand the program to an ultimate goal of 200 home keyers. These additional workers will be hired from outside the company.
Requirements: Since there are no telecommunications available, all recruiting will have to be done within the township of London. The only requirement will be a typing speed of 45 wpm. Experienced applicants will spend two days in-house learning to use the Multitech PC. Those with no experience in data entry will spend an additional 3 days in the company's standard training program. There is no pay for time spent in training. Each worker goes into the office to pick up the work and receive instructions. When the job is finished, he or she returns the work on disks (which are provided).
Provisions: The cottage keyers are all treated as part-time employees, not independent contractors. Each works a minimum of 20 hours a week. No one works over 30 hours a week at any time so the part-time status remains intact. There are no benefits due to this part-time status; however, the company is looking into ways of providing some benefits as the program progresses. In the meantime, there are production bonuses offered in addition to the guaranteed hourly wage. The equipment, Multitech PCs, are provided at no charge.

AQUARIUS PEOPLE MATERIALS, INC., Box 128, Indian Rocks Beach, FL 34635.
Positions: Contract programmers. Company publishes educational software for all grade levels. Original programs will be considered for publication. Contracts are

available for conversions.
Requirements: Must be very experienced with IBM or Radio Shack equipment.

ARTSCI, INC., P.O. Box 1848, Burbank, CA 91505.
Positions: Contract programmers to translate programs between IBM and Macintosh.
Programmer's guidelines are available only to those who send acceptable resumes.
Requirements: Resume and references required.
Provisions: Pays by the project.

ARTWORX SOFTWARE COMPANY, 1844 Penfield Rd., Penfield, NY 14526.
Positions: Programmers are contracted to do conversions from other computers to major
brand computers.
Requirements: Resume, work samples, and references required.
Provision: Pays by the job.

ATC SOFTWARE, 804 Jordon Lane, Huntsville, AL 35816.
Positions: Contract programmers. Original programs are considered for publication;
any type of business application software for AT&T, IBM, or CP/M computers. Only
programs written in C, BASIC, Cobol, dBase or Fortran will be considered. Also assigns
contracts for programming in these languages. There are programmers guides for coding
available for each of the five languages for $20 each or $79 for all five.
Requirements: Extensive knowledge and experience required. Resume and references
required.
Provisions: Pay methods vary.

AWARD SOFTWARE, 130 Knowles Drive, Los Gatos, CA 95030.
Positions: Contract programmers write data management programs to company
specifications.
Requirements: Prefers local programmers. Must have extensive knowledge of BIOS
and IBM, NEC, Sperry, or Heath/Zenith. Submit resume and references.
Provisions: Pay methods vary according to project.

BANTAM ELECTRONIC PUBLISHING, 666 Fifth Ave., New York, NY 10003.
Positions: Typesetting of book manuscripts.
Requirements: Must be local resident. Equipment, experience, and references are
required.

BELJAN, LTD., 2870 Baker Road, Dexter, MI 48130.
Positions: Beljan has been using home workers in its book typography business for 30
years. There are now 6 typesetting input operators and 2 proofreaders.
Requirements: Must be local resident in order to pick up and deliver work. Fast and
accurate typing skills required.
Provisions: Computers and training provided. Work comes from overflow from the
plant and is part-time only.

BIONIC FINGERS, 312 South Adams #3, Glendale, CA 91205.
Positions: Medical transcribers.
Requirements: Minimum of three years experience in general, acute care, and hospital
medical transcription is required. Must own word processor and transcribing machine
(standard or micro okay). Must live in the area.
Provisions: Pays by the line. Some benefits available. Courier service picks up and

Close Up: F-International

F-International, Berkhamsted, England, is not only the single largest company in the world that employs primarily home-based workers, but it is also one of the oldest to do so.

It was founded in 1962 by Steve Shirley, who was at the time a Sr. Assistant Programmer at ICT. She was also expecting her first child.

Even back then, the world of computer programming moved so fast that a career could be ruined in the time it takes to have a baby. Since there were no opportunities for her to continue work, Mrs. Shirley started her own computer consultancy and software house, F-International. ("F" stands for freelance.)

Today, 24 years later, the company has over 1,200 workers, 90% of whom are home-based. Positions for programmers, spec writers, estimators, sales executives, telemarketers, and managers are included.

Employees are recruited through ads placed in the trade press and also through recommendations of friends and client's friends. Publicity brings in applicants, too. Sometimes, posters are used touting the flexibility of home work as an enticement to would-be employees.

Though the firm has an open-door policy regarding new applicants, the requirements are by no means lax.

Even with a tremendous shortage of qualified computer personnel, a minimum of four years of experience is required. Just as important is the requirement of credibility. F-International needs to know that its people can work with a minimum amount of supervision. 13.5 years of experience is average for their personnel.

In return, workers have as much flexibility as they need. They have the unique opportunity to progress in their careers in whatever way they see fit. For women this has proven to be particularly important, and women here move into management positions much faster than in conventional companies.

What holds the company together in a fast-paced industry when its employees are spread throughout several countries? In any one month there are 250 projects going on for about 150 clients at at time! A self-designed management auditing system keeps the company machine running smoothly. The gears which turn and mesh together are committees representing every aspect of the business. They meet regularly to discuss management, project, and operational problems. All the committees work with each other at some point and issue follow-up reports. Everybody knows what's going on all of the time, so there's no room for slippage. All of this internal communication is an absolute must for the success of the company.

And it works. Annual growth is a healthy 30% and F-International is looking to expand throughout the rest of Europe with new services, such as their newly designed telecommunications networks.

At the same time, the rest of the world is watching. Delegations from all over—Australia, Japan, the U.S.--have come to learn from these pioneers of telecommuting.

Spokeswoman Rosie Symons says, "The home work force will grow quite quickly in the next five to ten years, mostly due to the availability of cheaper equipment."

Having an established model of success like F-International can't help but speed the process.

delivers work as far away as Orange County, "but only for top notch transcribers!".

BI-TECH ENTERPRISES, INC., 10 Carlough Road, Bohemia, NY 11716.
Positions: Contract programmers write communications and database software according to company specifications for Radio Shack, IBM, and Epson computers.
Requirements: Must be local resident. Extensive experience required. Submit resume and references.
Provisions: Pays by the project.

BLACK DOT, INC., 6115 Official Road, Crystal Lake IL 60014.
Positions: Typesetting input operators. Company has a very long waiting list.
Requirements: All operators are independent contractors and own their own equipment. Previous typesetting experience is required. Local residents only.

BLUE CROSS/BLUE SHIELD OF MARYLAND, 1946 Greenspring Drive, Timonium, MD 21093.
Positions: Cottage keyers (data entry operators) for coding health forms.
Requirements: Local residents only. Considerable experience is required.
Provisions: Part-time work only; partial benefits.

BLUE CROSS/BLUE SHIELD OF SOUTH CAROLINA, Columbia, SC 29219.
Positions: Local cottage keyers (data entry operators) for coding health claims. Full-time, 8-hour days. Openings are offered first to in-house employees, who are preferred for their company experience, but will also hire from outside applicants. Prefers to train in-house for 6 to 12 months if possible. Currently has over 100 workers.
Requirements: Must live in the area.
Provisions: Pays by the line on computer. Training and equipment (including computer and modem) is provided. Home workers are considered part-timers and receive virtually no benefits; employer/employee relations are excellent, however, and the program is considered by all parties concerned to be very successful. Inquires are welcome, but you should expect to be put on a waiting list.

BOYD PRINTING COMPANY, INC., 49 Sheridan Avenue, Albany, NY 12210.
Positions: Typesetting input operators.
Requirements: Must be local resident. Experienced operators with own equipment only.
Provisions: Pays by the word.

BRAUN-BRUMFIELD, INC., 100 North Staebler Rd., Ann Arbor, MI 48106.
Positions: Typesetting input operators for book typography.
Requirements: Local residents only. Experience and equipment required.
Provisions: Pays by the keystroke.

B/T COMPUTING CORPORATION, Box 1465, Euless, TX 76039.
Positions: Contract programmers. Company publishes business software for Macintosh.
Requirements: Thorough knowledege of Macintosh and Assembly language programming. Submit resume, work samples, and references.
Provisions: Pays royalties.

BUREAU OF OFFICE SERVICES, INC., 3815 N. Cicero, Chicago, IL 60641.

Positions: About 55 home-based workers do typing, transcription, and word processing for business customers.
Requirements: Must own PC and be experienced. Local residents only.

BUSINESS GRAPHICS, 3314 Baser N.E., Albuquerque, NM 87107.
Positions: Typesetting input operators.
Requirements: Must be local resident. Experience and computer required.

CARLISLE COMMUNICATIONS, 2530 Kerper Blvd., Dubuque, IA 52001.
Positions: Typesetting input operators. Currently has 17 home keyers.
Requirements: Must live in Dubuque in order to pick up and deliver manuscripts and disks. Must be excellent typist with high rate of accuracy.
Provisions: Training and equipment provided. Pays by the character.

CATERED GRAPHICS, 9823 Mason Avenue, Chatsworth, CA 91311.
Positions: Typesetting input operators for book typography.
Requirements: Local residents only. Must be experienced in this business. Must own IBM equipemnt. Apply with resume.

CHECKMATE TECHNOLOGY, INC., P.O. Box 250, Tempe, AZ 85281.
Positions: Contract programmers and technical writers. Company manufactures peripherals such as RAM disks and memory cards for the Apple IIE series, Macintosh, and IBM. Software is needed by company to enhance marketability of programs written to company specifications and also for conversion from Apple programs to others. Technical writers may be needed for documentation.

CIRCLE GRAPHICS, INC., 7484-K Candlewood Rd., Harmans, MD 21077.
Positions: Typesetting input operators. Company has 12 operators on call.
Requirements: Must be local resident in order to pick up and deliver work. Computer required; any brand okay.
Provisions: Pays by the character. Will train for company code.

COGHILL COMPOSITION COMPANY, 1627 Elmdale Avenue, Richmond, VA 23224.
Positions: Typesetting input operators. Company handles all types of commercial typesetting jobs.
Requirements: Must own IBM compatiable and have telecommunications capabilities. Local residents only.
Provisions: Pays by the character.

COMMERCIAL PRINTERS, 3 Hilltop Road. Norwich, CT 06360.
Positions: Typesetting input operators. Company uses combination of courier and telecommunications to transfer work.
Requirements: Local residents only. Must be fast and accurate typist. Prefers people with computer experience.
Provisions: Equipment provided. Operation is small so opportunities are limited.

COMPANION HEALTHCARE, 300 Arbor Lake Drive, Suite 800, Columbia, MD 29223.
Positions: Medical reviewers.

Requirements: Must be registered nurse and own a personal computer and a modem.
Provisions: Workers are independent contractors but retirement program is available.

HOMER   BY RICH TENNANT

COMPUTER CENTRAL CORPORATION, 1 Westbury Square, St. Charles, MO
63301.
Positions: Computer Central has been using home-based data entry operators since
1969. While 20 people do work in the office, about 50 work at home.
Requirements: Must be local resident. Must pick up and deliver own work daily. Must
be able to type 60 wpm accurately. Must be able to work five hours a day.
Provisions: A two-day training session is provided to learn the equipment and work
procedures. PCs are provided. Social Security and unemployment insurance coverage
is provided. Pays piece rates which equals about $4 an hour. There is an opportunity to
earn more with production bonuses for fast and accurate keyboarders.

COMPUTER SUPPORT SERVICES UNLIMITED, 10573 West Pico Blvd., Suite
215, Los Angeles, CA 90064.
Positions: This is a service bureau for customer support reps. Reps will work as on-call
consultants either directly for this company or subcontracted to other companies.
Expertise in any hardware or software (especially dBase and word processors) will be
considered. Some freelance programming will be assigned as well.
Requirements: No experience as a customer support rep is necessary. For the time
being, opportunities exist only in the state of California; can be anywhere in the state. To
be considered, send your name, address, phone number, and request an application
questionnaire.
Provisions: Pays a percentage of the contract. Company president, Judith Woods says,
" I am building a network of people I can call upon (at home). Flexible scheduling will
be offered so this work won't interfere with any other work the rep might be doing."

COMPUTERWARE, Box 668, Encinitas, CA 92024.
Positions: Freelance and contract programmers. Computerware has been publishing
software for Radio Shack and other 6809 computers since 1975.
Originally all programs were entertainment oriented, now they are mostly business.
Software is now being written for IBM PCs as well. All programming is done in

Assembly language. Freelancers are encouraged to submit programs with documentation for consideration. Also assigns programming contracts.
Requirements: Freelancers can request Computerware's "Authorship Guidelines" before submitting program. All others submit resume, samples, and references.
Provisions: Pay methods vary.

CREATIVE GRAPHICS, INC., P.O. Box 6048, Allentown, PA 18103.
Positions: Typesetting input operators and proofreaders. Currently has 12 home keyers.
Requirements: Local residents only. Must be fast and accurate typist.
Provisions: Will train on terminal "only if we think they're worth it" . Provides Radio Shack equipment.

CREATIVE SOFTWARE, 101 1st St., #454, Los Altos, CA 94022.
Positions: Contract programmers for freelance submission of original educational and personal programs. Some conversions from computer to computer. Works with Apple and IBM computers.
Requirements: Submit finished bug-free program.

CYBERTRONIX, INC., 1171 Tower Rd. Schaumburg, IL 60173.
Positions: Cybertronix conducts surveys for market and social research by telephone. The difference here is that all of the telephone polling is accomplished with automatic telemarketing through the use of a central computer connected by hardware and software to thousands of personal computers. The PCs are owned and operated by independent "field coordinator licensees" in 90 locations nationwide. The job of setting up the computer in the morning and tabulating the results at the end of the day amounts to less than one hour of work each day. The results are sent via modem to the central computer daily.
Requirements: The basic cost of becoming a Cybertronix licensee is $6400 plus the cost of an Apple II computer system if you don't have one already. There is an additional annual fee of $240. Applicants must have a record of financial and personal stability and be currently employed full-time. Send resume.
Provisions: A minimum of $200 a month in business is guaranteed by the company and each licensee's area coordinator is supposed to provide an additional $500 worth of business. A network of salespeople is working to provide more. In addition, each licensee is encouraged to solicit new accounts.

DATA COMMAND, Box 548, Kankakee, IL 60901.
Positions: Contract programming. Company publishes high quality educational programming for the top five computers.
Requirements: Innovative thinking is most important here. New ideas in educational programming are highly sought after. You can merely submit a great idea for a new program or submit a resume and references for possible contract assignments to company specs.

DILITHIUM PRESS, Box 606, Beaverton, OR 07975
Positions: Company publishes educational and business programs for five top computers. All programs are written by freelancers.
Requirements: Send proposal with work samples and SASE.

DIRECT DATA, 1215 Francis Dr., Arlington Heights, IL 60005.
Positions: Direct Data utilizes the services of about two dozen independent contractors

that they call "professional personal computer operators." The actual work performed includes mostly word processing and desktop publishing.
Requirements: Must be a local resident. Equipment and experience are a must.

DISCWASHER, 4310 Transworld Road, Schiller Park, IL 60176.
Positions: Contract programmers and technical writers. Programming is usually conversion work, but company also assigns programs written to client's specifications. Technical writers are occasionally used for documentation.
Requirements: Must own and have thorough knowledge of Apple, IBM, Atari, Commodore, or CPM computer. Resume should indicate knowledge and experience with languages and operating systems. Include previous work experience and references.
Provisions: Pays by the job or by the hour.

EDWARDS BROTHERS, INC., 2500 State Street, Ann Arbor, MI 48106.
Positions: Typesetting input operators, proofreaders, and layout for book typography business.
Requirements: Local residents only. Must have necessary skills.
Provisions: Equipment and specific training provided. Home workers are considered company employees.

ELECTRONIC ARTS, 1820 Gateway Dr., San Mateo, CA 94404.
Positions: Contract programmers for conversion work. Also regularly backs talented software developers on original programs. Company mainly produces entertainment software for the home market. Some technical writing is assigned for documentation.
Requirements: Must have experience on equipment owned. Prefers Apple, Atari, IBM, or Commodore. Must have fervent interest in company's products. "We look for someone specifically suited to the project."

ELITE SOFTWARE DEVELOPMENT, INC., Drawer 1194, Bryan, TX 77806.
Positions: Contract programmers for program components such as algorythms. Currently has pool of six.
Requirements: Must own and have experience with IBM-AT or clone. Also has some CPM 8-bit work. Prefers programmers who properly test their work and are capable of writing their own documentation.
Provisions: Generally pays by the hour, total sum not to exceed predetermined amount.

ELIZABETH TYPESETTING COMPANY, 26 North 26th St., Kenilworth, NJ 07033.
Positions: Typesetting input operators for book typography. Work is transferred via modem and FAX.
Requirements: Local residents only. Accurate keyboard skills required.
Provisions: Equipment is provided. Pays by the character.

EN FLEUR CORPORATION, 2494 Sun Valley Circle, Silver Spring, MD 20906.
Positions: Contract programmers for program sub-routines.
Requirements: Should own and be extremely familiar with MacIntosh, HP, or IBM. Assembly is the language most often used. Send work samples with resume. All work must be well documented.
Provisions: Pays by the job.

EPS GROUP, INC., 1501 Guilford Ave., Baltimore, MD 21202.
Positions: Typesetting input operators for book typography. Currently has 8 home keyers.
Requirements: Local residents only. Skilled keyboarders only.
Provisions: Equipment and courier provided when necessary. Pays by the character.

EXSPEEDITE PRINTING SERVICE, 12201 Old Columbia Pike, Silver Spring, MD 20914.
Positions: Typesetting input operators for book typography.
Requirements: Must be local resident in order to pick up and deliver work. Experience and computer equipment required.
Provisions: Work is part-time from overflow. Pays by the character.

FEDERATION OF THE HANDICAPPED, Automated Office Services, 211 West 14th St., 2nd Floor, New York, NY 10011.
Positions: Automated Office Systems is the newest of the Federation's programs for homebound disabled workers. It is similar to the typing/transcription department, except that all workers use computers and telecommunicaitons equipment to perform the work.
Requirements: All positions require evaluation through lengthy interviews and personal counseling. All workers must live in New York City.
Provisions: Automated Office Services provides training in word processing procedures. Computers, telecommunication equipment and a phone-in dictation system are provided. All positions pay piece rates.
Disability insurance counseling is provided.

FIELD PREMIUM, INC., 385 Pleasant St., Watertown, MA 02173.
Positions: Data entry operators. Work consists of computer data entry (mostly names and addresses for mail order fulfillment). There are currently 21 home workers.
Requirements: Experience is required. Must be local resident.
Provisions: Equipment and pick up and delivery are provided. Pays piece rates.

GRAPHIC TYPESETTING, 5650 Jillson St., Los Angeles, CA 90040.
Positions: Typesetting input operators for work in textbook typography. Currently has 25 operators working all over the U.S.
Requirements: Must be former employee or come with recommendation from another book typography firm.

GREAT NECK TYPESETTING & DESIGN, 81 Middle Neck Rd., Great Neck, NY 11021.
Positions: This growing typesetting company is always on the lookout for experienced typesetters for text input. Work is book manuscript input only.
Requirements: Must have experience working on Veritype typesetting machine. Machine will be supplied. Work is delivered once a week and home worker must get it back to the plant once a week, therefore worker must live within a reasonable distance.
Provisions: Pays by the hour: $9 to $12 depending on ability.

GUILD PRINTING COMPANY, INC., 380 West 38th St., Los Angeles, CA 90037.
Positions: Typesetting input operators for book typography.
Requirements: Must be former in-house employee.

HARD SYSTEMS, 200 Stonehenge Lane, Carle Place, NY 11514.
Positions: This data processing service specializes in keeping inventories for major department stores. More than 400 home-based data processing employees and their managers work throughout Nassau and Suffolk counties.
Requirements: Must live in one of the two counties mentioned. Must own a personal computer. There is a 24-hour turn-around requirement and workers must pick up and return their work to the coumpany if they live in Nassau County or to a manager's home if they live in Suffolk County.
Provisions: Pays piece rates (by the line). Pay ranges from $4.50 to $10 an hour depending on the speed of the individual worker. Managers receive a base salary plus a 10 percent override on workers. This can amount to $10,000 to $15,000 for a 94-day cycle. This work is very seasonal and is therefore not available all the time. The best times to apply are July and August and again in January and February.

HRM SOFTWARE, 175 Tompkins Ave., Pleasantville, NY 10570.
Positions: Computer programmers for freelance submissions, computer to computer conversions, and company-directed programming. HRM publishes only interactive home education programs
Requirements: Experience programming on Apple, Commodore, or IBM. Freelancers can submit finished programs for consideration. All others submit resume, samples, and references.

ICOM SIMULATIONS, 1110 Lake Cook Rd., Buffalo Grove, IL 60090.
Positions: Contract programmers write original business application software according to company specifications.
Requirements: Thorough knowledge and experience required. Submit resume, references, and work samples.
Provisions: Pay methods vary.

IMPRESSIONS, INC., P.O. Box 3304, Madison, WI 53704.
Positions: Typesetting input operators for book typography.
Requirements: Local residents only. Excellent keyboarding skills are required. Must own computer equipment.
Provisions: Hours are flexible. Pays by the character.

IMPRINT PRODUCTS, 70 Randall Ave., Rockville Center, NY 11710.
Positions: This is a mail order house that sells printed products of all kinds to businesses. Home-based data entry operators input names, addresses, and codes onto customer orders.
Requirements: Must be a local resident on Long Island. The three requirements, according to management, are speed, accuracy, and the available time to do the work. There is a 24-hour turn-around on all work.
Provisions: Training is provided in the office. For those without a computer (MS/DOS only), PCs will be provided. Pays piece rates for each order completed, plus bonus for each additional item.

INTELLIGENT MACHINES, 1440 West Broadway, Missoula, MT 59802.
Positions: Contract programmers and technical writers. Programmers write software according to company specifications. The company primarily produces business software for most major computers. Technical writers write manuals.

Requirements: Resume and references required for both positions.
Provisions: Pays by the hour and by the job.

INTELLIGENT MICRO SYSTEMS, INC., 1249 Greentree Lane, Narberth, PA 19072.
Positions: Contract programming of utility programs for AT&T, IBM and Macintosh.
Requirements: Extensive knowledge and experience with operating systems and languages. Must live on East Coast.

ISLAND GRAPHICS, 1 Harbor Drive, Sausalito, CA 94965.
Positions: Computer programmers used to develop computer graphics.
Requirements: Must be local resident. Experience is required.
Provisions: All equipment is supplied by the company. Employees are salaried. 10% of company employees work at home. 'We are an opportunity based company."

J & L GRAPHICS, INC., 418 Root Street, Park Ridge, IL 60068.
Positions: Typesetting input operators for book typography.
Requirements: Local residents only. Must be experienced, skilled operator with own computer equipment.
Provisions: Courier service provided. Pays $0.55/1,000 characters.

JOURNAL GRAPHICS, 267 Broadway, New York, NY 10007.
Positions: Journal Graphics transcribes about 40 news and talk show from TV. Home workers are assigned certain shows to tape, then transcribe onto personal computers, and transmit the transcripts via modem to company headquarters where they are printed out. Workers here are independent contractors with their own computer hardware.
Requirements: Tests are given to judge spelling, vocabulary, typing speed and accuracy, and general intellegence. Must own personal computer. Only local residents should apply. Send letter of interest.
Provisions: Word processing and communications software is provided. Pays flat fee per show transcribed.

KJ SOFTWARE, INC., 12629 N. Tatum Blvd., Suite 208, Phoenix, AZ 85032.
Positions: Freelance programmers and technical writers on contract. Company produces only management training programs with workbooks for IBM computers.
Requirements: Programmers can submit finished programs for consideration. Technical writers submit resume, samples, and references.
Provisions: Programmers are paid royalties. Writers are paid by the project.

LAKE AVENUE SOFTWARE, 650 Sierra Madre Villa, Suite 204, Pasadena, CA 91107.
Positions: Contract programmers and technical writers. Company develops accounting software for any size business using dBase III on IBM compatibles. Contract programmers are usually called upon to modify existing programs. Technical writers are used on occasion to write manuals. Most workers are local, but some are out of state. Work is handled through the transfer of disks; no telecommunications available at this time.
Provisions: Both positions pay by the job.

LASSEN SOFTWARE, INC., Box 2319, Paradise, CA 95967-2319.
Positions: Contract programmers and technical writers. Company produces business

utility software, some of which is specifically useful for the home-based business person. Contract programmers are used mostly for conversions. Technical writers are used for documentation and copy writing.

Requirements: Programmers should first send for programming guidelines. Both positions require resumes and samples of previous work.

Provisions: Pays by the job.

THE LEARNING COMPANY, 6493 Kaiser Dr., Fremont, CA 94555.

Positions: Contract programmers and technical writers. Company produces educational software with an emphasis on graphics and sound. Contract programmers are used for conversions from computer to computer. Technical writers produce manuals.

Requirements: Exceptional ability in working with graphics and sound effects is especially sought in programmers. Must be very familiar with IBM, Commodore, and Apple computers. Must be local resident. Ability to meet deadlines is important Writers should be experienced and their experience should be documented in their resumes.

Provisions: Pays by the job.

LEARNING WELL, 200 South Service Road, Roslyn Heights, NY 11577.

Positions: Contract programmers for conversions and programs written to company specifications. Company publishes educational programs for Apple, Commodore, and IBM.

Requirements: Thorough knowledge and experience programming in Assembly language on one of the mentioned computers. Submit resume, samples, and references.

LETTER PERFECT WORD PROCESSING CENTER, 4205 Menlo Drive, Baltimore, MD 21215.

Positions: Company operates a mailing center and publishes three newsletters for businesses in mail order. About a dozen home-based word processors and typists work mostly on mailing lists and the company's two monthly newsletters.

Requirements: Must be Baltimore resident. Must own PC and have experience using it. Word Perfect software is preferred. Typing speed of 100 to 110 wpm is average among workers here.

Provisions: Will train on Nutshell software. Pays piece rates which run from $10 to $20 an hour, much higher than in-house rates.

LIFT, INC., P.O. Box 1072, Mountainside, NJ 07092.

Positions: Lift, Inc., is a nonprofit organization that trains and places physically disabled people as home-based computer programmers for corporate employers. In the past 10 years, program participants have been placed with 52 major corporations.

Requirements: Applicants must have a severe but stable disability, such as MS or impaired limbs. Pilot programs for blind and deaf workers are underway, too. Standard aptitude tests are applied to find traits as motivation, drive, self-control, and an aptitude for computer programming. Occassionally the candidate already has some training, but prior training is not necessary for entry into the program. Each candidate is trained to specifically meet the needs of the corporate client using whatever language and equipment the employer chooses. Most candidates are trained in systems programming and business applications.

Provisions: Upon completion of training, the programmer will work under contract with Lift for one year. The salary is comparable to that of any other entry level programmer, with medical and life insurance provided. After the year is up, the corporate employer then has the option of employing the programmer directly. The placement record has been exceptional. Lift operates in 15 states now, but expansion is underway, with plans to include all 50. Qualified persons are encouraged to apply from any urban location. (All workers are required to go into the employer's office at least once a week and most corporations are located in densely populated areas.)

E.T. LOWE PUBLISHING COMPANY, 2920 Sidco Drive, Nashville, TN 37204.
Positions: Typesetting input operators for book typography.
Requirements: Local residents only. Experience and equipment required.
Provisions: Pays by the character.

MARILYNN'S SECRETARIAL SERVICE, 207 E. Redwood St., Baltimore, MD 21202.
Positions: Occasional overflow work is available for word processors to type manuscripts, legal briefs, resumes, and general business documents.
Requirements: Baltimore residents only. Must have PC with Word Perfect 4.2. Several years of experience is required. Send resume.

MARYLAND COMPOSITION CO., INC., 6711 Dover Road, Baymeadow Industrial Park, Glen Burnie, MD 21061.
Positions: Typesetting books, catalogs, and directories is done here by a pool of independent home keyboarders and is proofread by another pool of homeworkers.
Requirements: Keyboarders need good typing skills only; must be fast, but it is much more important to be accurate. Must be available for a minimum of 20 hours a week and live nearby. Workers pick up their own work.
Provisions: Company provides 40 to 50 hours of initial training. PCs are loaned to workers. Pays an hourly rate for the first six months, then the rate changes to a formula based on quality, quantity, and difficulty. "We look for people who have kids and can't get out to go to a full-time job. Usually their motivation is not money so much as it is getting out into the mainstream. We try to satisfy their needs by offering a flexible situation that we can all live with." Unfortunate last minute update: there is a backlog of applicants and no hiring plans. (This company will be deleted from future editions.)

MAVERICK PUBLICATIONS, P.O. Box 5007, Bend, OR 97701.
Positions: Keyboarding and proofreading. This is a small book producing company, established in 1968, that uses cottage labor where economics make it advantageous. An optical character reader is used to transfer manuscripts to magnetic disks. Computerized photo-typesetting allows corrections to be made on a video screen.
Requirements: Must be local resident.

MCFARLAND GRAPHICS & DESIGN, INC., P.O. Box 129, Dillsburg, PA 17019.
Positions: Typesetting input operators for mass market book typography. Currently has 8 operators working full-time and another 4 part-timers handle overflow.
Requirements: Uses former typesetters only. All are independent contractors. Local residents only. Must be disciplined. New applicants are tested.
Provisions: "We are different in that we pay an hourly rate. If an operator is getting paid by the character, there is too much stress built into the situation. They're likely to skip over problems rather than stop and call for help. In order to make a program like this work, there has to be a trust factor and a lot of give and take."

MICROPROSE SOFTWARE, INC., 180 Lake Front Dr., Hunt Valley, MD 21030.
Positions: Company uses contract programmers for conversion work and is always open

to freelance submissions of original softward, particularly productivity tools.
Requirements: Must be nearby resident. Freelancers should send letter describing finished program on disk along with documentation. Contract programmers, send resume. Both should be thoroughly experienced and work with their own Apple, Atari, Commodore, or IBM.
Provisions: All programmers are paid on a royalty basis.

MOD-KOMP CORP., 749 Truman Ave., East Meadow, NY 11554.
Positions: Mod-Komp is a typesetting company that uses home-based keyboarders and proofreaders to type manuscripts, books, magazines, and directories from typewritten copy into the computer. Although the keyboarders are actually typesetting input operators, the company insists that any good typist is qualified to do the work and "can be taught in an hour and a half how to use the computer".
Requirements: Applicants must be local residents. Computers are available to those who do not own their own. For those that do, MS/DOS is preferred, but CPM is alo acceptable. Disc swapping is preferred, but company does have modem capabilities and will use modem transmission of work for rush orders.
Provisions: Pays 40 cents per 1000 characters if computer is supplied by company; pays 46 cents per 1000 characters if worker owns computer. There is currently a backlog of applicants, but the company is expanding rapidly and is interested in hearing from more qualified applicants.

MOLECULAR, INC., 251 River Oaks Parkway, San Jose, CA 95134.
Positions: Contract programmers and technical writers. Company produces multi-user software packages for Concurrent CPM 86, 3.1 and Xenix 3.0 Programmers write according to company specifications. Technical writers handle documentation and copy writing.
Requirements: Send resume and references. Must be local resident.
Provisions: Pays by the job.

MONARCH/AVALON HILL GAME COMPANY, 4517 Hartford Road, Baltimore, MD 21214.
Positions: Monarch/Avalon has been making adult board games for 30 years. Company now produces adult computer strategy games. Contract programmers are used for conversions from one computer to another and also for original program writing to company specifications.
Requirements: Must own and have experience with IBM, Apple II, Commodore 64, or Atari. Some game experience is preferred, particularly with "our type of games." Send resume and include references. Programmers are encouraged to send for free "Programmer's Guidelines."
Provisions: Pays by the job or royalties or a combination of both. Can live anywhere. "We have programmers as far away as Hungary." Currently has up to 25 contract programmers working at a time.

MONOTYPE COMPOSITION COMPANY, 2050 Rockrose Avenue, Baltimore, MD 21211.
Positions: Typesetting input operators for book typography. This is a union shop, so in-house workers are guaranteed work first. Any overflow goes to independent contractors. There are about 6 full-time and another 12 on-call home keyers on the roster.
Requirements: Local residents only. Must own computer equipment and have experience.

Provisions: Pays by the character.

MOUNTAIN VIEW PRESS, Box 4656, Mountain View, CA 94040.
Positions: Freelance programmers. Publishes hundreds of programs of all types for all types of computers. All programs are FORTH language programs.
Requirements: High level experience writing in FORTH with resume, samples and references to prove it. Send along with proposal.

MUTUAL SERVICE LIFE INSURANCE COMPANY, 2 Pine Tree Drive, St. Paul, MN 55112.
Positions: Claims processors. Work comes from hospitals, doctors, dentists, and other medical clients. Currently has 15 home workers.
Requirements: Must have demonstrated good claim quality. "I'm not likely to let anyone work outside of the office setting if they won't be able to meet our quality standards." Must pay own phone charges incurred on the job. 10 hours is required in-office every quarter for staff meetings. There is no pay for this time, but any extra time beyond the required 10 hours will earn the specified hourly rate. Must be local resident.
Provisions: Equipment is provided (IBM 3161 computer terminals are hooked up to the company mainframe). Pays on a per claim basis. Minnesota Workman's Comp is provided.

NETWORK TYPESETTING, 220 Bank of Nebraska Mall, Center Mall, 42nd Center, Omaha, NE 68105.
Positions: Input operators that key in formats for typesetting. Workers are independent contractors. Currently has six input stations. "We would welcome inquires from high quality input people."
Requirements: Although actual experience is not required, quality of work is important. Need IBM PC with Wordstar and a 50,000 word (minimum) spelling checker; sometimes a modem and/or printer is also necessary. "You should understand the business and the importance of doing quality work." Must live in Omaha.
Provisions: Equipment is supplied if necesssary. Pays by the job. No benefits. "Out input people are highly paid, more than in-house workers."

NORTH SHORE MEDICAL TRANSCRIBING, 18 Federal Lane, Coram, NY 11727.
Positions: Medical transcription of discharge summaries and operating reports.
Requirements: Must own PC and have experience. Local residents only.
Provisions: Work is part-time, flexible hours. Pays piece rates up to $400 a week. (Has about 10 home workers; turnover is low. There is a waiting list).

NPD, 900 West Shore Road, Port Washington, NY 11050.
Positions: NPD is one of the largest market research firms in the country. They have begun to employ home-based data entry operators to process batches of source documents. The operators are divided into groups of 20 each, with a supervisor for each group. Supervisors are also home-based and are treated the same as in-house data entry supervisors with salaries, benefits, etc. They are provided with PCs for their homes, but do not do data entry work.
Requirements: Good typing skills are necessary. Must be local resident. Must attend quarterly meetings. Must pick up and deliver work about every three days.
Provisions: PCs and all necessary supplies are provided. Training is provided in NPD office for one to two weeks. Work is part-time, therefore, only sick leave and vacation

benefits (prorated) are provided; no insurance benefits. Pays piece rates equal to that of in-house workers. Applicatons are accepted, but there is a waiting list.

ORANGE CHERRY MEDIA, P.O. Box 390, Pound Ridge, NY 10576.
Positions: Freelance and contract programmers. Company publishes highly graphic educational programs for Apple, Atari, IBM, and Commodore computers.
Requirements: Freelancers can submit either finished program with documentation or proposal with samples and resume. Contract programmers are sometimes assigned to write to spec; submit resume, samples, and references.

OREGON SOFTWARE, INC., 6915 S.W. Macadam Avenue, Portland, OR 97219.
Positions: Technical writers for user manuals.
Requirements: Must be local writer with minimum five years experience in computer documentation. Submit resume, work samples, and references.
Provisions: Pays hourly rate.

OUTER OFFICE, 10005 Old Columbia Rd., Columbia, MD 21046.
Positions: Word processors.
Requirements: Local residents only. Equipment and several years of experience are required.
Provisions: Some overflow work is available, but there is a waiting list at this time.

PARKS STORIE, INC., 2880 Holcomb Bridge Road, Building b9, Suite 539, Alpharetta, GA 30202.
Positions: This company contracts computer programmers and support people such as technical writers (for software documentation) to work out of their homes for other companies. Disabled employees are placed whenever possible.
Requirements; Applications from experienced workers, particularly disabled ones, are welcome.

PARKWOOD COMPOSITION SERVICE, 1345 South Knowles Avenue, New Richmond, WI 54017.
Positions: Typesetting input operators, proofreaders, and layout for book typography.
Requirements: Local residents only. Experience and equipment required.
Provisions: All workers are independent contractors with no guarantees of continuous work. Work flow is very seasonal.

PEMBLE ASSOCIATES, 36 Park Avenue, Ossining, NY 10562.
Positions: Pemble Associates is looking for computer consultants and others knowledgable in computers to act as distributors for a time and billing software package for the legal industry. "Innertrack" is a PC compatible (only) package designed for both single use and multiuser systems. The product sells for $695 (single user) up to $2795 (multiuser) and the dealer receives a discount (profit) up to 40%.
Requirements: Dealers must purchase a dealer demo package with which they receive free technical support via phone and/or modem (user gets free technical support for the life of the product).

PERSONAL COMPUTER SUPPORT GROUP, INC., 4540 Beltway Drive, Dallas, TX 75244.
Positions: Contract programming and engineering.
Requirements: Send a resume.

POLARWARE, P.O. Box 31, Geneva, IL 60134.
Positions: Freelance programmers write all types of programs for the home computer user. Contract programmers for conversions.
Requirements: Experience programming for Apple, IBM, Macintosh, Commodore, or Atari. Freelancers can submit finished program with documentation for consideration. Contract programmers submit resume and references.

PONY-X-PRESS, 2050 Fairwood Ave., Columbus, OH 43207.
Positions: Typesetting input operators, proofreaders, and layout for book typography. Currently has 15 regulars on the roster.
Requirements: Local residents only. Must possess necessary skills. Operators must own computer equipment.
Provisions: "Although most of our home workers are former employees, we will try new people. They must have a word processor and be very familiar with their own equipment and software. If someone comes to us claiming to be an input operator, we'll assign one trial project. We will teach them our code. It's been customized for our type of work here so that it's very streamlined." All work is overflow.

> "It's really nice to be able to kick back when I want to. I can go out and mingle with my goats and geese and not worry about work for awhile. It'll get done."
>
> --Paul Farr, Remote Control

PORT CITY PRESS, INC., P.O. Box 5754, Baltimore, MD 21208.
Positions: Typesetting input operators for book typography.
Requirements: Local residents only. Experience and equipment required.
Provisions: Pays by the character.

PUBLISHERS CLEARING HOUSE, 382 Channel Dr., Pt. Washington, NY 11050.
Positions: Data entry operators work on PCs at home entering names and addresses and other data for mailing lists.
Requirements: Local residents only. Experience, speed, and accuracy are required.
Provisions: Pays piece rates. There is currently a waiting list of 6-9 months because the turnover is so low among the home-based workers.

QUEUE, INC., 338 Commerce Dr., Fairfield, CT 06430.
Positions: Contract programmers for writing educational software for Apple and/or IBM computers. Freelance programmers also do conversions and programming to company specifications.
Requirements: Local people are definitely preferred. Apply with resume and references or work samples. Quality of work is very important.
Provisions: Pays by the job or royalty. Inquiries are welcome.

QUICK KEY DATA, 58 Cardinal Lane, Hauppauge, NY 11788.
Positions: Quick Key Data is a data and word processing service in Long Island, New York, which also acts as an organization of home-based, freelance professionals, For an

annual listing fee of $25, home workers in upstate New York and Long Island, can receive subcontracted assignments for secretarial services and/or database management.
Provisions: Payment is worked out from contract to contract, but typically Quick Key Data takes 20 to 30 percent of the billed amount. Home workers also receive, upon being listed, a manual which explains how to set up as an independent contractor, a monthly newsletter called Home-Office, and helpful information on setting up home offices, advertising, finding work, billing, taxes, etc. President, Janice Curran, says, "I feel that home work is essential for the survival of people on Long Island, and in most of the country, especially single parents who cannot afford child care, people who need to supplement their own or their spouse's incomes, and the handicapped."

R M S BUSINESS SERVICES, 210 West Pennsylvania Ave., Suite 30, Towson, MD 21204.
Positions: Word Processors with minimum two years experience in medical, legal, and general business.
Requirements: Local residents only. Must own IBM PC or compatible with Word Perfect 5.0 or 5.1 Send resume.

REPRODUCTION TYPOGRAPHERS, 244 West First Avenue, Roselle, NJ 07203.
Positions: Typesetting input operators for book typography. All operators are independent contractors and can work for other companies simultaneously.
Requirements: Must be experienced operators with own equipment. Local residents only. Must pick up and deliver own work.
Provisions: All work is overflow from the plant. Pays by the keystroke.

RESEARCH INFORMATION SYSTEMS, 1991 Village Park Way, Suite 205, Encinitas, CA 92024.
Positions: This company is about two years old now and provides a unique and valuable service to professionals in the medical and bio-medical fields. It is a software company that produces a weekly subscription service whereby about 800 medical journals are indexed into an overall table of contents. Home-based workers input critical information such as title, author, and reprint address, from journals or photocopies of title pages, onto disks. The disks are then returned to the company where they are checked for errors by the company's computer. The work is transported via Federal Express and there is a one week turn-around. All of the 10 home-based indexers are women, mostly with children. They are independent contractors, working their own schedules. Some have their own independent word processing businesses and have other clients.
Requirements: Must own PC (MS/DOS only). Must be local resident and have experience and references.
Provisions: Training is provided. Software is also provided. Pays piece rates. The company is growing steadily, but there is very little turnover so opportunities are limited.

RESOURCE SOFTWARE INTERNATIONAL, 330 New Brunswick Avenue, Ford, NJ 08863.
Positions: Contract programmers work on various assignments writing new programs to company specs or modifying existing ones.
Requirements: Must have experience programming in Assembly language on Apple, IBM, HP, or Radio Shack. Submit resume, samples, and references. Prefers programmers on East Coast.
Provisions: Pays by the project.

Close Up: Appalachian Computer Services

London is a town of 7,000 cradled in the hills of Southern Kentucky. It is home to **Appalachian Computer Services,** a data processing service bureau.

A common problem among service bureaus is the ebb and flow of work as contracts come and go. Stabilizing the workflow is a constant source of frustration for managers in this situation. There is also the cost of keeping enough employees on the payroll to handle peak workloads even though they may not be needed some of the time.

Appalachian Computer Services is among a growing number of service bureaus that have solved these problems with a home work program. Last summer a pool of cottage keyers was formed out of former in-house employees. Most of them had left their jobs because they needed to be at home with their families. All were considered valuable employees and were highly recommended.

The cottage keyers are all treated as part-time employees rather than independent contractors. Each works a minimum of 20 hours a week. Peak periods push the hours up to 30 hours a week. No one works over 30 hours a week at any time so the part-time status remains intact. This suits the workers well since none are available for full-time work. The disadvantage, however, is the lack of benefits for part-time work. Marietta Bargo,

project supervisor, says the company is looking into ways of providing benefits as the program progresses.

In the meantime, there are production bonuses offered in addition to the guaranteed hourly wage. The equipment—Multitech PCs—are provided at no charge.

There is no on-line work involved. Each worker goes into the office to pick up the work and receive instructions. When the job is finished, he or she returns the work on disks (which are also provided).

So far, Ms. Bargo says, the program is successful. The workflow is being handled smoothly, the keyers are happy with the arrangement and company overhead is down.

Now that Appalachian Computer Services is sure the home work program is the solution they've been looking for, plans are underway to expand the program to 200 home keyers. These additional workers will be hired from **outside** the company. Since no telecommunications are available, all recruiting will have to be done within London.

The only requirement will be a typing speed of 45 wpm. Experienced applicants will spend two days in-house learning to use the Multitech PC. Those with no experience in data entry will spend an additional 3 days in the company's standard training program. There is no pay for time spent in training.

Carolyn Hyde
Data Entry Operator
Blue Cross/Blue Shield of SC

"The best thing about working at home is being able to work my own hours, not being confined to a 9 to 5 job. The pay is better too. Since I get paid by the line, all I have to do is work more to get paid more. It's nice to get paid for what I do."

RIGHT BROTHERS SOFTWARE, 1173 Niagra St., Denver, CO 80220.
Positions: Right Brothers is a new software publishing company looking for good educational programs for the Color Computer I, II, and III. Especially wants thought provoking, problem solving, courseware for higher education levels. Programs are highly interactive and are games only if there is also a strong educational value.
Requirements: Thorough knowledge of BASIC and Assembly languages (only). Submit disk, printed listing, and any other support materials available.
Provisions: Programs will be analyzed for commercial value and if accepted will offer standard royalty of 12-15%.

RIGHT ON PROGRAMS, 755 New York Ave., Huntington, NY 11743.
Positions: Contract programmers for computer to computer conversions. Company produces educational programs for Apple, IBM, and Commodore. Also accepts freelance submissions.
Requirements: Must be highly qualified. Submit resume and references.

ROXBURY PUBLISHING COMPANY, P.O. Box 491044, Los Angeles, CA 90049.
Positions: Freelance home-based typesetters are used by this textbook publisher.
Requirements: Must have typesetting equipment (not PC; this is not embedding, this is actual typesetting). Los Angeles residents only. Minimum of five years experience. Send resume and indicate equipment type.
Provisions: Pay method varies. Inquiries welcome from qualified people, but there is a waiting list.

THE SAYBROOK PRESS, INC., P.O. Box 629, Old Saybrook, CT 06475.
Positions: Typesetting input operators for book typography. Currently has 8 home keyers.
Requirements: Local residents only. Must be accurate typist. Must pick up and deliver own work.
Provisions: Training and equipment provided. Pays by the character.

THE TIM SCOTT CORPORATION, 96 St. James Ave., Springfield, **MA** 01109.
Positions: The Tim Scott Corporation is in the business of exporting/importing goods and services. Goods include a variety of products from rare books to office supplies. Services include computer programming for small businesses and information services for foreign businesses wanting to do business in the U.S. The company has a specific work-at-home program designed for women, handicapped, or welfare persons with no transportation, and women with small children. Men may also take advantage of the option. No training is needed and the company will provide all the required equipment. Benefits are the same as with other employees with very few exceptions. Jobs vary so always request a current job opening listing. Employees currently hired may also apply, but first choice will always be given to unemployed persons or an employed woman with the company who is expected to have a child within 12 months.
Requirements: Must be local resident.

SECRETEAM, 455 Sherman St., Suite 120, Denver, CO 80203.
Positions: SecreTeam's home-based workers handle word processing, transcribing, desktop publishing, and other office support skills.
Requirements: Denver residents only will be considered. Must own IBM PC or compatible. Must have good typing skills and excellent command of English. Word processing experience required (WordPerfect and Microsoft Word preferred). Home workers are independent contractors.
Provisions: Transcriptions equipment is provided if necessary. Pays by the word/line/page. Send resume.

SELEX, 10 Carlisle Drive, Livingston, NJ 07039.
Positions: Software developers. Company develops highly interactive text on any subject. Some technical writers.
Requirements: Must own and have thorough knowledge of major brand PC and printer. Send list of equipment availability with letter of interest.
Provisions: Pays royalty plus other benefits.

SET TYPE, 1717 West Beltline, Madison, WI 53713.
Positions: Typesetting input operators.
Requirements: Local residents only. Experience and own equipment required.
Provisions: Pays by the character.

TOM SNYDER PRODUCTIONS, INC., 123 Auburn St., Cambridge, MA 02138.
Positions: Contract programmers and software engineers. Company produces educational games for Apple, Atari, Commodore and IBM. Most of the available work is conversion from machine to machine.
Requirements: Send resume and work samples.
Provisions: Pays by the job or hourly rate of $10 to $40 and hour.

SOUTHWEST TRANSCRIPTION CENTER, 10714 Fenwick Rd., San Diego, CA 92126.
Positions: Both in-house and at-home medical transcribers are used by Southwest. All work is done on computers (IBM compatible) using WordPerfect and Writing Assistant.
Requirements: Only experienced medical transcribers with strong medical terminology and the proper equipment will be considered. Must live in San Diego. Work can be transmitted via modem or hand delivered, but there is a 24-hour turn-around requirement.

SPAR BURGOYNE MARKETING & INFORMATION SERVICES, 10925 Valley View Rd., Suite 102, Eden Prairie, MN 55344.
Positions: Spar is a service bureau that collects data about retailers in the field and then has home-based data processors enter the information from handwritten form onto disks. The home keyers send the disks to company headquarters to be printed out in report form for clients. About a dozen home keyers work as independent contractors, averaging 20 hours a week. This could mean some weeks there is no work and others there is up to 55 hours of work.
Requirements: Must be Minneapolis resident and able to type accurately.. The company is particularly interested in young mothers who might otherwise be without work options.
Provisions: Training in software and procedures is provided in the company offices. Pays $5.50 an hour.

SPSS, INC., 444 North Michigan Avenue, Suite 3000, Chicago, IL 60611.
Positions: Contract programmers and technical writers. Programmers do conversions of business graphics software. Technical writers are used for documentation and promotional materials.
Requirements: Programmers must have experience with mainframe or super-minis. Applicants for both positions must send resume and previous work samples.

STRATEGIC SIMULATIONS, INC., 675 Almanor Ave., Sunnyvale, CA 94086.
Positions: Contact programmers for computer to computer conversions. Company publishes over 100 games for Apple, Atari, and Macintosh computers.
Requirements: There is a lot of conversion work available. However, only programmers with a high level of proviciency and ownership of both computers will be considered. Submit resume and references. Include request for current conversion needs.

STSC, INC., 2115 E. Jefferson St., Rockville, MD 20852.
Positions: Contract programmers do conversion work and write original programs to company specifications. Company works with IBM compatible or UNIX operating systems and produces vertical market applications software for specific business, professional, and educational markets.
Requirements: Area residents only. Programmers must have at least three years of experience in APL programming plus experience in systems analysis, documentation, or project management.
Provisions: Pays hourly rates.

STYLISTS SOFTWARE, Box 916, Idaho Falls, ID 83402.
Positions: Contract programmers and technical writers. Programmers do some conversions and some original programs written to company specificatons. Company produces business and typesetting packages for 68,000 UNIX clones and Macintosh.
Requirements: Must be extremely familiar with Macintosh, Assembly and C languages. Technical writers must be local residents.
Provisions: Pays by the job.

TEKTRONIX, INC., Box 4600 MS 92-680, Beaverton, OR 97075.
Positions: Company publishes thousands of programs that are programming tools for software engineers. All programs are written in C language for AT&T, Compaq, DEC,

Close Up: At Home Professions

Do you know what a notereader-scopist is? It is a little known profession, usually done at home, that is in great demand. And a training and placement firm called At-Home Professions wants to teach you all about it.

A notereader-scopist is someone who prepares typed transcripts from court reporters' stenotype notes. Stenotype is a form of shorthand written on a machine which creates words according to phonetic syllables or sounds. In the past, most court reporters had to perform lengthy dictation of their notes onto a tape recording for a transcriber to type from. A notereader-scopist is trained to work directly from stenotype notes, eliminating the entire dictation process and saving the court reporter substantial time. There is even a computer system, called a CAT (Computer Aided Transcription) which can read some of the transcription work and make the job easier.

At-Home Professions is the first program to train people in their own homes to do a job that will also be done at home. According to Operations Manager Cole Thompson, this program has been so successful the company is planning on offering training for other at-home careers in the future.

The training program is designed to be completed in 18 weeks, but you can study at any rate of speed that is comfortable for you. The program is divided into 5 study units. Each section costs $430 and includes textbooks and study materials. Also included in the tuition is access to instructors via toll-free hotlines. In California, there are regular workshops open in some areas (at no additional cost), so students can consult with instructors in person. This service is optional, however; attendance is not required.

No experience is required to enroll in the program. The most important skill for this job is good English. Typing speed is only important to the notereader-scopist,

not the court reporter who will do the hiring. Since payment is based on production, speed will determine how much the notereader-scopist will earn. What the court reporter will look for is accuracy.

Much of this work is still being done on ordinary typewriters and a typewriter is the minimum equipment required. For those who want to increase productivity (and thereby increase earnings), the ultimate tool is the CAT. A CAT leases for about $125 to $150 a month - which can be a good investment considering the potential return. At the minimum rate of pay, annual earnings for notereader-scopists ranges from a low of $20,000 per year for a slow typist to a high of $36,000 per year for a speedy one.

Tuition in the At-Home Professions program also buys lifetime career counseling and job placement assistance. There are 50,000 court reporters nationwide, each needing 2 to 4 notereader-scopists. It is essential to live in a major metropolitan area if you are working on a typewriter, and easier to get work there in any case, but if you lease a CAT, living in other parts of the country does become an option. According to Cole Thompson, court reporters around the country have been sending floppy discs to graduates of the program in California to be completed on CATS because it is difficult to find experienced workers. Thompson says a good notereader-scopist with a CAT could live in the boonies of their choice and work by exchanging floppies. Modems and fax machines haven't emerged as a major factor in exchanging work yet, but that could quickly change.

At-Home Professions is based in California and actively recruits there, but anyone living in the continental United States can participate in the program. For more information, write At-Home Professions, 12383 Lewis St., Suite 103, Garden Grove, CA 92640.

Wanda Welliver
Typesetting Input Operator
Network Typesetting
Omaha, NE

"I worked at home for eight years as a typist and never even saw a computer. When I met my boss, he explained typography to me and said if I could type 100 words a minute, the job was mine. A couple of months later, I was completely comfortable working with Wordstar on my new IBM PC. Now I make a lot more money than I would just typing. But, even more important than that is the freedom. I really don't want to go back out there."

and IBM. Contract programmers write programs according to company specifications. **Requirements:** Must be highly experienced., Submit resumes and references.

TELE VEND, INC., 111 Croydon Rd., Baltimore, MD 21212.
Positions: Freelance and contract programmers. Company publishes business and financial programs for HP, IBM, Radio Shack, and Zenith computers.
Requirements: Prefers local programmers. Freelancers should submit finished program with complete documentation. All others submit resume.
Provisions: Pays royalty.

TOWSON WORD PROCESSING, 603 Washington Ave., Towson, MD 21204.
Positions: Word Processors handle legal and medical transcription.
Requirements: Local residents only. Must own PC with word Perfect 4.2 and a transcriber (standard or micro). Three to five years experinece is required. Good work is very important. Send resume noting available hours and equipment.

TYPETRONICS, 2094 Atwood, Madison, WI 53704.
Positions: Typesetting input operators.
Requirements: Local residents only. Experience and equipment required.
Provisions: Pays by the keystroke.

THE ULTIMATE SECRETARY, 18231 Los Alimos St., Northridge, CA 91326.
Positions: Medical and x-ray transcribers.
Requirements: Must live in the Valley and be experienced. Must own word processor (and have experience using it) and transcribing machine with either standard or micro cassettes.
Provisions: Training provided. For now workers will have to pick up and deliver their own work, especially during the training period, but a courier service is planned for the near future. Turnaround time on x-ray material is 24 hours and 48 hours on all others.

Work can be part-time or full-time. Pays by the line.

UNIBASE DATA ENTRY, 835 East 4800 South, Salt Lake City, UT 84107.
Positions: This is a data entry service bureau that employs several hundred home-based keyboarders.
Requirements: Must be a Salt Lake City resident, have basic knowledge of keyboarding skills, and perform at the level of 10,000 keystrokes per hour including both letters and numbers (that's about 55 wpm typing with no errors).
Provisions: Training is provided over a six week period in the head office. Training continues with the "clients" until the worker reaches 99.9% accuracy, then the work can be taken home from that point on. Work is picked up and delivered daily and this is done on a rotational basis by members of a car pooling group of home workers living within close proximity to each other. Home workers are included in company social functions. Home workers are paid per item keyed in which amounts to between $6 and $8 an hour for good workers.

UNISON, 2174 Seymour Ave., Cincinnati, OH 45237.
Positions: Company is looking for home-based sysops (administrators) for private online networks such as Catholic Charities.
Requirements: Send letter of interest along with resume and references.

UNITRON GRAPHICS, INC., 47-10 32nd Place, Long Island, NY 11101.
Positions: Typesetting input operators for book typography.
Requirements: Experience and equipment required. Local residents only.
Provisions: Pays by the keystroke.

UNIVERSITY GRAPHICS, INC., 11 West Lincoln Avenue, Atlantic Highlands, NJ 07716.
Positions: University Graphics provides services to the book publishing industry and has three pools of home workers: keyboarders for typesetting with embedded code, proofreaders, and page makeup people who key in data to the mainframe. Currently has over 70 home workers.
Requirements: Keyboarders must type 50 to 60 wpm with a low error rate. Proofreaders must have good English skills, "maybe an English major". Only local residents.
Provisions: Training is provided. Keyboarders are provided with IBM PCs; others receive terminals which are hooked up to company's mainframe. Pays piece rates. "We were one of the first in the composition industry to use cottage labor. Now it's becoming the norm because it helps stabilize costing in an industry which is cyclical in nature. By using home workers, we can keep tight controls on our costs and overhead. Inquiries are always welcome."

VICKERS STOCK RESEARCH CORP., 226 New York Ave., Huntington, NY 11743.
Positions: Data entry.
Requirements: Must be local resident. All home-based workers are independent contractors and must own PCs. Experience and references are required.
Provisions: Pays piece rates.

WAVERLY PRESS, INC., Guilford & Mt. Royal Avenues, Baltimore, MD 21202.
Positions: Waverly Press has been using home keyers for over 10 years to embed code for typesetting medical and scientific publications. This is a high volume operation

typesetting over 250,000 pages a year.

Requirements: Applicants must type fast and very accurately. "Some are surprised at the level of skill required for this work. This is not just a typing job." Must live in the area. Also has a pool of proofreaders; must be able to read at a certain rate (about 27,000 characters per hour while simultaneously checking for errors in the copy. A test is given upon application).

Provisions: Initial training is conducted in the plant for six weeks. Workers are then supplied with 640 K IBM PC compatible, dual disk drives, modified text editor, furniture, miscellaneous office supplies, and "an endless supply of manuscripts." Pay is dependent upon accuracy with 3 different rates: low, medium, and high. "Two thirds of our keyers are in the high range." Pays by the keystroke with the complexity taken into consideration; the computer is programmed to measure the work. Piece work with no benefits except a pension plan is available to those with over 1,000 hours a year. Daily van service is available to those who need it.

J. WESTON WALCH, Box 658, Portland, ME 04104.
Positions: Company publishes educational courseware. Freelance programmers can submit finished program with documentation for consideration. Contract programmers are also used for conversions and modificatons.
Requirements: Freelancers should send only proposal. Contract programmers should submit resume, work samples, and complete information describing particular expertise.

WENGER CORPORATION, 555 Park Drive, Owatonna, MN 55060.
Positions: Contract programmers for conversion, modifications, and original programming to company specifications. Company publishes educational programs on the subject of music only. All programs are written by freelancers.
Requirements: Submit resume, samples, and references.

WESTCHESTER BOOK COMPOSITIONS, 40 Triangle Center, Yorktown Heights, NY 10598.
Positions: Typesetting input operators.
Requirements: Local residents only. Experience and equipment required.
Provisions: Pays by the character.

JOHN WILEY & SONS, INC., 605 - 3rd Ave., New York, NY 10158.
Positions: Contract programmers and technical writers. Company produces technical applications software for the engineering and scientific fields. Various types of work are contracted out to programmers, including conversions, testing, debugging, and some original development. Technical writers do documentation work.
Requirements: Must own and have thorough knowledge of Apple or IBM PC. Send resume, work samples, and references.
Provisions: Payment methods vary according to the situation.

WILLIAM BYRD PRESS, 2905 Byrdhill Rd., Richmond, VA 23261.
Positions: Typesetting input operators, proofreaders, and pasteup people. Company produces scientific, medical and other very technical journals. Currently has about 104 cottage workers.
Requirements: Experience is required. Must live in Richmond. Send resume with proof of experience.
Provisions: Workers are considered part-time employees. Pays piece rates depending on the difficulty of the project. No benefits. There is a waiting list.

Phil Neal
Contract Programmer, Maine

"I live in such a remote area I do as much as possible over the phone. I start each job by traveling to the worksite to do a requirement analysis and determine what needs to be done. I then report on what the client will need, how long it will take, and when they can expect parts of the system to be tested. From there, all the work is done strictly from my house. Living in such a remote area, it would be difficult to envision working in any other way."

THE WISCONSIN PHYSICIANS SERVICE, 1717 West Broadway, P.O. Box 8190, Madison, WI 53708.
Positions: Claims processors.
Requirements: Apply with resume. Must be local resident.
Provisions: Pays piece rates.

WOOLF SOFTWARE SYSTEMS, INC., 6754 Eton Avenue, Canoga Park, CA 91303.
Positions: Contract programmers and technical writers. Company develops business and communications software for most computer systems. Programmers do conversions and some original programming to company specifications.
Requirements: Both positions require resumes, references, and work samples.
Provisions: Pays by the hour.

YORK GRAPHICS SERVICES, INC., 3600 West Market Street, York, PA 17404.
Positions: Typesetting input operators and proofreaders for book typography.
Requirements: Local residents only. Operators must have good typing skills. Proofreaders must be detail oriented and have excellent English skills.
Provisions: All home workers are independent contractors and should understand that there are no guarantees of work assignments. All available work is overflow.

Opportunities in Office Support Positions

"Desk jobs" are among the fastest-growing categories of home work opportunities. Just about any kind of job that is performed in an office setting can just as easily be done at home. The availability of inexpensive office equipment combined with new telephone service options makes it easier now than ever before.

Some companies hire home office workers directly. More often than not, however, they are hired through service bureaus. For instance, insurance policies have been typed by home workers for many years. But the insurance companies have nothing to do with the hiring of home typists. Instead, the insurance companies contract with policy typing service bureaus. The service bureaus are responsible for all phasaes of the policy-typing process and do all the hiring and training of the home typists.

Service bureaus are popping up everywhere in the medical transcribing field. Medical transcribing is the top of the line for home typists. Not only is it the most financially rewarding of all home typing jobs—it is also an industry that is growing at a breakneck speed and there are more openings for jobs than most employers can fill.

The job involves typing doctors' reports and correspondence from cassette tapes. Employers often require several years of experience and test applicants to ensure they have a thorough knowledge of medical terminology. To get the necessary background, there are "Medical Secretary" courses available through community colleges and private vocational schools. A complete course takes from three to six months. But even then, you will need some practice in order to keep up with the 24-hour turnaround time required by most companies. One good way to gain some experience is to sign up with one or more temporary employment agencies. Explain what you're trying to do and ask to be assigned to any medical office jobs that come up.

Foreign language translation is included in this section because so much of the work requires office skills such as typing, proofreading, typesetting, and transcribing. Again, this is a field handled almost entirely by service bureaus. Most translators work at home and many work for service bureaus located in another state or even another country.

Translation is not a job for amateurs. It requires a high level of proficiency in a foreign language and some bureaus will only hire native language translators. It is also necessary to have special expertise in a given field in order to be able to work with the terminology peculiar to that field. For instance, if you are a translator specializing in the legal field, you would need an understanding of legal terminology not only in English, but in the foreign language as well.

Other requirements for this job might include a typewriter, computer, modem, facsimile machine, or transcribing machine.

AA INTERNATIONAL TRANSLATIONS & LINGUISTICS, 2312 Artesia, Redondo Beach, CA 90278.
Positions: Foreign language translators; all languages and all subjects.
Requirements: Experienced native translators only. Send resume.

ACADEMIE LANGUAGE CENTER, 8032 West Third, Los Angeles, CA 90048.
Positions: Foreign language translations of documents.
Requirements: Certification required. Local residents only. Apply with resume.

ACCURAPID TRANSLATION SERVICES, INC., 806 Main St., Poughkeepsie, NY 12603.
Positions: Technical translators in all languages. Company specializes in business, engineering and scientific documents.
Requirements: Thorough knowledge of foreign language and English is required. Must also have experience in one of the three specialties. For translators outside the area, a computer and modem is preferred. Submit resume noting areas of technical expertise and type of computer and telecommunicatons equipment.
Provisions: Pays by the word on most contracts.

ACTION TRANSLATION & INTERPRETATION BUREAU, 7825 W. 101st, Palos Hills, IL 60465.
Positions: Foreign language translators work in all languages and subjects.
Requirements: Thorough knowledge of both foreign language and English is required. Some particular of expertise is also necessary. Residents on Northern Illinois only. Submit resume and references.

ACTIVE TRANSLATION BUREAU, 155 W. 68th St., Apt. 919, New York, NY 10023.
Positions: This is a very old translation bureau that handles all languages and all subjects. Native language translators handle literary, chemical, electronics, commercial, medical, legal, technical and industrial documents.
Requirements: Must be native language translator. Minimum five years professional translating experience required. Submit resume with references.
Provisions: Pay rates vary with different projects.

AD-EX TRANSLATIONS INTERNATIONAL/USA, P. O. 2008, Menlo Park, CA 94026.
Positions: Translators and some technical writers for translation of technical, sales, and legal documents, as well as literature, into any major language, or from other language into English. Word processors and typesetters also used, but only those with foreign language expertise. Work is sent via the U.S. mail, Federal Express, or telecopiers.
Requirements: Only experienced, skilled professionals will be considered. Must be versed in one or more industrial, scientific, technical, military, or biomed fields. Knowledge of foreign language is secondary, but must be thorough. Need typewriter or word processor. Send resume and work sample. Word processing capability and access to fax machine favored.
Provisions: Payment methods varies. 90% of staff works at home. Average 10 to 40 workers a day.

ADVANCE LANGUAGE SERVICE, 333 North Michigan Ave., Suite 3200, Chicago, IL 60601.

Positions: Translators and typesetters with foreign language expertise work in all languages and subjects.
Requirements: Experienced local translators only. Submit resume and references.

AF TRANSLATIONS, 324 N. Francisca, Redondo Beach, CA 90278.
Positions: Foreign language translation of general and technical documents. All major languages.
Requirements: Prefers to work with Southern California translators. Experience required. Apply with resume and references.

A I C I, P.O. Box 91301/Worldway Postal Ct., Los Angeles, CA 90009.
Positions: Freelance technical translators work at home for this translation service bureau.
Requirements: Must be able to work from and into English with French, German, Italian, Spanish, or Japanese. Will consider experienced translators only. Prefers computer users; any type. Apply with resume and references. Can Live anywhere.
Provisions: Pays by the word.

ALLIED INTERPRETING & TRANSLATING SERVICE, 7471 Melrose Ave., Los Angeles, CA 90046.
Positions: Foreign language translation of legal and medical documents. All languages
Requirements: Certification required. Los Angeles residents only. Apply with resume.

ALL-LANGUAGE SERVICES, INC., 545 Fifth Ave., New York, NY 10017.
Positions: Translators handle legal, technical, financial, medical and engineering documents.
Requirements: Prefers native language translators. Prefers New York residents because some projects require coming into headquarters. Resume and references required.
Provisions: Pay methods vary according to assignment.

ALPHA GAMA, 1 Scripp Dr., Suite 303, Sacramento, CA 95825.
Positions: Medical transcribers.
Requirements: CMT or qualified acute care experience is necessary. Must reside within the delivery area.
Provisions: Full-time or part-time work available. Pick up and delivery of supplies and finished work is available from Roseville to West Sacramento. Pays for production.

ALTRUSA LANGUAGE BANK OF CHICAGO, 332 S. Michigan Ave., Suite 1123, Chicago, IL 60604.
Positions: Foreign language translators. All languages; all subjects.
Requirements: Prefers native language translators; will accept certificaton instead. Submit resume and references.

AM-PM TRANSCRIPTIONS, 70 W. Huron, Room 1703, Chicago, IL 60610.
Positions: Transcribing of tapes from focus groups, round table discussion, etc.
Requirements: Minimum two years experience transcribing. Good keyboard skills required. Must live nearby.
Provisions: Provides word processors. Pays $1 to $2 per page depending on the project. (Workers average 15 to 18 pages per hour.) Currently has 10 transcribers.

ATI-AMERICAN TRANSLATORS INTERNATIONAL, INC., Box X, Stanford, CA 94309.
Positions: ATI is a leading international translation and interpretation service. Foreign language opportunities involve legal and technical fields. English word porcessing, transcription, and telemarketing opportunities also exist.
Requirements: Word processing and transcribing positions require ownership of an IBM-compatible computer, WordPerfect, fax machine, and modem. Telemarketers must have at least one year of full-time experience. Translators and interpreters must have at least five years of professional, full-time experience, and must focus on a specific industry.
Provisions: Word processors, transcriptionists, and interpreters are paid on an hourly basis. Telemarketers are paid by commission. Translators are paid on a cents-per-word basis.

BBT&T, 8920 Wilshire Blvd., Suite 404, Los Angeles, CA 90211.
Positions: Medical transcribers.
Requirements: Acute care experience necessary.
Provisions: Pick up and delivery available over large area of Los Angeles. Pays piece rates equal to about $12 an hour

BERLITZ TRANSLATION SERVICE, 660 Market Street, San Francisco, CA 94104.
Positions: Berlitz is a huge translation bureau with offices all over the country and in 23 foreign countries as well. Freelance translators in all languages work in all subject areas.
Requirements: Thorough knowledge of foreign language and English required. Only experienced translators are considered. Can live anywhere, but for those not near a Berlitz office, a computer and modem is preferred. Make note of equipment type on resume.
Provisions: Pays by the word.

BERTRAND LANGUAGES, INC., 370 Lexington Ave., New York, NY 10017.
Positions: Freelance translators handle engineering, scientific, medical, legal, commercial, financial, and some advertising documents.
Requirements: Prefers native language translators. Must have expertise in one of the areas mentioned above. Translators outside the New York area should have telecommunications capabilities. Submit resume and references.

BLESSING HOSPITAL, 1005 Broadway, Quincy, IL 62301.
Positions: Medical transcribers.
Requirements: Minimum three years experience required. Must have own equipment. Local residents only may apply.

BUREAU OF OFFICE SERVICES, 3815 North Cicero Avenue, Chicago, IL 60604.
Positions: Typing, transcription and word processing. Currently has 57 home workers.
Requirements: Must own good equipment and have at least three years experience. Must be local resident. Must obtain home worker certificate from the State Department of Labor.

BUFFINGTON'S BUSINESS SERVICES, 2905 W. 116th, Inglewood, CA 90303.
Positions: Medical transcribers.
Requirements: Must live in Inglewood area. At least five years medical transcribing

A Closer Look: Transcriptions Limited

With over 1,000 home-based medical transcribers associated with 27 offices around the country, Transcriptions Limited may be the largest home work organization in the U.S.

Founder and president Mark Forstein started the company in 1970, he says, "By happy accident." It is by no accident, however, that Transcriptions Limited reached its present level of success.

Forstein says home workers are a tremendous resource in the work force. Aside from the cost savings to employers like himself, he claims home workers are fiercely loyal and supportive of the work-at-home movement and each other.

Some transcribers have been with the company for many years. "These are mostly women who start out with us when they have young children. After the family is older, some of them want to get out of the house and back into the office routine for social contact. These women have been loyal to us and we return the trust by offering them the opportunity to come to work in our offices."

The offices, which are actually a separate business entity, handle any overload that comes up. Since the transcribers are independent contractors, they can refuse work at any time, for any reason. This gives them some latitude (and greatly reduced stress) within the structure which requires a 24-hour turnaround time as a rule.

The company operates on a seven-day week, 24 hours a day. It is managed by key people on a management pyramid.

Inquiries from experienced transcribers are always welcome, but you should be prepared to prove your worth. Experience in acute care would be best and you will be given an extensive test in medical terminology.

The training session lasts only for a few hours—just long enough to get an overview of how things work and what is expected. "We do not offer the luxury of on-the-job training."

If you know your stuff, though, you can make good money. Pay is based on production and varies depending upon the part of the country you are in. In California, average pay is more than $13 an hour and in Chicago, one woman made $60,000 last year.

You will need a typewriter and transcriber, but if you don't own one, Transcriptions Limited will rent it to you at a nominal fee. The same principle applies to pick-up and delivery; it is an option that is available for a small price if you choose. You can also choose the option of working part-time or full-time hours.

These options are the result of Forstein's efforts over the years to comply with any and all aspects of using independent contractors. "Nothing," he says, "has been left to chance."

experience is required.
Provisions: Pays piece rates.

CALIFORNIA REPORTING, 1049 Dolores St. #3, San Francisco, CA 94110.
Positions: Transcribers for court reporting firm. Work is part-time only.
Requirements: Experience is required. Must live in San Francisco. Word processor is required. Apply with resume.

CALIFORNIA TYPING EXCHANGE, P.O. Box 3547, Hayward, CA 94540.
Positions: Typists and transcribers for major metropolitan areas of California.
Requirements: Good typing/transcribing skills needed. Must own good typewriter.
Provisions: Pick up and delivery available within certain boundaries. Pays production rates.

CALLAGHAN & COMPANY, 3201 Old Glenview Road, Wilmette, IL 60091.
Positions: Manuscript typing for law book publisher.
Requirements: Must own good typewriter. Good typing skills required. Must be local resident. Must obtain home worker certificate from State Department of Labor.

CCA, INC., International Marketing Communications, 7120 Havenhurst Ave., #205/208, Van Nuys, CA 91406.
Positions: Technical translators and multilingual editors for computer manuals and data sheets.
Requirements: Must be highly experienced. Must own computer and modem. IBM compatible preferred; Macintosh okay. In general, Americans are used only for proofing and quality control work. Translators are usually native. Must be professionals, usually degreed. Being able to speak/write in foreign language not enough; technical expertise in a particular industry an absolute must. Time deadlines are critical.
Provisions: Work is transfered nationwide via telecommunications or, in some cases, using Federal Express. Freelance and retainer positions are available. Freelancers are paid on a per-word basis. "A good freelancer can make $50,000 a year.." Translators in all languages are invited to send resume with references.

CERTIFIED TRANSLATION BUREAU, INC., 2788 E. Gage Ave., Huntington Park, CA 90255.
Positions: Foreign language translators for all subjects.
Requirements: Experienced translators only; any language. Apply with resume and references.

CONTINENTAL TRANSLATION SERVICE, INC., 6 E. 43rd St., Suite 2100, New York, NY 10017.
Positions: Freelance translators handle technical manuals, legal documentation, marketing projects, and medical transcription in most foreign languages.
Requirements: Thorough knowledge of foreign language and English required. Must have expertise in one of the areas mentioned above. Submit resume. Prefers New York residents.
Provisions: Pay methods vary.

DAVID C. COOK PUBLISHING COMPANY, 850 North Grove Avenue, Elgin, IL 60120.

Steven Green
Owner, Green's Machine

Word processing businesses are popping up everywhere, but the field has a long way to go before reaching the saturation point. So says Steven Green, who operates Green'es Machine with his wife, Joy , from their Milwaukee home.

Steven and Joy have taken their word processing business to an exceptionally high level. Their clients are major corporations which they cultivated over a long period of time. They now have so much business, the work is formed out to 30 independent contractors in the Milwaukee area.

Steven thinks working at home is great, especially if you need a flexible schedule. But he warns about expecting to make a good living if you have inferior skills. "If you're not good enough, you'll fail. In the 'real world' of jobs, you can hide in the bureaucracy. As an independent contractor, you can't hide. You may think because on a typing test you type 90 words a minute, that means you're good. It doesn't. Typing different material from day to day is not the same as practicing a few paragraphs over and over. To make it as an independent word processor, you have to be better than good."

On the other hand, Steven says that at home, without the office rituals and distractions, you'll find you can accomplish in three hours the same work that used to take you eight hours. The other three hours (not to mention commuting time) can be spent any way you wish.

Positions: Manuscript typing and related clerical work.
Requirements: Must own good typewriter and have good skills. Must be local resident. Must obtain home worker certificate from State Department of Labor.

COSMOPOLITAN TRANSLATION BUREAU, INC., 53 W. Jackson Blvd., Suite 1260, Chicago, IL 60604.
Positions: Cosmopolitan is a very old translation bureau that handles all languages and subjects.
Requirements: Native translators are preferred, but will consider translators with absolute knowledge of a foreign language and good English skills. Must have a particular area of expertise for the terminology of that field (such as legal or medical). Chicago translators only. Submit resume and references.

DALE TYPING SERVICE, 8700 Old Harford Rd., Baltimore, MD 21236.
Positions: Medical transcribers.
Requirements: Local residents only. Minimum three years experience and equipment required.

DUN & BRADSTREET.
Positions: Commercial reporters.
Requirements: Work is available only to home-based freelancers in towns with less than 75,000 population. If this applies to you, contact the office in your town. Strong verbal and written communication skills are required.
Provisions: Pays by the report.

EURAMERICA TRANSLATIONS, INC., 257 Park Avenue, South, New York, NY 10036.
Positions: Freelance translators work in all languages on straight documentation, typesetting and audio-visual services. Especially needs translators with knowledge of automotive, high-tech, medical, financial, legal, or promotional material. Assignments are given on-line only.
Requirements: Thorough knowledge of foreign language "equal to a native" is required. A computer, modem and FAX is required for transmitting work. Submit resume and references. Note any special areas of expertise.
Provisons: Pays by the word.

EXCELLENCE TRANSLATION SERVICE, P.O. Box 5863, Presidio of Monterey, Monterey, CA 93940.
Positions: Foreign language translators for general and technical documentation. All languages.
Requirements: Thorough knowledge of foreign language and English required. Can live anywhere in California. Submit resume and references.

FEDERATION OF THE HANDICAPPED, 211 West 14th Street, 2nd Floor, New York, NY 10011.
Positions: The Federation operates the Home Employment Program (HEP) for home-bound disabled workers only. Within HEP there is a typing/transcription department.
Requirements: All positions here require evaluation through lengthy interviews and personal counseling. All workers must live in New York City.
Provisions: The workshop provides training plus any extra help necessary to overcome any unusual problems an individual might have. Pick up and delivery of supplies and finished work is provided regularly. Necessary equipment is provided. Pays piece rates. Disability insurance counseling is provided.

PAM FRYE TYPESETTING, 834 E. Rand Road, Mt. Prospect, IL.
Positions: Typing and proofreading.
Requirements: Must be local resident with skills and experience.

GLOBAL LANGUAGE SERVICES, 2027 Las Lunas, Pasadena, CA 91108.
Positions: Foreign language translators of general and technical documents. All languages.
Requirements: Prefers native language translators, but will consider certified translators. Some special area of expertise is required. Submit resume.

GLOBALINK, 9990 Lee Highway, Fairfax, VA 22030.
Positions: Foreign language translators for general and technical documents. All languages.
Requirements: Thorough knowledge of foreign language and good English skills are

required. Computer and modem is also required. All work is transferred via electronic mail and FAX. Submit resume along with equipment details. Can live anywhere.

GREEN'S MACHINE, 2031 North HiMount, Milwaukee, WI 53208.
Positions: Medical transcription, word processing, legal transcription, database development, and other typing. "We put forward a professional image on behalf of the independent contractors who would otherwise not be able to attract the top corporate clients we have." Currently has 30 home workers.
Requirements: Must live in Milwaukee. Typing skills are needed; accuracy is most important. Workers must own good typewriters. Workers must pick up and deliver their own work.
Provisions: Pays production rate equal to a minimum of $10 an hour.

HELEN'S LEGAL SUPPORT, 601 West Fifth, Los Angeles, CA 90071.
Positions: Legal transcribers handle overflow work only.
Requirements: Must own good equipment, have several years of legal transcribing experience, and references. Los Angeles residents only.
Provisions: Pay methods vary, but usually pays by the page.

HIGHLAND PARK HOSPITAL, 718 Glanview Ave., Highland, IL 60035.
Positions: Medical transcribers. This is a new and small operation and opporunities are limited.
Requirements: Minimum three years experience required. Must have proper equipment. Local resident only.

HOGARD BUSINESS SERVICES, INC., 462 S. Schuyler Ave., Bradley, IL 60915.
Positions: Typing and stuffing envelopes for this typing and mailing service.
Requirements: Must be local resident. Must obtain a home worker certificate from the Illinois. Department of Labor.

HOMEWORK COMPANY, 10210 NE 8th, Bellevue, WA 98004.
Positions: Policy typing, transcription, insurance rating and collating. Homework Company is a 35 year old company with 37 ofices west of the Mississippi. Currently has about 800 home workers.
Requirements: Workers are independent contractors and must supply own equipment for particular jobs; typewriter, transcription equipment, or calculator. Insurance raters need three years experience. Typists must be accurate.
Provisions: Training is provided. Choice of part-time or full-time. Pays piece rates for typing and transcribing. Pays hourly rate for insurance rating and collating.

HOOPER-HOLMES BUREAU.
Positions: Commercial reporters. Work consists of gathering information over the phone from businesses, usually for insurance company clients, then writing up the information in a narrative-style report. Company has 100 offices nationwide. Some use homeworkers, some do not. Look in your local phone book to see if there is an office near you. "In rural areas, it's common to have public servants like firemen and policemen do this to supplement their incomes. In this case, there may not even be an office."
Requirements: Excellent verbal and written communication skills required. Typewriter is needed.
Provisions: Training is provided. Workers are independent contractors and are paid per report.

HUNTER PUBLISHING, 950 Lee St., Des Plaines, IL 60016.
Positions: Miscellaneous clerical work in the circulation department. Opportunities are limited.
Requirements: Must be local resident. Must obtain home worker certificate from the Illinois Department of Labor.

ILLINOIS HOSPITAL JOINT VENTURES, 1151 Warrenville, Naperville, IL 60566.
Positions: Medical transcribers.
Requirements: Must be local resident. Extensive experience is required. Must own necessary equipment.
Provisions: Pays piece rates.

INDEX RESEARCH SERVICES, P.O. Box 3201, San Mateo, CA 94403.
Positions: Typing of reports from insurance adjusters after they have performed property inspections. Currently has over 15 home workers working from the company's three offices in San Mateo and Sacramento.
Requirements: Must have good typewriter and type at least 65 wpm. Must live near one of the three offices.
Provisions: Any extras such as transcription machines or supplies are provided. Work is part-time only. Workers are independent contractors and are paid on a per report basis with a guarantee of $5 to $6 an hour.

INLINGUA TRANSLATION SERVICE, 690 Market St., Suite 700, San Francisco, CA 94104.
Positions: Inlingua is a major translation bureau with more than 200 offices all over the world. Freelance translators handle legal, business, and medical documentation in all languages.
Requirements: A thorough knowledge of foreign language and English is required. Submit resume and note special areas of expertise.
Provisions: Pays by the word.

INTER TRANSLATION & INTERPRETING, 1840 North Winona, Los Angeles, CA 90027.
Positions: Foreign language translators for legal and insurance documents. Arabic, Armenian, Italian, Japanese, Russian, and Persian and Turkish languages.
Requirements: Native or certified translators only. Must be Los Angeles resident. Experience in legal and/or insurance field required. Submit resume and references.

INTERNATIONAL DOCUMENTATION, P.O. Box 67628, Los Angeles, CA 90067.
Positions: Freelance translators are used by this service bureau.
Requirements: Thorough knowledge of any language for all types of translating; technical writing, medical transcribing, booklets, brochures, etc. Experience is necessary.
Provision: Pays by the word. Work is transferred via modem or conventional methods.

INTERNATIONAL LANGUAGE & COMMUNICATIONS CENTERS, INC., 79 W. Monroe, Suite 1310, Chicago, IL 60603.
Positions: Freelance translators handle business documents.
Requirements: Must be expert in a foreign language and English. Experience working with business documents is required. Prefers translators with own computers. Must live in the Chicago area. Submit resume and references.

INTERNATIONAL TRANSLATION BUREAU, 123 West Fourth, Room 240, Los Angeles, CA 90013.
Positions: Foreign language translators for general documentation. All major languages.
Requirements: Experienced translators only. Prefers to work with Los Angeles area residents. Submit resume and references.

LEO KANNER ASSOCIATES, P.O. Box 5187, Redwood City, CA 94063.
Positions: Freelance translators in all languages work in all subject areas.
Requirements: Must be a West Coast resident. Only professional-level translators will be considered. Apply with resume and references.
Provisions: Pays by the word.

KEATING OF CHICAGO, INC., 715 S. 25th Ave., Bellwood, IL 60104.
Positions: Keating is in the business of selling commercial kitchen equipment. Home-based clerical workers handle the typing of orders. The home-based work force has not grown here for several years, so there is not much opportunity.
Requirements: Must be local resident.

KLINE'S DEPARTMENT STORE, INC., 515 W. 14th St., Chicago Heights, IL 60411.
Positions: This retail department store has home-based clerical workers handle miscellaneous paper work. There is a waiting list.
Requirements: Must be local resident. Must obtain a home worker certificate from the Illinois Department of Labor.

LAD TRANSCRIPTIONS, 17772 Irvine Boulevard, Suite 205, Tustin, CA 92680.
Positions: Medical transcribing.
Requirements: Minimum three years experience in basic four reports. Local residents only. Must own good typewriter and transcribing machine.
Provisions: Pays by the line.

THE LANGUAGE LAB, 211 E. 43rd St., New York, NY 10017.
Positions: Freelance translators work in all languages for clients in industry, law firms and government agencies.
Requirements: Only highly experienced professionals are considered. Submit resume and references.

LANGUAGE SERVICE BUREAU, 1601 Connecticut Ave., Suite 490, Washington, DC 20009.
Positions: Freelance foreign language translators.
Requirements: Experienced professionals only. Must be nearby resident. Submit resume and references.

LANGUAGES UNLIMITED, 4900 Leesburg Pike, Suite 402, Alexandria, VA 22302.
Positions: Freelance translators work in all languages on documentation for international businesses.
Requirements: Must be very experienced in foreign language translation and in working with business documents such as patents, taxes, or finance.
Submit resume and references.

LEADER TYPING SERVICE, 18 Caroline Ct., North Babylon, NY 11703.
Positions: Leader uses home-based typists to compile lists.
Requirements: Must live within the five surrounding areas of North Babylon, New York. Beyond knowing the keyboard, there are no typing speed requirements because piece rates are paid (per 1,000 characters typed). Typists must pick up and deliver their own work twice a week.
Provisions: Typewriters are provided. Pays $17 to $35 per 1,000 characters. "We always need typists. Home-based typists are hard for us to find."

LIBRARY OF CONGRESS, National Library Service for the Blind and Physically Handicapped, Washington, D.C. 20542.
Positions: Homebound disabled proofreaders in the Braille Development Section.
Provisions: A training program is available to teach blind people to proofread Braille materials. A certificate is awarded upon completion of the program. Work is farmed out to homebound workers from the Library's production department on a piece rate basis. Number of participants varies.

LINDNER TRANSLATIONS, INC., 29 Broadway, Suite 1707, New York, NY 10006.
Positions: Lindner is a 30-year-old translation bureau with freelance translators working in all languages. Areas include legal, medical, technical, chemical, financial, commercial and advertising.
Requirements: Must be proven professional with references. Prefers New York residents.
Provisions: Pays by the word on most assignments.

LINGUAMUNDI INTERNATIONAL, INC., P.O. Box 2206, Arlington, VA 22202.
Positions: Freelance translators; all languages. Company specializes in foreign language typesetting.
Requirements: Must be experienced professional translator with some area of technical expertise. Especially prefers translators with own computer equipment. Submit resume and references.

LINGUAASSIST, 4 DeHart Street, Morristown, NJ 07960.
Positions: LinguaAssist is a translation bureau that offers translation in 60 different languages. Freelancer translators handle technical and legal documentation, typesetting and printing services, and word processing services.
Requirements: Thorough knowledge of foreign language and English is required. Prefers local residents, but does have FAX capabilities for qualified translators outside the area. Submit resume.
Provisions: Pay varies according to project.

L.O.A.M., INC., 17549 Duvan Dr., Tinley Park, IL 60477.
Positions: About a hundred home-based clerical workers insert mailing pieces for this mailing service. There is a waiting list.
Requirements: Must be local resident. Must obtain home worker certificate from the Illinois Department of Labor.

MARKET FACTS, INC., 676 North St. Clair Street, Chicago, IL 60611.
Positions: Coding, keypunch, clerical, and statistical tabulation relating to market research work. Currently has 94 home workers.
Requirements: Must be local resident. Must obtain home worker certificate from State Department of Labor.
Provisions: Pay varies according to job functions.

MASS INSURANCE CONSULTANTS & ADMINISTRATORS, INC., 55 East Jackson, 8th Floor, Chicago, IL 60604.
Positions: Clerical work concerned with the handling of insurance claims.
Requirements: Must be local resident. Experience working in claims administration preferred. Must obtain a home worker certificate from Illinois Department of Labor.

MCGINLEY PROCESS SERVICE, 5922 S.W. 29th St., Miami, FL 33155.
Positions: Certified process servers. Company is setting up a nationwide network of process servers and related services.
Requirements: Certification is necessary where required by law. PC and modem are necessary. Send letter of interest.
Provisions: Can be located anywhere in U.S.

MECHANICAL SECRETARY, 38 W. 32nd St., New York, NY 10001.
Positions: Typists and transcribers. Work covers several areas: medical, legal, insurance, advertising and general business. Currently has 15 home workers and there is a very long waiting list.
Requirements: Must have good typing skills and own approved equipment. Experience is required. Send letter of interest. Must be resident of Manhattan, Brooklyn, or Queens.
Provisions: Pick up and delivery of supplies and finished work is provided. Pays production rates.

MOBILE STENO, 12439 S. Maple, 1st Rear, Blue Island, IL 60406.
Positions: General typing.
Requirements: Must be local resident. Experience and equipment required.

MODERN SECRETARIAL SERVICE, 2813 South La Cienega Avenue, Los Angeles, CA 90034.
Positions: Typists and word processors. Company specializes in insurance policy typing, but does all types of legal and general work. "We're always looking for good people."
Requirements: Must have good equipment and skills. Test will be given. Los Angeles residents only.

NEWSBANK, INC., 58 Pine Street, New Canaan, CT 06840.
Positions: About 20 indexers and proofreaders produce current affairs references from their home offices. The work is part-time; each works from 20 to 25 hours per week.
Requirements: Must be local in order to pick up and drop off work twice a week and attend meetings.
Provisions:; There is a three-month training period in-house for learning the company's indexing methods and how to use a personal computer. All equipment is provided.

NODEL/LEE ENTERPRISES, 17111 S. Wallace, South Holland, IL 60473.
Positions: Home-based workers insert coupons into envelopes for this direct mail advertising service.
Requirements: Must be local resident. Apply in person. Workers are called when work builds up.
Provisions: Pays piece rates.

NORTHWEST MAILING SERVICE, 5401 W. Grand, Chicago, IL 60639.
Positions: Miscellaneous clerical work involved in mailing services.
Requirements: Must be local resident. Must obtain home worker certificate from Illinois Department of Labor.
Provisions: Pays piece rates.

THE OFFICE CONNECTION, INC.,/NORTHWEST POLICY TYPING, 209 Dayton Ave., Suite 103, Edmonds, WA 98020.
Positions: Insurance policy typists and legal transcribers. Workers are independent contractors. Currently has about 100 home workers.
Requirements: Good typing skills are required. Accuracy is much more important than speed. 24-hour turn-around time is required with a five-day work week. Must own good typewriter. Apply with a typed letter of interest.
Provisions: Training is provided. The initial training sesssion lasts about a week in the company facilities; minimum wage is paid for training time. Pick up and delivery is provided daily. Semi-regular meeting are required to discuss changes in methods, new contracts, etc. Meeting time pays minimum wage plus car allowance. Pay for work is both by the hour for handling and by the piece for typing. Different rates are set for each type of form. "Our top typists average $15 an hour." Pays once a month. Work is available only in the Seattle area.

OMNILINGUA, INC., 2857 Mt. Vernon Rd., S.E., Cedar Rapids, IA 52403.
Positions: Native-speaking translators for work in many different fields. All languages are eligible.

Requirements: Expertise in any area of business is necessary.
Provisions: Can live anywhere. Pay methods vary. Inquiries are welcome from qualified translators.

PAPERWORKS, 816 South Illinois, Carbondale, IL 62901.
Positions: Typing of general business forms and correspondence.
Requirements: Must be local resident. Experience is required. Must own approved typewriter. All typists are given a two-hour typing test.
Provisions: Pays piece rates.

PARADISE MAILING, INC., 607 Harbor View Boulevard, Somerset, MA 02725.
Positions: Typing addresses on envelopes and flyers for direct mail processing.
Requirements: Good typing skills and typewriter are required. Must be local resident.
Provisions: Pays minimum wage..

PETERS SHORTHAND REPORTING CORPORATION, 3433 American River Drive, Suite A, Sacramento, CA 95825.
Positions: Court reporting and transcribing.
Requirements: Must be local resident. Some travel is required. Experience is necessary.
Provisions: Pays hourly, plus piece rates, plus expenses.

PHYSICIANS MEDICAL TRANSCRIBING, Chatsworth, CA (818) 938-1553.
Positions: Medical transcribers.
Requirements: Must live in or near the San Fernando Valley. Experience is required in acute care.
Provisions: Part-time hours only. Pays piece rates.

PREFERRED BUSINESS CENTERS, 875 N. Michigan, Suite 3614, Chicago, IL 60614.
Positions: General transcription.
Requirements: Must be experienced and have necessary equipment. Local residents only.

RSI, P.O. Box 5510, San Mateo, CA 94402.
Positions: Insurance inspectors/investigators. Independent contractors only.
Requirements: Extensive experience is required. Send resume. Must live in one of the Bay area counties.

SACRAMENTO PROFESSIONAL TYPISTS NETWORK, 9113 Sherrilee Way, Orangevale, CA 95662.
The Network got its start as the original chapter of Peggy Glenn's national home typing group. After the national group disbanded, the Sacramento Network continued as a support group, then eventually formed an organization with bylaws and regular meetings which are held on the second Thursday of each month. Members are professional home-based typists and word processors. Members refer clients and work to other members when there is overflow, rush jobs, jobs that are too big to handle, and in cases of illness or vacations. Often, one member will bid on a large job and then enlist the help of other members to do the job. "This is our lifestyle; it's called freedom," says chairwoman Janice Katz. Currently has 50 members. Inquires and new members are welcome.
Requirements: Only residents of Sacramento can participate. Annual dues are $25.

SCRIPTURE PRESS PUBLICATIONS, 1825 College Ave., Wheaton, IL 60187.
Positions: This religious publisher uses home-based clerical workers to proofread and assemble packets of printed materials.
Requirements: Must be local resident.

SECREPHONE, 248 Columbia Turnpike, Florham Park, NJ 07932.
Positions: Secrephone subcontracts medical transcribing work to home-based medical transcribers.
Requirements: Local residents only. Must own equipment and have minimum three years hospital experience. Send resume.

SH3, INC., 5338 E. 115th St. Kansas City, MO 64137.
Positions: Freelance translators for this service bureau.
Requirements: Thorough knowledge of French, German, Italian,, or Spanish. You must be experienced and able to provide telecommunications, IBM PC (or compatible) disks, or COM disks. Send resume.

SHERMAN HOSPITAL, 934 Center St., Elgin, IL.
Positions: Medical transcribing.
Requirements: Must be local resident. Equipment, good skills and a minimum five years experience are required.

SKRUDLAND PHOTO SERVICE, INC., 1720 Rand Rd., Palatine, IL 60074.
Positions: Typing, stuffing envelopes, and other clerical operations.
Requirements: Must be local resident. Must obtain home worker certificate from the State Department of Labor.

TIM SWEENEY & ASSOCIATES, 101 California St., Suite 300, San Francisco, CA 94111.
Positions: Tim Sweeney is a stock broker who conducts financial seminars around the Bay area. He uses home workers for bulk mail processing projects.
Requirements: Must live in San Francisco. Must be dependable for steady, part-time work. Work involves picking up supplies such as mailing labels, brochures, and envelopes, taking them home and stuffing them, then returning them for postage metering (they will be mailed from the office).
Provisions: Pays cash daily, $.03 or $.05 per envelope depending on the particular job.

TAYLOR PUBLISHING COMPANY, 1550 Mockingbird, Dallas, TX 75235.
Positions: Taylor Publishing is in the business of producing school yearbooks. About 500 independent contractors work full-time and part-time in the Dallas area. Some are home-based, some are not. The home-based work involves typing, proofing, stripping, and other jobs associated with publishing.
Requirements: Must be local resident. Applications are accepted only during June, July, and August.
Provisions: Pays piece rates for completed work associates.

TECHNICAL WRITING AND TRANSLATING ASSOCIATES, 5356 N. Bernard, Chicago, IL 60625.
Positions: Foreign language translators work as technical writers and editors in all languages.

Requirements: Thorough knowledge of foreign language and excellent English skills are essential. Technical writing expereince is required. Prefers to work with Northern Illinois residents. Submit resume and references.

TELECOMMUNICATIONS PROFESSIONAL DESIGN, P.O. Box 215684, Sacramento, CA 95821.
Positions: Home-based telemarketers are being sought in the Sacramento area for business-to-business calls. Workers take orders, set appointments, do surveys and market research. No sales calls.
Provisions: Training is provided in workshop area.

> "The whole idea of not wanting to lock a bunch of people up in a factory anymore ... that's what we're all about"
> --Martin Paul, Cofounder, DEVA

THUDIUM MAIL ADVERTISING COMPANY, 3553 North Milwaukee, Chicago, IL 60641.
Positions: Typing, labeling, inserting and other clerical operations involved in letter shop work. Currently has 38 home workers.
Requirements: Must be local resident. Must obtain home worker certificate from State Department of Labor.

TRANSET GRAPHICS, 520 North Michigan, Chicago, IL 60611.
Positions: Foreign langauge translators. Company specializes in graphic arts and typesetting services.
Requirements: Absolute knowledge of foreign language and English is required. Experience in typesetting industry also preferred. Will only consider translators with own computers and modems. Submit resume and references.

TRANSCRIPTIONS LIMITED.
Positions: Medical transcribers for hospital overflow work; discharge summaries and operative reports. Currently has over 1,000 home workers and 30 offices nationwide, including Los Angeles, San Francisco, Sacramento, Denver, and Chicago. If there is an office near enough for you to work for, you will find it listed in your local phone book.
Requirements: Acute care experience is required. A test in medical terminology is given to all applicants.
Provisions: Choice of part-time or full-time hours is available. Equipment is provided on a rental basis if necessary. Daily pick up and delivery of supplies and finished work is provided. Pays production rates that vary depending on the part of the country where you're located. Average hourly pay is about $13 an hour. Inquiries are always welcome from qualified transcribers.

TRANSLATING ASSOCIATES, 104 East 40th , New York, NY 10016.
Positions: Freelance translators work on assignments in all subject areas.

Requirements: Must be New York resident. Only highly professional translators with verifiable references will be considered. Prefers translators with writing and editing experience.
Provisions: Pays by the word.

TRANSLATION COMPANY OF AMERICA, INC., 10 West 37th, New York, NY 10018.
Positions: Translators, interpreters, and typesetters.
Requirements: Prefers native language translators. Must own typewriter or word processor. Expertise in a particular area of business is required. Send resume and references.
Provisions: Pays by the word.

TRANS-LINGUAL COMMUNICATIONS, INC., Quaker Tower, 321 N. Clark St., Suite 3140, Chicago, IL 60610.
Positions: Foreign language translators work in all subject areas. Company specialized in software and technical manual translation.
Requirements: Minimum five years verifiable experience as a professional translator is required. Must have own technical background. Prefers translators with own computer equipment. Can live anywhere.
Provisions: Pays by the word.

TRANS-LINK, 1850 Gaugh, Suite 701, San Francisco, CA 94109.
Positions: Translators in 55 different foreign languages handle freelance assignments in technical translation, international advertising and audio-visual dubbing.
Requirements: Absolute knowledge of foreign language and English is required. Must be West Coast resident, preferably California. Resume and references required. Note area of technical expertise.
Provisions: Pay methods very according to type of work.

TYPE-A-LINE, INC., 311 Woods Avenue, Oceanside, NY 11572.
Positions: Typing of labels, cards, envelopes, and some inserting for direct mail fulfillment company. Some OCR typing on computers also. Currently has 17 home workers and no applications are being taken as there is a very long waiting list.
Requirements: Typewriter and good typing skills are required. Must be local to either Oceanside or Brentwood in order to pick up and deliver supplies and finished work.
Provisions: Training is provided. If necessary and nearby, company will provide pick up and delivery services. Pays piece rates equal to about $5 an hour. "New York State is tough on home workers. The State demands 'good' reasons for being allowed to work at home. I'd like to hire more home workers, but unless you meet the requirements, I can't."

TYPE-A-SCAN, INC., 1358 Rockaway Parkway, Brooklyn, NY 11236.
Positions: Various kinds of typing in the mailing list industry, mostly involving address labels. Typing is converted to disk by use of an optical scanner in-house.
Requirements: Reliability is very important here. Typing speed of 60 wpm with a low error rate is required. Workers must pick up and deliver their own supplies and finished work. Currently has "many" home workers throughout Long Island, New York City and part of New Jersey.
Provisions: Pays piece rates. Company provides IBM Selectric typewriters. Training is provided. "We are unique in our methods. We are always looking for new people."

THE TYPING COMPANY, 129 E St., Suite B-4, Davis, CA 95616.
Positions: Typists and transcribers. Most work is academic; term papers, theses, dissertatons, application forms, tables, and grants. Now expanding into medical transcribing.
Requirements: Must have good typewriter and excellent skills. Davis residents only. Home workers pick up and deliver own supplies and finished work whenever they want to during the day.
Provisions: Some training is provided. Pays 60% of the fee paid to the company. The best typist earns up to $12 an hour.

UMI/DATA COURIER, 620 S. Third St., Louisville, KY 40202.
Positions: About 30 abstracters work at home as independent contractors. Home workers have been used here since 1976.
Requirements: Must live nearby in order to pick up the publications that you will be abstracting once a week. Reasonable good communication skills are needeed. Send resume.
Provisions: Computers are necessary for the job and the company does provide them.

BETTY VAN KEULEN, 18215 Jayhawk Dr., Penn Valley, CA 95946.
Positions: Medical transcribers.
Requirements: Hospital transcribing experience is requried. Must be local resident in order to pick up and deliver supplies and finished work. A good typewriter is necessary.
Provisions: If a transcriber isn't available, company will lease a transcriber at half price. Pays by the line.

VERNA MEDICAL TRANSCRIPTIONS, 156 Smithwood Avenue, Milpitas, CA 95035.
Positions: Medical transcribers for all types of medical records.
Requirements: Experience is necessary. Must own good typewriter and transcribing machine with either standard or microcassettes. Must be local resident in order to pick up and deliver supplies and finished work.
Provisions: Pays piece rates. Part-time or full-time work is available.

WCC, 40 Skokie Boulevard, Northbrook, IL 60062.
Positions: Translators for computer-aided technical translation into all major languages.
Requirements: Thorough knowledge of both English and foreign language. Some word processing experience. Apply with resume and references. Prefers local people.

WOMEN'S CLUBS PUBLISHING CO., 323 S. Franklin St., Chicago, IL 60606.
Positions: Miscellaneous typing and clerical work.
Requirements: Must be local resident. Must obtain home worker certificate from the Illinois Department of Labor.
Provisions: Pays piece rates.

WORDNET, P.O. Box 164, Acton, MA 01720.
Positions: Professional freelancers translate technical manuals and documentation in and out of all major languages.
Requirements: Must be experienced and skilled both in languages, technical verbage, and computers. Because translation projects are transmitted electronically all over the world, a computer and modem is required. Send resume.

WORLD WIDE, P.O. Box 2266, Culver City, CA 90231.
Positions: Medical transcribers for home work out of three Los Angeles offices. Currently has over 100 home workers.
Requirements: Must have experience and knowledge of medical terminology. Work will be for hospitals, clinics, doctors, and government. Must have good typewriter and transcribing machine. Los Angeles residents only.
Provisions: Specific training is provided. Pick up and delivery of supplies and finished work will be provided if necessary. Pays piece rates equal to about $12 an hour. Part-time or full-time hours available. Inquiries are welcome.

WORLDWIDE TRANSLATION AGENCY, 1680 North Vine, Suite 610, Holly-wood, CA 90028.
Positions: Foreign language translators work on a wide variety of documents.
Requirements: Los Angeles residents only. Must be experienced professional translator with resume and references.
Provisions: Pays by the word.

Opportunities Working With People

In this section you will find jobs that have but one basic requirement—the ability to work well with people. Both at-home and from-home jobs are included. At-home jobs include telephone surveying, customer service, fund raising, recruiting, and staffing coordination.

Telephone surveying involves calling consumers to ask specific questions about their buying habits, or more weighty questions of social significance. The names and numbers are supplied and the surveyor is paid for each call. The average pay works out to about $6 an hour. The work is not usually steady; it tends to come and go. This can be good for someone who cannot make a permanent commitment. If you want steady surveying work you should sign up with several companies in order to insure back-to-back assignments.

Customer service is a profession that is just beginning to come into its own. American companies are starting to realize the importance of listening to their customers and trying to satisfy their needs. A customer service representative is basically a problem-solver. The job requires an ability to listen and record customers' comments accurately.

Fund raising can also be an easy job. It doesn't pay as well as surveying, usually only minimum wage plus a small bonus for bringing in so-much in donations. It is, however, very easy work to get and it can be good experience leading to more sophisticated and higher-paying phone work.

Like customer service, staffing coordination is a fairly new opportunity for home workers. This work is found most often in the burgeoning health-care field. Agencies are used to fill the staffing needs of hospitals, nursing homes, and outpatients. Calls come in day and night, but most agencies don't keep their doors open 24 hours a day. After 5:00 on weekdays and on weekends, calls are forwarded to a staffing coordinator's home. It is the coordinator's job to dispatch nurses and home health care workers as they are needed during those hours. Most coordinators have electronic pagers, so they need not be completely homebound.

Field surveying is a job that is custom-made for someone with an outgoing personality. The word "field" indicates that most of the work is done outside-- which may mean in a mall, at a movie theatre, or door-to-door. The surveyor collects answers to survey questions in the field and then returns home to fill out the paperwork. It is perfect for the person that needs the flexibility that working from home offers, but who doesn't want to be stuck inside all the time.

Field surveyors work for market research firms and opinion pollers. They generally work as independent contractors, often working for more than one company at a time because each survey may last from only two days to two weeks on average and being on the roster at a number of companies makes steady work more likely.

ADULT INDEPENDENT DEVELOPMENT CENTER OF SANTA CLARA COUNTY, INC. 1190 Benton, Santa Clara, CA 95050.
Positions: Fund raisers request donations over the phone.
Requirements: Must be reliable and self-managing. Must live within Santa Clara County.
Provisions: Training is provided. Pays salary plus bonuses and fringe benefits.

AIS MARKET RESEARCH, 4974 N. Fresno, Bldg. 567, Fresno, CA 93726.
Positions: Field surveyers in the San Joaquin Valley.
Requirements: Must be resident of either Fresno or Modesto. Market research or similar experience required. Send for application.
Provisions: Work is part-time and sporadic. Pays by the survey.

ALL CITY LOCKSMITHS, 160 Del Vale, San Francisco, CA 94127.
Positions: Customer service/dispatchers for locksmiths. Job consists of answering incoming calls at home and determining whether dispatch is necessary.
Requirements: Need to be friendly, alert, and articulate. Locksmith knowledge is preferred. Company works on a 24-hour a day, seven day a week schedule, with home workers working on shift rotations. Calls are forwarded to workers' homes for duration of each shift period only. Must live in San Francisco.
Provisions: Complete training is provided. Commission paid on successfully concluded calls. Company is expanding.

AMERICAN RED CROSS, 2700 Wilshire Blvd., Los Angeles, CA 90057.
Positions: Telephone recruiters locate potential blood donors.
Requirements: Two years telemarketing experience required. Must be available Sunday through Thursday. Excellent comunications skills necessary. Los Angeles residents only. Send resume.
Provisions: Pays $4.63 an hour.

AMERICAN TELEMARKETING, INC., 3349 Cahuenga Blvd. West, Suite 5A, Los Angeles, CA 90068.
Positions: Market research is conducted solely over the phone. Part-time hours only. Work is available in most major metropolitan areas.
Requirements: Market research experience is preferred, but not required.
Provisions: Pays about $8 an hour.

AMVETS, 1111 Prospect, Indianapolis, IN 46203.
Positions: Fund raisers call for donations of clothing and household articles.
Requirements: Must live in Indianapolis.
Provisions: Pays hourly wage plus bonus plan.

A-ONE RESEARCH, INC., 2800 Coyle St., Brooklyn, NY 11235.
Positions: Field surveyers for market research studies.
Requirements: Must be resident of New York City or one of the immediate suburbs. Good communication skills and interviewing experience required.
Provisions: Work is part-time only. Pays by the survey.

ARTHRITIS FOUNDATION, 203 Willow St., Suite 201, San Francisco, CA 94109.
Positions: Telephone recruiters find volunteers to go door-to-door for donations. This

program repeats every fall and spring for about two months each time.
Requirements: Must live in the Bay area. Experience is not required, but the director says this work is very difficult and may not be suitable for newcomers. Must be available to work (call) during the evening hours of 6 to 9:30 pm.
Provisions: Pays $1.50 per recruitment.

LESLIE R. ASHER, 400 Second Ave., Suite 16b, New York, NY 10010
Positions: Field surveyers and some telephone interviewers for focus group recruiting.
Requirements: Work is only assigned to residents of metropolitan New York, Long Island, New Jersey, and Westchester County. Experience in market research required.

ATLANTA MARKETING RESEARCH CENTER, 3355 Lenox Rd., Suite 660, Atlanta, GA 30326.
Positions: Field surveyers and occasionally, telephone interviewers.
Requirements: Atlanta residents only. Experience preferred.
Provisions: Pays by the survey.

FRANCES BAUMAN ASSOCIATES, 23 Girard St.; Marlboro, NJ 07746.
Positions: Field surveyers and telephone interviewers for market research assignments.
Requirements: Must live in tri-state area of New York, New Jersey, or Pennsylvania. Experience required.
Provisions: Work is part-time on-call only. Pays by the survey.

BLIND & HANDICAPPED, P.O. Box 23771, Oakland, CA 94623.
Positions: Telemarketing of household products for fund raising.
Requirements: Must live in Northern California.
Provisions: Training is provided. Pays salary or commission.

BURKE INTERNATIONAL RESEARCH CORPPORATION, 420 Lexington Ave., New York 10001.
Positions: Market researchers for field surveys only.
Requirements: Some experience in market research is required. Will consider workers who have worked with the public in some capacity. The primary requirement is the ability to communicate effectively.
Provisions: Training and supplies are provided. Pays per survey. Write for field supervisor in your area; major urban centers only.

BUSINESS TREND ANALYSTS, 2171 Jerrico Trunpike, Commack, NY 11725.
Positions: Market research.
Requirements: Must be a local resident. Good communication skills and some experience in market research is required.

CALIFORNIA AMVETS, 747 Twelfth Ave., San Diego, CA 92101.
Positions: Fund raisers telephone for donations of household discards to be sold through thrift shops. Also has locations in El Cajon, Fresno, and Oceanside.
Requirements: Must be dependable and have good speaking skills. Must live in local area.
Provisions: Choice of part-time or full-time; hours flexible. Pays guarantee of minimum wage plus bonus plan. Training provided.

CALIFORNIA COUNCIL FOR THE BLIND, 8700 Reseda Blvd. #208, Northridge, CA 91325.
Positions: Fund raisers telephone for donations of household discards.
Requirements: Must be resident of greater Los Angeles area. Good phone manner necessary.
Provisions: Pays $6 an hour plus bonus plan.

CAMERON MILLS RESEARCH SERVICE, 2414 Cameron Mills Rd., Alexandria, VA 22302.
Positions: Field surveyers and telephone interviewers for market research projects.
Requirements: Must live in Washington, D.C., Northern Virginia, or nearby Maryland. Some experience working with the public necessary.
Provisions: Pays by the survey.

CANCER FEDERATION, San Jose, CA. (209) 287-3088.
Positions: Telemarketers call for household discards in fundraising effort. Work 5 hours each evening, 5 days a week.
Requirements: Some telemarketing experience is required. Must live in Northern California.
Provisions: Training is provided. Pays guaranteed salary plus bonuses.

CAR-LENE RESEARCH, Deerbrook Mall, Deerfield, IL 60015.
Positions: Field surveyers and telephone interviewers for market research assignments.
Requirements: Must live in Deerfield, IL; Pomona, CA; Santa Fe Springs, CA; Northbrook, IL; Hanover, MA; Dallas, TX; or Richardson, TX. Market research experience is required.
Provisions: Pays by the survey.

CERTIFIED MARKETING SERVICES, INC., Route 9, P.O. Box 447, Kinderhook, NY 12106.
Positions: Market Research surveys are conducted nationwide by independent, part-time field workers.
Requirements: Must be over 18 years of age. No experience is required, but good organization and communication skills are helpful. Write for information.
Provisions: Hourly wage, travel expenses and reimbursables.

CHAMBERLAIN MARKET RESEARCH, 1036 Oakhaven Rd., Memphis, TN 38119.
Positions: Field surveyers.
Requirements: Memphis residents only. Experience required.
Provisions: Pays by the survey.

CHECK II MARKET RESEARCH, 900 Osceola Dr., Suite 207, West Palm Beach, FL 33409.
Positions: Field surveyers.
Requirements: Local residents only. Experience is preferred.
Provisions: Work is part-time only. Pays by the survey.

CONSUMER OPINION SEARCH, INC., 10795 Watson Rd., St. Louis, MO 63127.
Positions: Field surveyers.

Requirements: St. Louis residents only. Good communication skills required.
Provisions: Pays by the survey.

DAKOTA INTERVIEWING SERVICE AND MARKET RESEARCH, 16 Vista Dr., Minot, ND 58701.
Positions: Opinion polls are conducted in the field and on the telephone.
Requirements: Local residents only. Good communication skills required. Must be able to follow directions exactly.
Provisions: Work is part-time, on-call only.

> "We make much more money than other employment counselors . . . up to $1,000 a week."
> --Escrow Overload

DALE SYSTEM, INC.,1101 Stewart Ave., Garden City, NY 11530.
Positions: Market research surveys are conducted in the field by means of purchases and observations in movie theatres, bowling alleys, restaurants, retail stores, and many other business establishments. Positions are part-time only..
Requirements: Experience in market research is preferred, but other experience dealing with the public could suffice. Need to live in one of the company's sampling areas. Send letter of interest requesting name and address of field supervisor nearest you.
Provisions: Pays per survey, plus reimbursements for related expenses.

DAVIS AND DAVIS RESEARCH, INC., 214 Van Gogh, Brandon, FL 33511.
Positions: Market research surveys are conducted in the field.
Requirements: Must be local resident. Experience required.
Provisions: Must be available for assignments as they come in. Pays by the project.

DAVIS MARKET RESEARCH SERVICES, INC.,23801 Calabasas Rd., Calabasas, CA 91302.
Positions: Field surveyers.
Requirements: Local residents only. Previous experience working with the public required.

D.C. MARKET RESEARCH, 936 North Second St., Springfield, IL 62702.
Positions: Field surveyers.
Requirements: Experienced interviewers only. Must be local resident.
Provisions: Pays by the project.

DELAWARE INTERVIEWING SERVICE, 811 Sunset Terrace, Dover, DE 19901.
Positions: Field interviewers for market research surveys. Surveys are conducted in Delaware and nearby parts of Maryland only.
Requirements: Interviewing experience required. Must live in one of the sampling points.

DENNIS RESEARCH SERVICE, INC., 3502 Stellhorn Rd., Fort Wayne, IN 46815.
Positions: Market research surveys are conducted in Northern Indiana by independent part-time field surveyers.
Requirements: Must be resident of Fort Wayne or South Bend. No experience is required, but good communication skills are a must.
Provisions: Pays by the survey.

DEPTH RESEARCH LABORATORIES, INC., 1103 Albemarle Rd., Brooklyn, NY 11218.
Positions: Field interviewers for various market research and opinion poll surveys. All are conducted in the greater New York City area.
Requirements: Interviewing experience is required. Send for application.
Provisions: Pays by the survey.

DISABLED AMERICAN VETERANS, 273 E. 800 South, Salt Lake City, UT 84111.
Positions: Telemarketers use the phone to ask for donations of household articles.
Requirements: No experience required. Must live in Salt Lake City.
Provisions: Pays minimum hourly wage plus bonus plan.

DISABLED AMERICAN VETERANS OF COLORADO, 8799 North Washington, Denver, CO 80229.
Positions: Fund raisers call for donations of household discards to be sold through thrift stores.
Requirements: Denver residents only. Must have good phone voice and self-discipline.
Provisions: Training provided. Pays small hourly wage plus bonus plan.

EVELYN DREXLER INTERVIEWING SERVICE, 8807 Bridlewood Dr., Huntsville, AL 35802.
Positions: Market research surveys are conducted by field surveyers and telephone interviewers in Northern Alabama and Southern Tennessee.
Requirements: Must live in one of the sampling areas. Previous experience is preferred.

C.B. DUPREE ASSOCIATES, 3 Rathburn Rd., #6, Niantic, CT 06357.
Positions: Field surveyers and telephone interviewers conduct market research surveys.
Requirements: Must be local resident. Market research experience required.

EL CAMINO MEMORIAL PARK, 5600 Carol Canyon Rd., San Diego, CA 92121.
Positions: Telemarketers conduct surveys over the phone.
Requirements: Experience dealing with the public. Must live in San Diego.
Provisions: Training is provided. Pays salary plus bonus.

ELECTROTEL, 3810 Pierce, Wheat Ridge, CO 80033.
Positions: Phone surveyers work on a variety of projects.
Requirements: Experience is required. Must be self-motivated. Local residents only.
Provisions: Training is provided in office for one week. Pay based on performance.

ESCROW OVERLOAD, 4417 Sarah Street, Burbank, CA 91505.
Positions: Middle managers - i.e., recruiters, are completely home-based. Escrow Overload is a temporary help service operating from San Diego to Ventura, California. All home workers are considered independent managers. All have professional offices set up in their homes complete with waiting rooms for new applicants, WATS lines and

Close Up: NORC

Founded in 1941, NORC is the oldest survey research organization established for non-commercial purposes. NORC is a not-for-profit organization affiliated with the University of Chicago.

Survey research is the collection of accurate, unbiased information from a carefully chosen sample of individuals.

Some organizations do opinion polls, asking people to rate the performance of public officials, for example. Others do market research, asking about such things as the products people use. NORC does social science research, asking about people's attitudes and behavior in areas of social concern, such as education, housing, employment (and unemployment), and health care.

NORC's clients include the American Cancer Society, Harvard University, the Rockefeller Foundation, the U.S. Dept. of Labor, and the Social Security Administration to name just a few. Nowhere will you find higher standards of quality in research of this kind.

To date, NORC has conducted more than 1,000 surveys. This may not sound like a lot considering the thousands that are conducted for companies like Gallup. Unlike Gallup, though, NORC's surveys are "longitudinal," meaning the same people are surveyed over long periods of time. Over 900 part-time NORC interviewers are located in cities, towns, and rural areas throughout the United States. Many, but not all, are home-based. Each assignment is on a temporary, per-project basis. The average project lasts about 6 months. All interviewers must be available to work at least 20 hours a week. 40 hour weeks are common.

About half of the people working for NORC have been with the company at least 5 years. That's an outstanding record in an industry where rapid employee turnover is the norm. Nevertheless, NORC is constantly seeking more qualified interviewers—especially in hard-to-staff metropolitan areas such as New York, Chicago, Los Angeles and Miami.

Field Director Miriam Clarke says "We look for someone who is people-oriented, outgoing, and somewhat aggressive. Someone who does not like to be tied to a desk is a good candidate actually. Being able to follow instructions precisely is important, too."

An hour and a half of general training is provided at a central location. After that, project briefings are handled by mail and phone.

The pay range depends upon where you live, but the entry level base rate is $4.50 an hour and up, depending upon experience. Any particular qualifications, such as foreign languages, pay extra. Pay raises come once a year and are based on performance.

file cabinets. On-line computer systems are being added. Work consists of interviewing new job applicants, phoning new accounts, and placing employees.
Provisions: Pays commission. "The down side to working at home is the long hours, since we're responsible for virtually all aspects of the business in our respective areas. The up side is we make much more money than other employment counselors because the company's overhead is so low. We make $2 per hour booked, up to $1000 a week." (The $2 per hour is earned for each temporary placed, so the recruiter earns $80 for a 40 hour placement.)

E-Z INTERVIEWING, P.O. Box 951, Farmington, CT 06032.
Positions: Field surveyers.
Requirements: Local residents only. Must have interviewing experience.

FACTS 'N FIGURES, Panorama Mall, Suite 78B, Panorama City, CA 91402.
Positions: Market research and public opinion surveys are conducted by field surveyers and telephone interviewers.
Requirements: Must be resident of greater Los Angeles. Interviewing experience is required.
Provisions: Pays by the survey.

FAR WEST RESEARCH, INC., 438 25th Ave. #4, San Francisco, CA 94121.
Positions: Market researchers conduct surveys on the telephone at home. Surveys are conducted in major metropolitan areas on the West Coast only.
Requirements: Must have market research experience. Must live in one of the company's sampling areas.
Provisions: Pays by the survey.

FIELD RESEARCH, INC., 234 Front St., San Francisco, CA 94111.
Positions: Market research surveys are conducted in the field mainly in California.
Requirements: Experience is preferred. Must live in one of the sampling areas.
Provisions: Pays by the survey.

GEORGE FINE RESEARCH, INC., 220 N. Central Park Ave., Hartsdale, NY 10530.
Positions: Market research surveys are conducted both in the field and over the phone.
Requirements: Experience is preferred. Must live in one of the company's sampling areas.
Provisions: Pays by the survey.

FOGARTY MARKET RESEARCH, 4828 Ronson Ct., Suite C, San Diego, CA 92111.
Positions: Market research by phone only. Work consists of phone interviewing part-time; some is temporary, some is ongoing.
Requirements: Must live in San Diego.
Provisions: Training is provided. Pays by the survey.

GALLUP POLL, 47 Hulfish Street, 100 Palmer Square, Suite 200, P.O. Box 310, Princeton, NJ 08542. Attn: Field Dept.
Positions: Market researchers for field research. Across the country, there are 360 sampling areas. Market researchers conduct surveys in the field (usually door-to-door), returning home only to do the "paperwork." There are almost 2,000 of these home-based

researchers around the U.S. This work is permanent part-time. It is conducted during weekends, approximately 1 - 2 weekends per month.

Requirements: No experience required and no age restriction for persons over 18. You need only to be able to read well, talk with people and have a dependable car. Send work experience, address and phone number with letter of interest.

Provisions: An applicant must complete sample work which is tested and graded before job begins. After a person is accepted as an interviewer, Gallup's techniques are self-taught using an Interviewer's Manual and by communicating with the Field Administrator in the Princeton Office. All workers are independent contractors and are expected to meet minimum quotas. Pays an hourly wage plus expenses. "We're always looking for responsible people, especially permanent part-timers."

GARGAN & ASSOCIATES, P.O. Box 12249, Portland, OR 97212.
Positions: Market research and public opinion surveys are conducted by field surveyers and telephone interviewers.
Requirements: Experience is preferred. Must live in Astoria, Portland, Salem, Albany, Eugene, Bend, Coos Bay, Roseburg, or Medford.
Provisions: Pays by the survey.

L. TUCKER GIBSON AND ASSOCIATES, INC., 1046 Central Parkway S., San Antonio, TX 78232.
Positions: Field surveyers and telephone interviewers for market research studies.
Requirements: Must be experienced local resident. Bilingual applicants only.

GIRARD & GIRARD CREATIVE CONCEPTS, 22260 Parthenia St., Canoga Park, CA 91304.
Positions: Field surveyers and telephone interviewers for market research.
Requirements: Interviewing experience is required. Residents of Los Angeles only.

LUANNE GLAZER ASSOCIATES, INC., 98 Ocean Dr. East, Stamford, CT 06902.
Positions: Field surveyers and telephone interviewers for market research.
Requirements: Must be local resident. Excellent communication skills and ability to follow directions explicitly required.
Provisions: Training is provided. Pays by the survey.

RUTH GOLDER INTERVIEWING SERVICE, 1804 Jaybee Rd., Wilmington, DE 19803.
Positions: Field interviewers for market research.
Requirements: Interviewing experience required. Must live in Chester or Delaware County, Pennsylvania, or Salem County, New Jersey.

AURELIA K. GOLDSMITH MARKETING RESEARCH SERVICES, INC., 1279 Guelbreath Lane, #204, St. Louis, MO 63146.
Positions: Field surveyers and telephone interviewers.
Requirements: Local residents only. Interviewing experience preferred.

GOOD SHEPHERD HOME FOR MENTALLY RETARDED, Denver, CO (303)232-7697.
Positions: Telephone fund raisers call for donations of household good and donations.
Requirements: Denver residents only. Must be dependable and sincere. To apply, you must call, do not write. Must be available to work early mornings and evenings.
Provisions: Training is provided in a 2 hour interview/orientation. Names to call are provided. Pays commission per pick up scheduled, averages $3.50 to $6.50 an hour.

LOUIS HARRIS AND ASSOCIATES, 630 Fifth Ave., New York, NY 10020.
Positions: Market researchers and opinion surveyers are needed in the field.
Requirements: No experience is necessary. Louis Harris has "several hundred" sampling areas and it is necessary to live in one of them. Write and ask for an application which will be kept on file. When something comes up, you will be called. If you are ready for work, you will receive your instructions over the phone. How you go about completing the assignment from there is up to you.
Provisions: Pays by the survey, about $10 to $44 per survey.

HARVEY RESEARCH ORGANIZATION, INC., 600 Perinton Hills Office Park, Fairport, NY 14450.
Positions: Interviewers to work as independent contractors on continuing assignments. Work is available in all major cities. There are 50 to 100 interviewers in each sampling area. Most interviews are conducted in the field.
Requirements: Experience is necessary. Write a letter of interest. You will be sent an application, then a sample survey to complete before being hired permanently .
Provisions: Pays by the survey.

HAYES MARKETING RESEARCH, 7840 El Cajon Blvd., Suite 400, La Mesa, CA 92041.
Positions: Field surveyers and telephone interviewers for market research.
Requirements: Local area residents only. Experience required.
Provisions: Pays by the survey.

HEAKIN RESEARCH, INC., P.O. Box 146, Olympia Field, IL 60461.
Positions: Field surveyors conduct market research survey in 15 areas.
Requirements: Experience is preferred. Must be resident of Los Angeles, Sacramento, San Francisco area, Chicago, Kansas City, Baltimore, Independence, Pittsburgh, Memphis, or Houston.

PAT HENRY ENTERPRISES, 8505 Tanglewood Sq., #101, Chagrin Falls, OH 44022.

Positions: Market research surveys are conducted in the field and over the phone.
Requirements: Market research experience required. Must be resident of Northeastern Ohio.

HOSPICE OF SAN FRANCISCO, 225 - 30th, San Francisco, CA 94121.
Positions: Staffing coordinator for non-office hours.
Requirements: Experience in medical staffing required. Must live in San Francisco. Good phone manner important. Knowledge of medical terminology preferred.
Provisions: Pays hourly rates.

IDEAS IN MARKETING, 14100 N. 46th St., #207K, Tampa, FL 33613.
Positions: Market research surveys are conducted in the field and over the phone.
Requirements: Market research experience is required. Must be resident of Tampa, St. Petersburg, Sarasota, Orlando, or Lakeland.

ILLINOIS AMVETS, 4711 W. 137th St., Crestwood, IL 60445.
Positions: Fund raisers phone for donations of household articles.
Requirements: There are 10 locations in Illinois; you must reside in one of them. No experience necessary outside of good speaking ability.
Provisions: Part-time hours are flexible. Pays commission for every pick-up; averages about $4.50 and hour.

INFORMATION RESOURCES, INC., 150 N. Clinton, Chicago, IL 60606.
Positions: Market research interviewers and supervisors. Interviewers conduct surveys by phone. Supervisors are home-based. Company is growing rapidly and is assigning many new areas in addition to the major cities covered now.
Requirements: Must have good communication skills and work well independently. Interviewers should write letters of interest. Supervisors need to send resume.
Provisions: Interviewers are paid by the project. Supervisors are paid a salary and benefits.

ISAAC RESEARCH, INC., P.O. Box 989, Columbus, IN 47202.
Positions: Market research surveys are conducted in the field and over the phone.
Requirements: Interviewing experience is required. Local residents only.

J & R FIELD SERVICES, INC., 747 Caldwell Ave., North Woodmere, NY 11581.
Positions: Field surveyers.
Requirements: Market research experience is required. Must be local resident.

JACKSON ASSOCIATES, 3070 Presidential Dr., #123, Atlanta, GA 30340.
Positions: Field and telephone interviewers for market research surveys.
Requirements: Experience required. Must be local resident.
Provisions: Pays by the survey.

JAPAN EXCHANGE SERVICES, 20705 Mansel Ave., Torrance, CA 90503.
Positions: Home-based coordinators are needed by this nonprofit educational organization. Responsibilities include finding host families for Japanese students, coordinating activities and tours. Work is part-time starting in March and ending in August each year. A second opportunity exists for area representatives that recruit host families for the academic year. The bulk of recruiting occurs from January through June. Throughout the rest of the year, it is the rep's responsibility to monitor the exchange student's progress

by keeping in contact with the school and the student.

Requirements: Must be responsible, have time and energy, and current community involvement is preferred.

Provisions: Area coordinators are paid $100 per student placement plus bonuses for initial paperwork. Also pays for parties, etc. Area reps are paid $380 per student. This is broken down to a split between placement and supervision. Japan Exchange Services is open to inquiries from any area in the country, but some will be screened out on a variety of criteria.

KELLY SERVICES, INC.
Positions: Staffing coordinators. Kelly relies on home-based staffing coordinators to take calls and dispatch temporary personnel during the night as a service to clients who operate on 24-hour shift rotations.

Requirements: Some experience in personnel placement is required. Write to locate the office nearest or find it in the phone book, then apply directly to that office.

Provisions: Positions are considered part-time only. Pays flat salary.

THE KIDNEY FOUNDATION.

Positions: Fund raising on a local level. Work involves calling for donations of household items.

Provisions: Training provided. Pays hourly wage plus bonuses. The Kidney Foundation has branch offices in every city. Call the one nearest you for more information.

LOS ANGELES MARKETING RESEARCH ASSOCIATES, 5712 Lankershim Blvd., North Hollywood, CA 91601.
Positions: Field interviewers.

Requirements: Interviewing experience required.

Provisions: Pays by the survey.

MARKET INTELLIGENCE RESEARCH CORPORATION, 2525 Charleston Road, Mountain View, CA 94043.
Positions: Freelancers write market research reports for various industries including telecommunications and medicine.

Requirements: Experience is required. Apply with resume and clips.

Provisions: Pays by the contract.

MARKET INTERVIEWS, 33029 Schoolcraft, Livonia, MI 48150.
Positions: Field surveyers conduct market research studies in dozens of sampling areas around the country.

Requirements: Must be experienced surveyer. Must live in one of the sampling areas. Send for application.

MARKET RESEARCH SERVICES OF DALLAS, 2944 Motley Dr. #207, Mesquite, TX 75150.
Positions: Local field surveyers and telephone interviewers are contracted by out-of-town market research firms to conduct surveys in the Dallas area.

Requirements: Good communication skills are necessary. Prefers some kind of experience dealing with the public.

Provisions: Work is part-time on-call only. Pays by the job.

Close Up: CSI Telemarketing

Consumer Surveys, Inc., more commonly known as C.S.I. Telemarketing, is growing steadily and now has over 1,200 home workers according to president Sam Gower.

C.S.I. developed a unique program for its clients several years ago called Precision Target Marketing. It combines market research with telemarketing in a two-step technique that is designed to increase a manufacturer's market share of a given product.

Here's how it works. A C.S.I. interviewer calls a consumer living within the immediate area of a particiapating store and asks questions like "What kind of toothpaste do you use?" to discover what brands of various groceries they use and, more importantly, in which supermarket they shop. If the consumer responds that they use Ivory Soap, drink Pepsi-Cola and have never tried a steak sandwich, C.S.I. will then mail the customer a packet of money-saving coupons for Dove, Coke and Steck-Umm Sandwich Steaks—all C.S.I. clients.

If the customer says they shop at the participating market, only those coupons are sent. But, if they shop elsewhere, an additional coupon good for a discount at the participating market will be included as well.

The result is that the client company is able to identify its competitor's customers for the first time. By targeting those customers with high value coupons, there is a much greater return. And for the supermarkets, there is an immediate increase in customer traffic, too.

C.S.I. interviewer Jean A. has worked from her New York home for five years now. Her perspective on how people feel about being called is interesting because she herself was called at home and surveyed. As a matter of fact, that's how she found out about C.S.I. in the first place. She found the whole thing so interesting, she sent the company a letter asking for information. She then applied for work and was taken on as an independent contractor.

"One of the best things about this," says Jean, "is we are not selling anything. We are offering something of value to the customers, so they are very receptive. It doesn't take much of their time, maybe 3 minutes. It's extremely rare that anyone hangs up."

Jean says she works for a few hours in the morning and a few hours in the afternoon and sometimes for a couple of hours in the evening. She is paid for each survey completed. Since she is an independent contractor, she can work as little or as much as she likes, but there are bonuses available for high levels of production and she likes to reach a certain plateau each week. The result for Jean is about $1,000 a month.

C.S.I. operates in Los Angeles, San Diego, Dallas, Detroit, Chicago, Boston, Philadelphia, Miami, Albany, New York, and Newark.

MARKETING FORCE, 805 Oakwood, Rochester, MI 48063.
Positions: Marketing Force conducts market research surveys in the field in sampling points around the country. Currently has over 18,000 surveyers and 1,500 supervisors on roster.
Requirements: Good communication skills and the ability to follow directions to the letter are most important. Send for application and ask for name and address of nearest field manager.

MARKETING INVESTIGATIONS, INC., Osborne Plaza, 1106 Ohio River Blvd., Box 343, Sewickley, PA 15143.
Positions: Field surveyers for market research studies.
Requirements: Interviewing experience required. Must live in Pittsburgh area.

J.B. MARTIN INTERVIEWING SERVICES, INC., 4695 Main St., Bridgeport, CT 06606.
Positions: Field surveyers.
Requirements: Market research experience required. Local surveyers only.

MARY LUCAS MARKET RESEARCH, Marietta Plaza, 13250 New Halls Ferry Road, Florissant, MO 63033.
Positions: Field surveyers and telephone interviewers.
Requirements: Market research experience is required. Must be resident of greater St. Louis area.

B.J. MAYERSON INTERVIEWING SERVICE, 928 East Hampton Rd., Milwaukee, WI 53217.
Positions: Field surveyers and telephone interviewers.
Requirements: Market research experience required. Must be local resident.
Provisions: Pays by the survey.

MAZUR/ZACHOW INTERVIEWING, 4319 North 76 Street, Milwaukee, WI.
Positions: FIeld surveyers and telephone interviewers.
Requirements: Market research experience required. Must be Milwaukee resident.

T. MCCARTHY ASSOCIATES, INC., Penn-Can Mall, 5775 South Bay Road, Syracuse-Clay, NY 13041.
Positions: Market research surveys are conducted in the field and over the phone.
Requirements: Must be local resident. Interviewing experience is required.
Provisions: Pays by the survey.

MEDICAL PERSONNEL POOL, 2050 Spectrum Blvd., Ft. Lauderdale, FL 33309.
Positions: This franchised agency is a nursing staff placement agency with office coast to coast. In some areas where "satellite offices" operate in outlying area, home-based staffing coordinators are used to take incoming calls and dispatch nurses to work assignments. In some offices, this is done only at night and on weekends.
Requirements: Some phone experience is preferred. Staffing experience is also preferred, but not necessary. Must be self-directed. Write to find the office nearest to you or look it up in your local phone book.

MENTOR, The Columbia Commons, 256 Columbia Turnpike, Suite 102, Florham Park, NJ 07932.

Positions: Home care for young people, ages 3 - 18, with psychiatric and substance abuse problems.
Requirements: To be a "mentor" does not necessarily require formal education, but experience, an understanding of people and most of all, compassion. If you qualify, you will be assigned to one patient at a time to live in your home. You'll become a Mental Health Technician, and an integral part of an expert mental health team.
Provisions: Excellent compensation. Openings exist in seven states including Pennsylvania, Texas, New Jersey, Massachusetts, South Carolina, Illinois, and Maryland.

METROPOLITAN FINANCE CORPORATION, 1127-1131 W. 41st St., Kansas City, MO 64111.
Positions: Credit collections brokers for business-to-business accounts only.
Requirements: Some experience in the collections field is necessary.
Provisions: Good company support and training is provided. Pays commission. Can be located anywhere. All brokers are independent contractors.

MEYER CARE, 760 Market St., Suite 612, San Francisco, CA 94102. Offices also in Kansas City, Denver, and St. Louis.
Positions: Meyer Care is a home health care provider as well as a placement agency that dispatches medical personnel to nursing homes as needed. Home-based medical coordinators receive calls and assign staff to home care cases and facilities from home at night and especially on weekends.
Requirements: Home workers are also required to come into the office on Fridays for a few hours to help with clerical support since this is a peak day. California Regional Director, Harris Perles, says this is not a job for moonlighters, but rather someone who is home because of a need to care for family, for instance. Calls may come in at any time during the night and the coordinator has to be able to handle it properly with efficiency and genuine concern. "This takes a certain personality. It's hard for us to find the right kind of people."
Provisions: Some offices pay salary only; some pay an additional bonus. Electronic pagers are also provided, so the workers are not quite so homebound.

MISSIONS SURVEYS, 3771 Mt. Ariane Drive, San Diego, CA 92111.
Positions: Opinion surveys are conducted in the field and on the phone.
Requirements: Must be resident of Southern California and have good communication skills.

NATIONAL ANALYSTS, 1700 Market St., Philadelphia, PA 19103.
Positions: Opinion surveys are conducted in the field.
Requirements: Must live in one of the sampling areas. Experience is preferred.
Provisions: Training is provided. Pays by the survey.

NATIONAL OPINION RESEARCH CENTER, Social Science Research Center of the University of Chicago, 6030 South Ellis Avenue, Chicago, IL 60637.
Positions: Interviewers for long-term social science research projects. This nonprofit organization is the oldest research center in the country, founded in 1941. Research contracts come from government agencies and other institutional clients generally to study behavioral changes in specified areas of the population. There are 100 "area probability centers," plus studies are conducted in other locations specifically requested by the clients. All workers are considered part-time, temporary independent contractors though projects often last up to 14 months. Most work is done face-to-face, some is done

over the phone. Currently has over 700 interviewers and is actively seeking more, particularly in metropolitan areas.

Requirements: Must be available a minimum of 20 hours a week; some work 40 hours a week. Need to be people-oriented, independent, outgoing, somewhat aggressive, able to follow instructions precisely and pay attention to details. Send letter of interest.

Provisions: Training is provided; general training takes about a day and a half in the office. Project briefings are a combination of written materials and oral instructions over the phone. Pays starting salary of $4.75 plus expenses. Pay goes up with experience or with particular qualifications that may be hard to find. Annual increases are based on performance.

NORTHWEST CENTER FOR THE RETARDED, 1600 West Armory Way, Seattle, WA 98119.

Positions: Telemarketers to call for donations of household goods.
Requirements: Must be local resident.
Provisions: Training is provided. Pays hourly wage of $3.55 plus bonus plan.

OLSTEN HEALTH CARE SERVICES.
Positions: Staffing coordinators. Olsten now has over 300 offices nationwide in its health care services division. Each office has a minimum of two home-based staffing coordinators job sharing on a seven-days-on, seven-days-off routine. The job consists of taking calls during the day, at night, and on weekends to dispatch appropriate personnel for hospital and home health care positions.
Requirements: Some staffing experience or medical background is required. Write to locate the office nearest you, then apply directly to that office.
Provisions: Pays weekly salary plus placement bonuses.

OPINION RESEARCH CORPORATION, Opinion Park, Princeton, NJ 08540.
Positions: Opinion surveyers conduct interviews in the field in New Jersey only.
Requirements: Ability to communicate effectively with people is a must. Send letter of interest.
Provisions: Pays by the survey.

PROFESSIONAL RESEARCH ORGANIZATON, INC., 10 Corporate Hill Drive, Suite 100, Little Rock, AR 72205.
Positions: Market research surveys are conducted in the field and over the phone.
Requirements: Must be experienced. Local residents only.

PROFILE MARKETING RESEARCH, INC., 4020 S. 57th Ave., Lakeworth, FL 33463.
Positions: Field surveyers.
Requirements: Experience required. Southern Florida residents only.

PUBLIC REACTION RESEARCH, One Dillion Rd., Kendall Park, NJ 08824.
Positions: Public opinion surveys are conducted in the field and over the phone.
Requirements: Some kind of interviewing experience is required. Must be resident of greater Princeton area.
Provisions: Pays by the job.

PURPLE HEART SERVICE FOUNDATION.
Positions: Part-time telemarketers solicit for donations.

Requirements: Must work well with the public. Personal interview will be required. Look for the office nearest you in your local phone book and contact that office directly.
Provisions: Hours are flexible. Pays commission of between $5 and $10 an hour.

Q & A RESEARCH, INC., 1701 Sunrise Hwy, Bay Shore, NY 11706.
Positions: Field surveyers.
Requirements: Market research experience required. Must be local resident.
Provisions: Pays by the survey.

RESEARCH TRIANGLE INSTITUTE, Hanes Building, Research Triangle Park, Raleigh, NC 27601.
Positions: Interviewers for opinion research surveys conducted primarily in the field. Research Triangle is a nonprofit social research organization operating nationwide.
Requirements: Good communication skills needed. Send letter of interest.
Provisions: Pays hourly rate in some areas, pays by the survey in others. Training is provided.

THE ROPER ORGANIZATION, 566 Boston Post Road., Mamaroneck, NY 10543.
Positions: Opinion surveyers conduct research within sampling areas around the country. All research is conducted in the field.
Requirements: No opinion surveying experience is necessary, but experience involving some kind of public contact is preferred. Write and ask for name and address of nearest field supervisor.

SAGE SURVEYS, INC., Soundview Lane, Port Washington, NY 11050.
Positions: Field surveyers and telephone interviewers.
Requirements: Interviewing experience is required. Must be resident of New York City or one of the nearby suburbs.

SALEM SERVICES, 21 Poe Road, Thornwood, NY 10594.
Positions: Field surveyers and telephone interviewers.
Requirements: Experienced surveyers only. Must be resident of Westchester or Rockland County.
Provisions: Pays by the job.

SALT LAKE ANIMAL SOCIETY, 1151 South Redwood Road, Suite 108, Salt Lake City, UT 84104.
Positions: Telemarketers call for donations.
Requirements: Must live in Salt Lake City.
Provisions: Training is provided. Pays commission and bonus plan.

SANDIA MARKETING SERVICES, 923 Coronado Mall, N.E., Albuquerque, NM 87110.
Positions: Field surveyers.
Requirements: Market research experience preferred. Must be local resident.
Provisions: Pays by the survey.

SANTELL MARKET RESEARCH, INC., 300 Mt. Lebanon Boulevard, Suite 2204, Pittsburgh, PA 15234.
Positions: Field surveyers.
Requirements: Market research experience preferred. Must be local resident.
Provisions: Pays by the survey.

SHUGOLL RESEARCH, 7455 Wisconsin Ave., Bethesda, MD 20814.
Positions: Market researchers conduct public opinion interviews over the phone and in person.
Requirements: Must be assertive and able to communicate clearly. Projects are part-time and temporary. Must be local resident.

SIMMONS MARKET RESEARCH BUREAU, 380 Madison Ave., 5th Floor, New York, NY 10017.
Positions: Opinion surveyers conduct research in the field. Both surveyers and their supervisors are home-based.
Requirements: Must live within one of the Simmons' survey areas. Send letter of interest and ask for the name and address of the field supervisor closest to you.
Provisions: No experience is necessary. Must attend short training sessions which are conducted regularly within survey areas all over U.S. Pays by the survey.

SOUND IDEA PRODUCTIONS/HPRP, Attn: Personnel Dept. 1-PR, 6547 N. Academy Blvd., Suite 548, Colorado Springs, CO 80918.
Positions: The title of the home-based position with this company is "Human Resource Assistance Representative."
Requirements: Experience in human resource management, public relations or sales and management helpful, but not required. Must enjoy working with and helping others.
Provisions: If selected, you will be trained and certified by the company to work in your area. You can work with complete flexibility and independence. Earnings can go as high as $900 part-time, even higher full-time.

SURVEY CENTER, INC., 505 North Lake Shore Drive, Chicago, IL 60611.
Positions: Market research surveys are conducted in sampling points around the country. Field interviewers and their supervisors work part-time on-call.
Requirements: Write and request name and address of nearest field supervisor.
Provisions: Pays by the survey.

TAYLOR INTERVIEWING SERVICE, 1026 Horseshoe Rd., Augusta, GA 30906.
Positions: Field surveyers and telephone interviewers.

Requirements: Market research experience preferred. Must be Augusta resident.

TAYLOR MANAGEMENT SYSTEMS, 9242 Markville, Dallas, TX 75243.
Positions: Telephone recruiters locate fund raiser volunteers.
Requirements: Telemarketing experience required. Must be Dallas resident.
Provisions: Pays piece rates based on number of volunteers recruited.

TAYLOR RESEARCH, 3990 Old Town Ave., Suite 210A, San Diego, CA 92110.
Positions: Field surveyers.
Requirements: Market research experience required. Must be San Diego resident.
Provisions: Pays by the survey.

TEMPOSITIONS, Home Health Care Division, 150 Post St., San Francisco, CA 94104.
Positions: Staffing coordinator for evenings and weekends.
Requirements: Experience in medical staffing required. Must live in San Francisco.
Provisions: This is part-time work only.

TEXAS GULF MINERALS AND METALS, INC., 1610 Frank Akers Road, Anniston, AL 36201.
Positions: Buyers. Company recycles catalytic converters. Home-based buyers locate and purchase used catalytic converters which will in turn be sold to the company.
Requirements: Write for complete details.
Provisions: Pick up is provided weekly. Pays weekly. Training is provided. Can be anywhere in U.S.

TRENDFACTS RESEARCH/FIELD SERVICES, 31800 Northwestern Highway, Suite 380, Farmington Hills, MI 48018.
Positions: Field surveyers work part-time on-call in Michigan only.
Requirements: Market research experience required.
Provisions: Pays by the survey.

TRI-COUNTY RESEARCH, 3 Rexal Court, New City, NY 10956.
Positions: Field surveyers and telephone interviewers.
Requirements: Market research experience required. Must live in Westchester, Rockland, Bergen, Passaic, or Upstate New York.

UCPA, 11401 Rainier Avenue South, Seattle, WA 98178.
Positions: Fund raising involves calling for donations of reusable household items.
Requirements: Must live in greater Seattle area.
Provisions: Pays base salary plus bonus plan. Benefits include paid vacation. Hours can be part-time or full-time. Training is provided.

UNITED CEREBRAL PALSY, 1217 Alhambra Blvd., Sacramento, CA 95816.
Positions: Fund raising by phone. Job consists of calling for donations of household discards for about four hours a day.
Requirements: Must live in Sacaramento.
Provisions: Pays hourly wage plus bonus plan.

VALLEY RESEARCH & SURVEY, 2241 S. 250th E., Bountiful, UT 84010.
Positions: Field surveyers and telephone interviewers.

Requirements: Market research experience required. Salt Lake City residents only.

VALUE VILLAGE PROJECT OF THE NATIONAL CHILDREN'S CENTER, INC., 525 Rhode Island Ave. N.E., Washington, D.C. 20002.
Positions: Telephone fund raising.
Requirements: Must be local resident. Must be articulate and able to work well with the public.

VETERANS' REHABILITATION CENTER, 9201 Pacific Avenue, Tacoma, WA 98444.
Positions: Fund raisers phone for donations of household items, clothing, etc.
Requirements: Must come to Tacoma for short training session. (Can live in Seattle.)
Provisions: Paid training is provided. Pays guaranteed hourly wage. Inquiries are welcome.

VIETNAM VETERANS OF AMERICA FOUNDATION, Ventura, CA (800) 827-2013.
Positions: Fund raisers phone for donations of household items to be sold in thrift stores.
Requirements: No experience required. Must have good speaking voice. Local residents only. Apply by calling.
Provisions: Pays guaranteed minimum wage plus bonus plan. Training is provided.

VISION SERVICES, 9709 3rd Ave. N.E., Ste. 100, Seattle, WA 98115.
Positions: Phone work for nonprofit agency that offers programs to the blind and visually impaired. No sales is involved.
Requirements: Must live in Seattle. Touchtone phone required.
Provisions: One week of training is provided at headquarters. Pays $3.75 per hour. After four months a bonus plan is added.

WALKER RESEARCH COMPANY, 8000 Knue Road, Indianapolis, IN 46250.
Positions: Opinion surveyers conduct field interviews within sampling areas around the country.
Requirements: Send letter of interest asking for name and address of nearest field supervisor.
Provisions: Training is provided. Pays by the survey.

WEST STAT, 1650 Research Boulevard, Rockville, MD 20850.
Positions: Interviewers conduct social research surveys in the field.
Requirements: Must be able to attend training session.
Provisions: Training is provided. Write for the location of the nearest office.

WESTERN MEDICAL SERVICES, 690 Market St., Ste. 502, San Francisco, CA 94104.
Positions: Answering service staff.
Requirements: Excellent communication skills are necessary. Some medical knowledge is required. Must live in the local calling area of San Francisco. Work is part-time, evenings only.
Provisions: Pays hourly wage.

WHITE VACUUM COMPANY, 215 Brownsville Rd., Pittsburgh, PA 15210.
Positions: Telemarketers do customer service work.

Requirements: Must apply in person (must live in Pittsburgh); after initial application all contact is done via the mail.
Provisions: Training is provided. Customer list is supplied. Work is part-time; three hours a day, five days a week. Pays salary plus commission.

WORLD EXCHANGE, White Birch Road, Putnam Valley, NY 10579.
Positions: World Exchange needs Program Directors for its exchange student program. This year 1,000 students will be arriving from France, Japan, Spain, and Holland and U.S. students will be sent to England, France, Spain and Holland for one month cultural exchange. Program Directors find and interview host families on a part-time, seasonal basis.
Requirements: Experience helps, but is not necessary. World Exchange is looking for people who are "internationally minded"; ability to work well with people and various civic organizations is important. Can live within 300 miles of Los Angeles or San Francisco on the West Coast; and anywhere from Southern Florida to the Canadian Border on the East Coast.
Provisions: Compensates for each placement.

Homeworker Profile
Charlene Weiss, Salaried Manager

As a mother of two children, Charlene Weiss was working in a big office in Chicago when her husband was transferred by the Air Force to Arizona. Her employer, National Opinion Research Center (NORC), saw no reason why she shouldn't take her job with her since over 800 NORC interviewers work from their homes all around the country.

Working in an extra room at home was a new experience for Charlene, who was accustomed to commuting to the office "downtown." With the aid of a personal computer and modem (and, of course, the indispensible telephone) she was able to keep in close contact with the Chicago office and NORC employees all over the country.

After only three years, Charlene was promoted to a position that has made her administratively responsible for the 800 interviewers and their 80 supervisors. Her work involves talking to supervisors about their staffing needs, developing materials for the field management staff, putting out procedural memos, and other supervisory duties.

NORC is fairly typical of market research and opinion poll companies. A person can start working part-time, temporarily, from home, making a small supplemental income. But there is always room for upward mobility. Charlene certainly proved that. She has the highest supervisory position in her company with the corporate salary to prove it.

Industrial Home Work

Industrial home work is the kind of work that most people think of when you mention home work. It is work that is usually performed in a factory setting or sometimes in an office. It generally requires no special skills and therefore it doesn't generally pay very well.

It is simply a myth that this is the most common type of home work. Actually, it is the least common type of home work, because industrial home work is illegal in many states and some types of industrial home work are prohibited by federal labor laws as well. The states that do allow it have very strict standards and certification procedures. In Illinois, for example, any employer who wishes to hire home workers must obtain certification not only for the company, but for each and every employee as well.

All industrial home work is done locally. It is impossible for this type of work to be transported from one location to another, partly because of the labor laws. Also, it is not economically feasible to pay to transport materials to and from a worker's home, pay the worker, and expect to make a profit. Most of the time, an industrial home worker must pick up and deliver the materials and finished work himself. In rare instances, a courier service is set up within a short radius of the employer's factory or office.

As the manufacturing sector of our economic base continues to shrink, so will industrial home work. There is not very much of it available now, and there will be even less available in the future.

ADCRAFT MFG., CO., 2535 S. 25th Ave., Broadview, IL 60153.
Positions: Hand assembly of specialty advertising products. Home-based workforce is on the decline here, so opportunities are limited.
Requirements: Must be local resident. Must obtain home worker certificate from Illinois Department of Labor.
Provisions: Pays piece rates.

ALLEN SHOE COMPANY, INC., 53 Falmouth St., Attleboro, MA 02703.
Positions: Work is very specialized; French cord turning for shoe manufacturer. There are currently no home workers being hired.
Requirements: Some experience specific to this work is necessary. Must be local resident.
Provisions: Machinery is provided by the company. Piece rates equal approximately $4 an hour.

ALLISON ELECTRONICS, INC., 406 West Fairway, P.O. Box "B". Big Bear City, CA 92314.
Positions: Electronic assemblers. Loading only, no soldering, of PC boards and ICs. There are currently 28 home workers at Allison.
Requirements: Experience preferred, but not required. Must be local resident.
Provisions: Pays piece rates based on production. Will accept applications, but has a waiting list.

ANGLER'S CHOICE FISHING PRODUCTS, INC., 411 Centerville Road, Gordonville, PA 17529.
Positions: Hand assembly of various fishing tackle components.
Requirements: Must be local resident. Must qualify as Pennsylvania industrial home worker (be either disabled or need to care for invalid family member).
Provisions: Pays piece rates.

ASHLAND PRODUCTS, 10910 S. Langley, Chicago, IL.
Positions: Hand assembly.
Requirements: Must be a local resident. Must obtain a home worker certificate from the Illinois Department of Labor.

AT&T BELL LABORATORIES, 200 Park Plaza, Naperville, IL.
Positions: Hand assembly.
Requirements: Must be local resident. Must obtain a home worker certificate from the Illinois Department of Labor.

AURA BADGE COMPANY, Clayton Ave., Clayton, NJ 08312
Positions: Hand assembly includes inserting pins into cello buttons and acetate badgeholders.
Requirements: Must be local resident in order to pick up and deliver supplies and finished work. No experience or equipment is required.
Provisions: Pays salary and basic benefits provided by law. Currently has 15 home workers.

BIRCH CUTTING CORPORATION, Crown Avenue & Birch Streets, Scranton, PA 18505.
Positions: Hand assembly.

Requirements: Must be local resident. Must qualitfy as Pennsylvania industrial home worker (be either disabled or need to care for invalid family member).
Provisions: Pays piece rates.

BY RICH TENNANT

BROOKLYN BUREAU OF COMMUNITY SERVICE, Program for the Handicapped, 285 Schemerhorn Street, Brooklyn, NY 11217.
Positions: This is a non-profit organization offering many services to the elderly and handicapped citizens of Brooklyn. Home work involves manual assembly of products such as novelties and pharmaceuticals. Products are chosen for suitability - i.e., must be small enough to store in an apartment for a week at a time, light enough to carry up stairs, and suitable for quality control by the individual worker.
Requirements: Must be an elderly or handicapped resident of Brooklyn.
Provisions: Training and supplies are provided. Pick up and delivery of supplies and finished work are provided on a weekly basis. Pays piece rates. Has advocate on staff to insure SSI and disability insurance benefits are protected.

BUTACO CORPORATION, 6051 South Knox, Chicago, IL 60629.
Positions: Butaco is a producer of advertising specialties. Home workers assemble metal pins into lithographic buttons. Currently has 27 home workers.
Requirements: Must be local resident. Must obtain home worker certificate from Illinois State Department of Labor.
Provisions: Pays piece rates.

CADIE PRODUCTS CORPORATION, 100 Sixth Avenue, Paterson, NJ 07524.
Positions: Packaging small items produced by the company.
Requirements: Must be local resident. No machinery or experience needed.
Provisions: Pays piece rates.

ANTHONY D. CAPONIGRO CO., 124 Eisenhauer Blvd., Roseto, PA 18013.
Positions: Hand assembly.
Requirements: Must be local resident. Must qualify as Pennsylvania industrial home

worker (be either disabled or need to care for invalid family member).
Provisions: Pays piece rates.

CARTRIDGE ACTUATED DEVICES, INC., 123 Clinton Road, Fairfield, NJ 07006.
Positions: Soldering and some bridgewiring of explosive devices.
Requirements: Must be local resident in order to pick up and deliver supplies and finished work. Must own a microscope as prescribed by the company.
Provisions: Training is provided. Pays piece rates, but workers are full employees with basic benefits provided by law. Inquiries welcome.

CENTRAL ASSEMBLY COMPANY, INC., 1110 West National Avenue, Addison, IL 60101.
Positions: Light assembly and packaging of small products.
Requirements: Must be local resident. Must obtain home worker certificate from Illinois State Department of Labor.
Provisions: Pays piece rates. Work availability fluctuates according to availability of contracts.

CENTRAL-SHIPPEE, INC., 46 Star Lake Avenue, Bloomington, NJ 07403.
Positions: Manual assembly of color cards, swatching, inserting and mailing;. Central-Shippee is a swatch manufacturer. Home workers put together the swatch cards from provided samples.
Requirements: Must be local resident.
Provisions: Training is provided. Pick up and delivery also provided. Pays piece rates.

COMPONENT PLASTICS, 700 W. Tollgate Road, Elgin, Il.
Positions: Hand assembly and light inspection. This company has only four home workers and the opportunities are nil.
Requirements: Must be local resident. Must obtain a home worker certificate from the Illinois Department of Labor.

CONDON INDUSTRIES, INC., 175 Paterson Ave., Midland Park, NJ 07432.
Positions: Inspection and cutting of woven labels.
Requirements: Must be local resident.

CONSOLIDATED INDUSTRIES OF GREATER SYRACUSE, INC., 541 Seymour St., Syracuse, NY 13204.
Positions: Electrical and electronic assembly of small parts; collating and mechanical assembly packaging; mailing and office services; and handicrafts. Currently has 30 home working participants; anyone qualified is welcome to apply.
Requirements: Applicant must go through an extensive evaluation process, since all the home work is issued to disabled workers only. Must live in the greater Syracuse area.
Provisions: "Homebound Program" provides complete and ongoing training, plus as much counseling as is needed for each individual. Pick-up and delivery of supplies and finished work is provided weekly. Pays piece rates.

COOPERATIVE MARKETING, 731 Racquet Club Dr., Addision, IL.
Positions: Hand work involved in mailing projects.
Requirements: Must be local resident. Must obtain a home worker certificate from the Illinois Department of Labor.

CORD CRAFTS, INC., 530 Mt. Pleasant Ave., Dover, NJ 07801.
Positions: Hand assembly of plant hangers. Currently has over 70 home workers.
Requirements: Must be local resident in order to pick up and deliver supplies and finished products.
Provisions: Training is provided. Pays piece rates.

COTTAGE INDUSTRIES, 3698 Haven Ave., Ste B, Redwood City, CA 94002.
Positions: Electronic asembly of PC boards and harnesses. There is no soldering; only stuffing of boards and harness pulling.
Requirements: Workers are independent contractors and must have business licenses. Must supply own tools, pick up and delivery, etc. Local residents only. Experience is also required.
Provisions: Pays piece rates. Current number of home workers is small. Company has had more in the past, but orders at this time are mostly too big to handle outside the plant on time schedules provided by contracts.

CYMATICS, INC., 31 W. 280 Diehl Rd., Naperville, IL 60540.
Positions: Circuit board assembly for electronics manufacturer.
Requirements: Must be local resident. Experience is required. Must obtain home worker certificate from Illinois Department of Labor.
Provisions: Pays piece rates.

DALY CO., 10606 1/2 S. Torrence Ave., Chicago, IL 60617.
Positions: Hand assembly of small products.
Requirements: Must be local resident. Must obtain home worker certificate from Illinois Department of Labor.
Provisions: Pays piece rates.

DAVCO, INC., 42 Walnut Street, Haverhill, MA 01830.
Positions: Hand assembly of shoe findings. There are currently 23 home workers.
Requirements: Must be local resident.
Provisions: Pick up and delivery provided. Pays piece rates equal to minimum wage.

DIVERSIFIED TEMPORARY SERVICES, 27715 Jefferson Ave., #112, Temecula, CA 92390.
Positions: This agency has a contract with a manufacturer to hire home workers to assemble bows from ribbon and wire and package them. There are usually 6 to 12 home workers at any given time.
Requirements: Must be local resident.
Provisions: Pays piece rates.

DUBRO PRODUCTS, 480 Bonner Rd., Wauconda, IL.
Positions: Hand assembly.
Requirements: Must be local resident. Must obtain a home worker certificate from the Illinois Department of Labor.

EASTER SEAL SOCIETY OF METROPOLITAN CHICAGO, INC., 220 South State Street, Room 312, Chicago, IL 60604.
Positions: This is a not-for-profit program for handicapped Chicago residents. 38 home workers handle small packaging, light assembly, collating, and hand-addressing.

Requirements: Must be handicapped and live in Chicago.
Provisions: Training is provided. Pick up and delivery is provided. Pays piece rates.

FEDERATION OF THE HANDICAPPED, 211 West 14th Street, 2nd Floor, New York, NY 10011.
Positions: The Home Employment Program (HEP) is a workshop program which consists of industrial bench assembly (manual assembly work).
Requirements: All workers must live in New York City and have a disability. Requires evaluation through lengthy interviews and personal counseling before participating.
Provisions: The workshop provides training plus any extra help necessary to overcome any unusual problems an individual might have. Pick up and delivery of supplies and finished work is provided regularly. Pays piece rates. Disability insurance counseling is provided. Number of home workers fluctuates, but over 1000 have participated in the program since the early 60s and there are currently several hundred.

FINEST FASHIONS, INC., 3650 North Cicero Avenue , Chicago, IL 60644.
Positions: Product packaging for apparel wholesaler.
Requirements: Must be local resident. Must obtain home worker certificate from Illinois State Department of Labor.

FOUR WORD INDUSTRIES CORPORATION, 9462 Franklin Ave., Franklin Park, IL 60131.
Positions: Hand assemblers insert pins into the backs of metal buttons for this producer of advertising specialties. Currently has 18 home workers and opportunities are decreasing.
Requirements: Must be local resident. Must obtain a home worker certificate from Illinois State Department of Labor.
Provisions: Pays piece rates.

FOXON PACKAGING CORPORATION, 235 West Park St., Providence, RI 02901.
Positions: Home workers assemble string tags for this manufacturer. There are currently about 23 home workers.
Requirements: Must be local resident.

FULLER BOX COMPANIES, 150 Chestnut Street, North Attleboro, MA 02760.
Positions: Manual assembly involved in the production of steel set-up boxes and jewelry display boxes. Work consists of rimming, padding, tipping, wiring, and other assembly functions. Opportunities here are very limited.
Requirements: Must be local resident.
Provisions: Pick up and deliver of supplies and finished products is provided. Pays piece rates equal to about $4 an hour.

GERSON INDUSTRIES, 4501 Dell Avenue, North Bergen, NJ 07047.
Positions: Sewing covers for mattresses and boxsprings.
Requirements: Must be local resident and own industrial sewing machine. Production level experience is required.
Provisions: Training is provided. Pick up and delivery of supplies and finished work is provided.

GLASS REFLECTIONS, 350 North 3rd St., Newport, PA 17074.
Positions: Glass Reflections has been making high quality tiffany lampshades for ten

years. Home workers tape together the pieces with adhesive tape. No tools required.
Requirements: Must be local resident. Must qualify as Pennsylvania industrial home worker (be either disabled or need to care for invalid family member). Charges a $1.50 pick-up fee.
Provisions: Pays piece rates.

GORDON BRUSH MANUFACTURING COMPANY, INC., 2150 Sacramento Street, Los Angeles, CA 90021.
Positions: Assembly of hand tied brush parts.
Requirements: Must live nearby.
Provisions: Training is provided. Pays by the piece. There are only 5 home workers and there is a long waiting list.

GREENWOOD ENTERPRISES, INC., 9834 South Kedzie Avenue, Evergreen Park, Chicago, IL 60642.
Positions: Company manufactures novelty and custom design buttons. Hand assemblers insert pins into the backs of the buttons. Currently has19 home workers.
Requirements: Must be local resident. Must obtain home worker certificate from Illinois State Department of Labor.
Provisions: Pays piece rates.

HARPER LEATHER GOODS MANUFACTURING COMPANY, 2133 West Pershing Road, Chicago, IL 60609.
Positions: Light industrial work involved in the manufacture of pet supplies; packaging rawhide "bones", sewing cat and dog toys, and sewing cat collars.
Requirements: Must be local resident. Must obtain home worker certificate from Illinois State Department of Labor.

HAYMOSS MFG. CO. INC., 714 27th St., Union City, NJ 07087.
Positions: Hand cutting and hand beading embroidered pieces.
Requirements: Must be local resident. Experience is required.

HILDY LICHT CO., INC., 897 Independence #3B, Mountainview, CA 94043.
Positions: Electronic assembly; PC boards, reworking, etc. The company currently has 10 home workers.
Requirements; Must be local resident.

HYGIENOL COMPANY, INC., 73 Crescent Avenue, New Rochelle, NY 10801.
Positions: Hand assembly involved in the manufacture of powder puffs.
Requirements: Local residents only.
Provisions: Home work force is extremely small now, but at one time (before 1950) there were over 400. Company is considering revitalizing home work program.

INSULFAB PLASTICS, INC., 150 Union Ave., East Rutherford., NJ 07073.
Positions: Hand assembly of name plate badges.
Requirements: Must be local resident.

JACKSON SPRING & MANUFACTURING COMPANY, INC., 2680 American Lane, Elk Grove, IL 60007.
Positions: Packing parts.
Requirements: Must be local resident. Must obtain home worker certificate from Illinois State Department of Labor.
Provisions: Pays piece rates.

JOSEPH'S BROS. EMBROIDERY CORP., 6030 Monroe Place, West New York, NJ.
Positions: Sample mending of embroidery designs.
Requirements: Must be local resident. Experience is required.

KARELIS HEEL CORP., 417 River St., Haverhill, MA 01803.
Positions: Hand assemblers put fancy coverings on women's belts and heels.
Requirements: Must be local resident. Currently has only 3 home workers.

LANCASTER COUNTY ASSOCIATION FOR THE BLIND, 244 North Queen St., Lancaster, PA 17603.
Positions: This non-profit organization has both a sheltered workshop and, for those who are homebound, certain hand assembly work can be farmed out to home workers.
Requirements: Must be disabled worker in the Lancaster area.
Provisions: Pays piece rates.

GEO. LAUTERER CORP., 310 W. Washington, Chicago, IL 60096.
Positions: Hand assembly.
Requirements: Must be local resident. Must obtain home worker certificate from Illinois Department of Labor.
Provisions: Pays piece rates.

LENCO ELECTRONICS, INC., 1330 Belden St., McHenry, IL 60050.
Positions: Connecting and soldering wires onto transformers.
Requirements: Must be local resident. Must obtain home worker certificate from Illinois Department of Labor.
Provisions: Provides necessary hand tools. Pays piece rates.

LESANDE SHOE COMPANY, 81-87 Washington Street, Haverhill, MA 01830.
Positions: Stitching shoe parts. Currently has about 10 home workers and the number is decreasing.
Requirements: Experience is required. Must be local resident.
Provisions: Machinery is provided. Pays piece rates equal to about $5 and hour.

LEWIS SPRING CO., 2652 W. North Ave., Chicago, IL 60697.
Positions: Assembly and packaging.
Requirements: Must be local resident. Must obtain home worker certificate from Illinois Department of Labor. Currently has 17 home workers.

"A good freelancer can make $50,000 a year."
—CCA, Inc.

LIMALDI & ASSOCIATES, 165 Vanderpool Street, Newark, NJ 07114.
Positions: Hand inserting pins into metal buttons. Current number of home workers is 10, but that number fluctuates.
Requirements: Must be local resident.
Provisions: Pick up and delivery of supplies and finished work is provided. Home workers are salaried employees.

LMB HAND REHAB PRODUCTS, INC., 265 South Street, Suite B, San Luis Obispo, CA 93401.
Positions: Hand assembly of wire-foam hand and finger medicinal splints.
Requirements: Must be local resident.

LNL, R.D. #3, Bangor, PA 18013.
Positions: Garment sewing.
Requirements: Must be local resident. Must qualify as Pennsylvania industrial home worker (be either disabled or need to care for invalid family member).
Provisions: Pays piece rates.

MAR-DOL, INC., 29 W. Fullerton, Box 91, Addison, IL 60101.
Positions: Hand assembly.
Requirements: Must be local resident. Must obtain home worker certificate from Illinois Department of Labor.
Provisions: Pays piece rates.

MONTGOMERY COUNTY ASSOCIATION FOR RETARDED CHILDREN, Liberty Enterprises, P. O. Box 639, Amsterdam, NY 12010.
Positions: Affixing of labels, collating and folding of mailings, and stuffing envelopes. Also, some hand assembly of plastic parts.
Requirements: Must have verifiable disability that requires work at home. Must be local resident.

Provisions: Training is provided. Pick-up and delivery of supplies and finished work is provided. Pays piece rates.

MUENTENER EMBROIDERY CO., INC., 6904 Adams St., Guttenberg, NJ 07093.
Positions: Cutting out embroidered emblems.
Requirements: Must be local resident.

MYERS BROTHERS, 481 Paoli Ave., Philadelphia, PA 19128.
Positions: Hand assembly.
Requirements:: Must be local resident. Must qualify as Pennsylvania industrial home worker (be either disabled or need to care for invalid family member).
Provisions: Pays piece rates.

NATIONAL STAY COMPANY, INC., 680 Lynnway, Lynn, MA 01905.
Positions: Hand assembly of bows and vamps for shoes. Work is seasonal.
Requirements: Local residents only.
Provisions: Pays hourly rate of $3.50.

NORTH AMERICAN PLASTICS CORPORATION, P.O. Box 37, Lawrence, MA 01830.
Positions: Hand assembly work involved in the manufacture of plastic sleeves. Currently has 60 home workers.
Requirements: Must live within 25 mile radius of factory.
Provisions: Pays minimum wage.

PENT HOUSE SALES CORPORATION, 860 West Central Street, Franklin, MA 02038.
Positions: Hand assembly of shoe parts and accessories.
Requirements: Must be local resident.
Provisions: Pays minimum wage.

PHILLIPS MANUFACTURING COMPANY, INC., 190 Emmet Street, Newark, NJ 07114.
Positions: Company manufactures buttons.
Requirements: Home work is only distributed to contractors with valid state permit for redistribution.

PROMOTION SUPPORT SERVICES, 310 3rd St., Rock Island, IL.
Positions: Hand work involved in mailing projects.
Requirements: Must be local resident. Must obtain a home worker certificate from the Illinois Department of Labor.

R.C. COIL MFG. CO., 490 Mitchell Rd., Glendale Heights, IL.
Positions: Hand packing.
Requirements: Must be local resident. Must obtain a home worker certificate from the Illinois Department of Labor.

REGAL GAMES MANUFACTURING CO., 3714-16 W. Irving Park Rd., Chicago, IL 60618.
Positions: Hand assembly involving insertion of plastic chips in cardboard bingo cards. The company currently has about 8 home workers and opportunities are very limited.

Requirements: Must be local resident. Must obtain home worker certificate from Illinois Department of Labor.
Provisions: Pays piece rates.

RICHLAND SHOE CO., 30 North 3rd St., Womelsdorf, PA 19567.
Positions: Hand assembly.
Requirements: Must be local resident. Must qualify as Pennsylvania industrial home worker (be either disabled or need to care for invalid family member).
Provisions: Pays piece rates.

SAFECO CORPORATION, 6060 North Northwest Highway, Chicago, IL 60631.
Positions: Light assembly of small plastic and metal parts. Currently has about two dozen home workers.
Requirements: Must be local resident. Must obtain home worker certificate from Illinois Department of Labor.
Provisions: Pays piece rates.

SAMTEC, 1342 N. Market Blvd., Sacramento, CA 95834
Positions: Industrial homework involving electronic connectors. The company currently has seven home workers.
Requirements: Must be local resident.

THE SCREEN PLACE, INC., 90 Dayton Ave., Passaic, NJ 07055.
Positions: Color seperation of artwork.
Requirements: Must be local resident. Experience is required.

SCRIPTURE PRESS PUBLICATIONS, 1825 College Avenue, Wheaton, IL 60187.
Positions: Proofreading and packet assembly for religious publisher.
Requirements: Must be local resident. Good English skills required. Must obtain home worker certificate from Illinois State Department of Labor.

SHELTERED EMPLOYMENT SERVICES, INC., 600 N. 5th St., Philadelphia, PA 19123.
Positions: This non-profit agency offers both a sheltered workshop and a homebound work program for disabled workers in Philadelhhia. Work consists of hand assembly of small products and some typing.
Requirements: An intake worker will evaluate whether an individual qualifies for the program.
Provisions: Pays piece rates. Training is provided.

SHORELINE INDUSTRIES, 316 North 8th St., Bangor, PA 18013.
Positions: Sewing of shoulder pads.
Requirements: Must be local resident. Must qualify as Pennsylvania industrial home worker (be either disabled or need to care for invalid family member).
Provisions: Sewing machines are provided when necessary. Pays piece rates.

SKILLS UNLIMITED, INC., 405 Locust Avenue, Oakdale, NY 11769.
Positions: Hand assembly of various items. Currently has 35 home workers in program.
Requirements: Only people with catastrophic disabilities may apply. One to four weeks evaluation and state certification is required. Must live within 15 mile radius of headquarters.

Closeup: Village of the Smoky Hills

Village of the Smoky Hills is an award-winning cottage industry center in Osage, Minnesota. Fifteen buildings nestled amid 67 acres of pine forest showcase every imaginable type of handcraft.

Founder Lorelei Kraft came up with the idea in 1984 as a way to employ her neighbors without forfeiting the clear air and natural beauty of the area. At that time, unemployment was over 20%; the area was the poorest in the state. Kraft says she was inspired by Rockefeller's Appalachian quilting project, but rather than send the handcrafted products away to be sold, she gave the plan a whole new twist. She envisioned a village so unique it would not only attract customers, but would charge admissions to cover the cost of personal appearances by the craftspeople.

It took two months to develop the original business plan, during which time Kraft and 11 other social activists formed The Founding Mothers, Inc. From that point, it took only five months to locate the land, apply for a loan, get a zoning variance, build the complex, interview and train employees to run it, and open to the public.

Over 350 local artisans bring their products from home to be displayed and sold. The Village takes care of inventory, staffing clerks, advertising, etc. Everything is of high quality; nothing "plastic" is accepted.

Each building houses something different; Woodworking, Stenciling, Pottery, Indian Arts, Mrs. Santa's House, Bake Shoppe, Candle-Dipping, Quilting, Stained Glass, "Country," Old-Tyme Photo, and Ice Cream Parlor.

If this sounds like just another cutesy shopping center, it's far from it. In addition to displaying the crafts, the group demonstrates how they are made. The Pavilion in the center of The Commons features special demonstrations throughout the summer. There's soap-making, birchbark weaving, making tea from common plants, spinning and weaving, chainsaw sculptures, tole painting, basketmaking, silver-smithing, and more.

Visitors are invited to get involved, too. Want a souvenir T-shirt? Stencil your own! Or dip your own candles, or grind your own flour at the Bake Shoppe. The biggest project so far has been the erection of an authentic log cabin.

The key to the Village's success is participation. 20,000 visitors were expected the first year, but 100,000 came from all over to get involved in all the fun activities. For that, the Village won the State Travel Marketing of the Year Award, swept the top awards at the 1984 Minnesota Tourism Conference, and won the Regional Development Award for outstanding tourism

Provisions: Training is provided, as well as ongoing help and support. Skills Unlimited will set up the home work station, provide transportation to the central facilities for training as needed, and pick up and deliver supplies and finished work regularly. Pays piece rates.

SONOCO PRODUCTS CO., 1874 S. 54th Ave., Cicero, IL 60650.
Positions: Hand assembly of small products.
Requirements: Must be local resident. Must obtain home worker certificate from Illinois Department of Labor.
Provisions: Pays piece rates.

STERLING SPRING CORP., 5432 W. 54th St., Chicago, IL 60638.
Positions: Hand assembly and packaging.
Requirements: Must be local resident. Must obtain home worker certificate from Illinois Department of Labor.
Provisions: Pays piece rates.

STUART SPORTS SPECIALTIES, P.O.Box 13, Indian Orchard, MA 01151.
Positions: Hand assembly of fishing tackle components.
Requirements: Experience preferred. Must be local resident.
Provisions: Pays $4 an hour.

SUPERIOR SPRING STAMP CO., 5200 N. Otto, Chicago, IL 60656.
Positions: Hand assembly and packaging.
Requirements: Must be local resident. Must obtain home worker certificate form Illinois Department of Labor.
Provisions: Pays piece rates.

SWIBCO, INC., 4820 Venture Rd., Lisle, IL 60532.
Positions: Hand assembly of jewelry onto plastic cards and packaging.
Requirements: Must be local resident of Lisle. Must obtain a home worker certificate from the Illinois Department of Labor.

TEKTEST, 225 North Second Avenue, Arcadia, CA 91006.
Positions: Industrial homework involving electronic test connectors. The company currently has nine home workers.
Requirements: Must be local resident.

TELEDYNE ISOTOPES, 50 Van Buren Avenue, Westwood, NJ 07675.
Positions: Two types of work are performed at home. One is the assembly of badge cases and the other is slicing of ultrathin discs.
Requirements: Must be local resident. Prefers referrals.
Provisions: Equipment is provided as necessary.

THREE W MFG. CO., 1016 Springfield Road, Union City, NJ 07083.
Postitions: Light assembly work involving carding and bosing of costume jewelry.
Requirements: Must be local resident.

TIFFANY & CO., 801 Jefferson Rd., Parsippany, NJ 07054.
Positions: Pre-packaging and ribboning of gift items.
Requirements: Must be local.

TOMORROW TODAY CORPORATION, P. O. Box 6125, Westfield, MA 01085.
Positions: Hand work consists of tying bows and working with flowers to make decorations. Currently has 23 home workers.
Requirements: Must be local.
Provisions: Pays minimum wage.

TRUCOLOR FOTO, 5374 Linda Vista Rd., San Diego, CA 92110.
Positions: Trucolor has only four industrial home workers handling photofinishing.
Requirements: Must be local resident with experience.

UNITED CEREBRAL PALSY ASSOCIATION OF WESTCHESTER COUNTY, INC., King St. and Lincoln Ave. in the Town of Rye, NY; mailing address P.O. Box 555, Purchase, NY 10577.
Positions: Hand assembly of various items on subcontract basis. Program is for homebound disabled workers only.
Requirements: All home workers must be approved by the U.S. Dept. of Labor which generally requires a doctor's statement. Local residents only.
Provisions: The screening is tight, but once the program is there, there is a lot of support available. Each participant is assigned a vocational trainer and a counselor that meet with the worker at least once a month after the initial training is completed. Pick up and delivery of supplies and finished work is provided. Any tools and/or equipment necessary for the work are provided. Pays piece rates. Inquiries are welcome from Westchester County and from throughout Connecticut. Some work is opening up in the computer field, too.

WEILER BRUSH CO., INC., One Wildwood Drive, Cresco, PA 18326.
Positions: Hand assembly.
Requirements: Must be local resident. Must qualify as Pennsylvania industrial home worker (be either disabled or need to care for invalid family member).
Provisions: Pays piece rates.

WEST COAST BRUSH COMPANY, 433 Lanzit Ave., Los Angeles, CA 90061.
Positions: Assembly of hand tied stainless steel wire brushes.
Requirements: Must live nearby.
Provisions: Training is provided. Home workers are reqular employees and are paid a salary plus basic benefits. There are currently only four home workers and opportunities are nil.

WORKSHOP INDUSTRIES, INC., 400 Clay Ave., Jeannette, PA 15644.
Positions: This is a non-profit organization offering employment opportunities to disabled workers within a 50-mile radius of Jeannette. Work consists of hand assembly of various small products.
Provisions: Training is provided.

YORK SPRING COMPANY, 1551 North La Fox Street, South Elgin, IL 60177.
Positions: Assembly and packaging springs for manufacturer. Home based work force has grown to 51.
Requirements: Must be local resident. Must obtain home worker certificate from Illinois State Department of Labor.
Provisions: Pays piece rates.

Opportunities in Sales

The field of sales has long been a traditional from-home opportunity. Today, most salespeople have offices at home and some even conduct all their business from home.

Sales may be the only true opportunity to earn an executive level income with literally no educational requirements or experience. It is particularly good for women, who often report doubling or tripling their income after leaving other types of jobs. It also allows for a maximum amount of flexibility in terms of time spent and when it is spent.

What does it take to be a good salesperson? Good communication skills are at the top of the list. You must truly enjoy talking to people to make it in sales. You must be careful to listen to them as well. Assertiveness is also important. This does not mean you must be aggressive or go for the "hard sell," but shrinking violets aren't likely to make it in this field. The toughest part of this job is handling rejection. Nobody likes rejection; some people are traumatized by it. But, it goes with the territory. The professional salesperson knows that with each rejection, he/she is one step closer to a successfully-closed sale.

Sales is a profession with its own set of rules, just like any other profession. The job basically consists of prospecting for customers, qualifying the prospect to make sure the potential customer is a viable prospect, making the presentation, overcoming objections, closing the sale, and getting referrals. A good company will teach you all you need to know about each of these steps. You can also find classes in salesmanship for both beginners and advanced students at community colleges and adult learning centers.

Many of the opportunities listed in this section have interesting ways of introducing the product. Home parties are especially fun and easy. Many home parties now seem more like classes than sales pitches with hands-on demonstrations in cooking, baking, needlework, and crafts. If you think you might be interested in a particular company, you can check it out first by hosting your own party. You'll not only be able to check out the company first hand, but you'll earn a bonus gift at the same time.

For those who want to be home all the time, telemarketing is the best bet. It is a marketing method that is mushrooming because it is more efficient and cheaper than face-to-face methods of selling. Telemarketing jobs rarely exceed four hours a day, but the pay can equal a full-time salary for a good communicator. For additional opportunities in telemarketing, look in your local newspaper "help wanted" ads.

ACCENTS INTERNATIONAL, 909 Commerce Circle, P. O. Drawer 11047, Charleston, SC 29411.
Positions: Direct sales of decorative accessories for the home. Most reps sell the products at exclusive showings in customers' homes.
Provisions: Pays commission. Training is provided.

ACT II JEWELRY, INC., 818 Thorndale Ave., Bensenville, IL 60106.
Positions: Direct sales of fashion and fine jewelry.

ADMAR ENTERPRISES, (202)364-0789.
Positions: Telemarketing, no sales involved. Cold call within your local area exchange to offer free gifts and give location of pick up.
Requirements: Can live anywhere within the greater Washington D.C., Baltimore area. Must be able to speak clearly and be self-assured.
Provisions: All telemarketers are independent contractors and can set own schedules from 9 am to 9 pm, part-time or full-time. Pays base salary from $200 to $600 per week. Company benefits are provided.

ALCAS CUTLERY CORPORATION, 1116 East State Street, P.O. Box 810, Olean, NY 147600-0810.
Positions: Alcas make cutlery, cookware, and tableware. The products are sold with the aid of mail order catalogs.
Provisions: Catalogs and other supplies are provided. Pays commission.

ALFA METALCRAFT CORPORATION OF AMERICA, 6593 Powers Ave., Suite 17, Jacksonville, FL 32217.
Positions: Direct sales of cookware. Reps can use any direct sales methods. Some reps have incorporated the sales of Alfa cookware into cooking classes in their homes.
Provisions: Pays commission.

ALOE MAGIC, Division of Exalo Tech, 2828 East 55 Place, P.O. Box 20423, Indianapolis, IN 46220.
Positions: Aloe Magic has an extensive line of aloe-based cosmetics and health and skin care products. Reps use a variety of direct sales methods.
Provisions: Pays commission.

ALOETTE COSMETICS, INC., P.O. Box 2346, West Chester, PA 19380.
Positions: Direct sales of skin care cosmetics.

AMER-I-CAN FIRE AND SAFETY CORP., Treavose Manor, 3779 Bristol Rd., Bensalem, PA 19020.
Positions: Direct sales of fire extinguishers.

AMERICAN HORIZONS, 11251 Phillips Parkway Drive East, Jacksonville, FL 32224.
Positions: Direct sales of skin care products and cosmetics.

AMWAY CORPORATION, 7575 East Fulton Road, Ada, MI 49355.
Positions: Amway is well known as the original multilevel organization. There are now five different divisions which include not only products but many services as well such as MTI Long Distance.

ARBONNE INTERNATIONAL, INC., (801) 561-4588.
Positions: Direct sales of European cosmetics and skin care products. Reps build customers bases using any direct sales methods that work for them.
Provisions: Training and ongoing managerial support is provided. Pays commission.

ARTISTIC IMPRESSIONS, INC., 240 Cortland Ave., Lombard, IL 60148.
Positions: Direct sales of art works.

AVACARE, INC., 19501 E. Walnut Dr., City of Industry, CA 91749.
Positions: Direct sales of "natural" cosmetics and skin, hair and health care products.
Provisions: Pays commission.

AVADYNE, INC., 2801 Salinas Highway, Monterey, CA 93953.
Positions: Direct sales of meal replacement formula and nutritional procducts.

AVON PRODUCTS, INC., Nine West 57 St., New York, NY 10019.
Positions: Avon, which is known for door-to-door slaes, rarely uses this method anymore. Instead, its huge number of reps uses telemarketing methods to arrange home parties and make appointments for exclusive showings.
Requirements: Reps are required to buy samples, hostess thank-you gifts, and necessary paperwork.
Provisions: Pays commission. Management opportunities are available.

BEAUTICONTROL, INC., 2101 Midway Road, P.O. Box 345189, Dallas, TX 75234.
Positions: BeautiControl primarily markets a cosmetic line that is tied into the "seasonal" method of color coordination. A secondary line of women's apparel is marketed in the same way. In 1985, the company topped $30 million in gross sales. BeautiControl does not use the party plan method of direct sales, but rather focuses on one-on-one sales. This is accomplished through intensive training, personal development, and corporate support of the consultants, A free color analysis is offered to potential customers; this has proven to be the company's most powerful marketing tool.
Requirements: A one-time investment of $500 is required.
Provisions: Personal earnings are reported in the company's monthly in-house publication, "Achiever", and typically range from $12,000 down to $3,700 per month after being in the company for about two years. It is not unusual for new Consultants to earn $100 to $200 per day.

BEN'S MEATS, 260 Islip Ave., Islip, NY 11751.
Positions: This company sells and delivers customized monthly meat orders. Home-based telemarketers sell the service over the phone. Work is part-time only.
Requirements: Must have some telemarketing experience. Residents of Suffolk County only will be considered.
Provisions: Training is conducted in the office for about two hours. Pays salary plus commissions and bonuses.

BON DEL CORPORATION, 3716 East Main Street, Mesa, AZ 85205.
Positions: Bon Del manufactures household bacteriostatic water treatment units. Independent reps sell the units direct by placing ads in local papers, through telemarketing, and sometimes with company provided leads.
Provisions: Training is provided. Pays commission.

✳ **BOOK OF LIFE,** 1414 Robinson Road, Grand Rapids, MI 49506.
Positions: Direct sales of educational publications.

BOSE CORPORATION, The Mountain Rd., Framingham, MA 01701.
Positions: Direct sales of acoustic wave music systems.

✳ **BRITE MUSIC ENTERPRISES, INC.,** Box 9191, Salt Lake City, UT 84109.
Positions: Direct sales of children's song books, casettes, and records.

THE BRON-SHOE COMPANY, 1313 Alum Creek Drive, Columbus, OH 43209.
Positions: Direct marketing of baby shoe bronzing services.

CALICO SUBSCRIPTIONS, P.O. Box 11, Milpitas, CA 95035.
Positions: Telemarketing for periodical subscription renewals.
Requirements: Must be in the Bay area or Silicon Valley.
Provisions: Pays commission only. "Our telemarketers make very good money. We're always looking for good phone people."

CAMEO COUTURES, INC., 9004 Ambassador Row, P.O. Box 47390, Dallas, TX 75247.
Positions: Home party sales of lingerie, cosmetics, and food supplements.
Provisions: Training is provided. Pays commission.

CAMEO PRODUCTS, INC., P.O. Box 590388, Orlando, FL 32859.
Positions: Cameo has been offering quality products and services for over 17 years now. The products are typically craft kits such as needlepunch, fabric painting, bow art, iron-on transfers, etc. Product demonstrators act as craft instructors in a home party style "class". Cameo offers more than just whoesale craft supplies. It entails a complete program of supplies, designs, products, training aids, and sales promotion representatives. Cameo representatives can choose the way they want to demonstrate and sell the products. Many reps sell directly to customers at crafts shows, fairs, open houses, and direct mail. Classes at adult community education centers, retirement centers, schools, and other institutions are also selling avenues.
Provisions: Minimum 25% commission for instructors. Commission plus override for managers.

CHAMBRE COSMETIC CORPORATION, P.O. Box 690370, San Antonio, TX 78240.
Positions: Direct sales of cosmetics and food supplements.
Provisions: Pays commission.

CHRISTMAS AROUND THE WORLD, P.O. Box 9999, Kansas City, MO 64134-9999.
Positions: Home party demonstrators and supervisors. Company markets an upscale line of gifts and ornaments. All work is transferred via UPS. No investment requirements of any kind.
Provisions: Full training is provided. Pays commission plus override.

CLUB WATERMASTERS, INC., 5670 W. Cypress St., Suite I, Tampa, FL 33607.
Positions: Direct sales of drinking water systems.

Sue Rusch
The Pampered Chef

"Working at home has lent tremendous flexibility to my family life. I can be a full time mother first, but a very successful business person as well. And best of all, I call the shots. I decide when to work, how much to work, and I can still be on the PTA and sit down on the floor to play with my kids. I used to be a personnel manager, but hour for hour, the rate of pay can't even come close to what I make now."

COLLECTORS CORNER, INC., AND AFFILIATES, 5327 W. Minnesota St., Indianapolis, IN 46241.
Positions: Direct sales of oil paintings and limited edition prints.

P.F. COLLIER, INC., Educational Services Division, 135 Community Drive, Great Neck, NY 11021.
Positions: Direct sales of encyclopedias.

CONCEPT NOW COSMETICS, 14000 Anson Street, Santa Fe Springs, CA 90670.
Positions: This 17 year old company has been selling an extensive line of skin care products primarily though party plan sales. Reps operate through the U.S., Mexico, Canada, Puerto Rico, and the Virgin Islands.
Requirements: A start-up kit with $325 requires a $65 investment.
Provisions: No set territories. Training is available and includes tapes, manual, presentation outline and company support. Car allowance is provided along with specified promotions. Pays commission only for reps and override for managers.

CON-STAN INDUSTRIES, INC., 19501 Walnut Dr., City of Industry, CA 91748.
Positions: Direct sales of cosmetics and food supplements.
Provisions: Pays commission.

CONTEMPO FASHIONS, 6100 Broadmoor, Shawnee Mission, KS 66202.
Positions: Direct sales of jewelry and accessories.

COPPERSMITH COMPANY, 410 E. College, P.O. Box 1000, Roswell, NM 88201-7525.
Positions: Coppersmith is a manufacturer of decorative home accessories including tableware and wall decor, all made out of copper. Reps use a variety of means to market the products: home parties, exclusive showings, one-on-one consultations, and catalog sales.

Provisions: Strong company support is provided. Pays commission.

CORNET PRODUCING CORPORATION, 4738 North Harlem, Schiller Park, IL 60141.
Positions: Inside sales of entertainment events to businesses. 20 hours a week.
Requirements: Experience in business-to-business sales is necessary.

COUNTRY HOME COLLECTION, 1719 Hallock-Young Rd., Warren, OH 44481.
Positions: Direct sales of decorative home products.

THE CREATIVE CIRCLE, 15711 So. Broadway, Gardena, CA 90248.
Positions: Party plan sales of needlework kits. Work involves conducting classes in needlework.
Requirements: $40 investment buys $90 worth of merchandise and paperwork supplies for three classes.
Provisions: Pays 25% commission plus incentives. Also provides thank you gifts for hostesses and premiums used during parties. Managerial opportunities available. "The beauty of our company is we have no quotas, set territories, or anyone looking over our shoulders."

CREATIVE MEMORIES, 2815 Clearwater Road, St. Cloud, MN 56302.
Positions: Party-plan sales of books, hobby products, photo albums, and photography products.

CREATIVE TREASURES, 6836 Duckling Way, Sacramento, CA 95842.
Positions: Creative Treasures is a home party business that markets quality handcrafts of all kinds. Home party demonstrators and their supervisors are home-based. Items are ordered from a sample that is provided by each crafter.
Requirements: Write a letter of interest.

D.E.L.T.A. INTERNATIONAL, 16910 West 10 Mile Road, Ste. 400, Southfield, MI 48075.
Positions: Direct sales of nutritional supplements.

DELUXE BUILDING MAINTENANCE, 760 Market St., San Francisco, CA 94140.
Positions: Telemarketing. Cold calls only.
Requirements: Experience is required. Must be resident of San Francisco.
Provisions: Pays commission only.

DEXI US, INC., 130 W. 42nd St. Bldg. 2900, New York, NY 10036.
Positions: Direct sales of cosmetics.

DIAMITE CORPORATION, 1625 McCandless Dr., Milpitas, CA 95035.
Positions: Now 13 years old, Diamite still offers groundfloor opportunities nationwide. Manufacturer of skin care and nutritional products with the latest technology for anti-aging and life extension. Innovative marketing plan through networking part-time or full-time. Product line has 100% customer money back guarantee.
Provisions: Training is provided in the form of literature and video tapes.

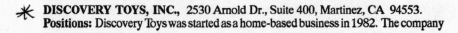

DISCOVERY TOYS, INC., 2530 Arnold Dr., Suite 400, Martinez, CA 94553.
Positions: Discovery Toys was started as a home-based business in 1982. The company

markets a line of educationally sound toys and accessories through home parties. Home party demonstrators and their supervisors are all home-based.
Requirements: Send letter of interest.
Provisions: Complete training is provided. Pays commission and override. Can live anywhere.

DONCASTER, Box 1159, Rutherfordton, NC 28139.
Positions: Doncaster trains women to be fashion consultants, "Selling the art of dressing well." Fashion Consultants present the Doncaster collection in private showing in their own homes four times a year. These fashions are considered to be investment quality and are designed primarily for career women.
Provisions: Training is provided. Pays commission. Management opportunities are available.

DUDLEY PRODUCTS COMPANY, 7856 McCloud Rd., Greensboro, NC 27409.
Positions: Direct sales of cosmetics using home parties as primary sales method.
Provisions: Training is provided. Pays commission and override for managers.

DUSKIN-CALIFORNIA, INC., 108E Star of India Lane, Carson, CA 90746.
Positions: Direct sales of household products. Primary focus is on dust control products. Reps use any method of sales they chose.
Provisions: Pays commission.

EFE' COSMETICS, LTD., 4940 El Camino Real, Los Altos, CA 94022.
Positions: Sales of cosmetics through home parties.

EKCO HOME PRODUCTS CO., 2382 Townsgate Road, Westlake Village, CA 91361.
Positions: Direct sales of cookware and cutlery.

ELAN VITAL, LTD., 6185 Harrison Dr., Ste. 1, Las Vegas, NV 89120.
Positions: Direct sales of nutritional supplements.

ELECTRIC MOBILITY CORPORATION, Number 1 Mobility Plaza, Sewell, NJ 08080.
Positions: This manufacturer of electric mobility three-wheelers uses a national network of independent reps to demonstrate and sell their products. All reps are home-based, but must travel to demonstrate the products to interested buyers because they are either elderly or handicapped.
Requirements: This is not hard sell; reps must be easy going, caring, efficient and very organized. Apply with resume.
Provisions: Leads are generated through national advertising and are prequailified by telmarketers before being sent to reps. Territories are assigned by zip codes. Commission are about $300 per sale.

ELECTROLUX CORP., 2300 Windy Ridge Parkway, Suite 900 South, Marietta, GA 30067.
Positions: Direct sales of vacuum cleaners, floor polishers, and attachments.

EMMA PAGE JEWELRY, INC., P. O. Box 179, Blairstown, NJ 07825.
Positions: Direct sales of jewelry.

EMMELINE COSMETICS CORPORATION, 3939 Washington Ave., Kansas City, MO 64111.
Positions: Direct sales of cosmetics.
Provisions: Pays commission.

ENCYCLOPAEDIA BRITTANICA, INC., Brittanica Centre, 310 South Michigan Ave, Chicago, IL 60604.
Positions: This is the largest company of its kind in the world. It also has a reputation for having the highest paid direct sales reps of any industry. Britannica is now sold through a variety of means, very little door-to-door effort is used.
Provisions: A two week training session is provided. In most areas, write-in leads are provided. Pays highest commission in the industry,. plus override for managers.

ENERGY SAVERS, INC., 101 Ridgeside Ct., Ste. 202, Mt. Airy, MD 21771.
Positions: Direct sales of energy conservation systems.

FAMILY RECORD PLAN, INC., 5155 North Clareton Dr., P.O. Box 3043, Agoura Hills, CA 91301.
Positions: Direct marketing of professional and amateur photography products.

FASHION TWO TWENTY, INC., P.O. Box 25220, Cleveland, OH 44202.
Positions: Direct sales of extensive line of quality cosmetics. Reps start by conducting home parties. After building an established clientele, home parties are usually replaced with prearranged personal consultations.
Requirements: There is usually a $15 fee to cover the cost of the manual and data processing. A new rep must also purchase the standard Show-Case kit. New consultants are expected to submit at least $150 retail orders per month.
Provisions: Pays commission. Management opportunities exist.

FIBER CLEAN, 966 Hungerford Dr. , Rockville, MD 20850.
Positions: Part-time telemarketing; PR work involves no sales, scheduling does require sales, but no cold calling.
Requirements: Local residents only. Schedulers must have telephone sales experience.
Provisions: PR work pays up to $6 an hour; schedulers receive salary of $20,000 a year. Full-time workers receive company benefits. Training is provided.

FINELLE COSMETICS, 137 Marston St., P.O. Box 5200, Lawrence, MA 01842.
Positions: Direct sales of cosmetics and skin care products.

FINISHING TOUCH BOUTIQUE, P.O. Box 231, Ringwood, NJ 07456.
Positions: Party-plan sales of home decorating accessories including country, Victorian, infant, and Christmas. All products in the 28 page catalog are sold year-round. This two-year old company has expanded rapidly into 14 states plus Puerto Rico and Hawaii.
Provisions: Kits are provided free. No delivery or collection. Management opportunities exist after recruiting only one individual. (At that point, commissions go up plus there are override commissions.) Pays about $25 per hour based on 30% commission. Bonus gifts for both reps and hostesses.

FORYOU, INC., 4235 Main St., Loris, SC 29569.
Positions: Direct sales of cosmetics, self improvement programs, and skincare products. The line is sold mainly through party-plan methods.

FULLER BRUSH COMPANY, 5635 Hanes Mill Rd., Winston-Salem, NC 27105.
Positions: Telemarketing program replaces old door-to-door methods.
Requirements: $29 fee to start. There are set production requirements.
Provisions: Leads are provided. Pays commissions of 25% to 50% plus many incentives. Extends $900 credit line after joining firm. Can live anywhere.

> "Our top typists average $15 an hour."
> —The Office Connection

FULLER INDUSTRIES, 3065 Center Green Dr., Boulder Co 80301.
Positions: Direct sales of cleaning products and house kitchenwares.

G & M MIND GAMES, INC., 2545 Valdina Dr., Beavercreek, OH 45385.
Positions: Sales of Old Testament non-denominational Bible game to churches, stores, and friends.
Provisions: Profit amounts to about $9.00 per game.

GARMENT PRINTERS, 2920 Arden Way, Sacramento, CA 95825.
Positions: Telemarketing in local business-to-business marketing program.
Requirements: Must live in Sacramento.
Provisions: Offers choice of part-time or full-time work.

GOLDEN PRIDE, INC., 1501 Northpoint Parkway, Suite 100, West Palm Beach, FL 33407.
Positions: Direct sales of health and beauty aids.

GOLDENWEST MEDICAL-NUTRITION CENTER, 400 Newport Center Dr., Suite 411, Newport Beach, CA 92660.
Positions: Marketing of weight loss and nutritional programs.

GROLIER INCORPORATED, Sherman Turnpike, Danbury, CT 06816.
Positions: Grolier is best known for publishing Encyclopedia Americana and has expanded into other educational publishing (such as the Disney series and Mr. Light). **Provision:** Training is provided in one-week classroom sessions. No leads, no territories. Sales are direct and usually accomplished by setting appointments by phone in advance of the presentation. Pays commission (about 23%) to reps plus override to managers. Some expenses such as phone and car are reimbursed on an individual arrangement with management.

THE HANOVER SHOE, INC., 118 Carlisle St., Hanover, PA 17331.
Positions: Hanover is over 50 years old and still markets its shoes primarily through the use of independent reps. Reps sell direct through any method they chose, usually by starting with friends and neighbors and building up an established pool of customers through referrals.
Provisions: A portion of the retail price is returned to the rep.

HEALTH-GLO, INC., 6689 Peachtree Industrial Blvd., Suite P, Norcross, GA 30092. (404)458-6072.
Positions: Direct sales of "natural" cosmetics. Reps use a variety of sales methods, but mostly home parties.
Provisions: Training is provided. Pays commission.

HEALTH-MOR, INC., 151 E. 22nd St., Lombard, IL 60148.
Positions: Health-Mor is the manufacturer of vacuum cleaners, specifically Filter Queen. Company provides advertising and reps follow up on specific leads.
Provisions: Training is provided. Pays commission.

HEART AND HOME, INC., 76 Commercial Way, East Providence, RI 02314-1006.
Positions: Direct sales of decorative accessories.

HERBALIFE INTERNATIONAL, 9800 La Cienega Blvd., P.O. Box 80210, Los Angeles, CA 90009.
Positions: Direct sales of weight control food products.

HERITAGE CORPORATION OF AMERICA, P.O. Box 401209, Dallas, TX 75240.
Positions: Catalog sales of food supplements.
Requirements: An initial purchase of the products is required.
Provisions: Pays commission.

HIGHLIGHTS FOR CHILDREN, INC., Parent and Child Resource Center, Inc., Representative Sales Dept., P. O. Box 269, Columbus, OH 43215.
Positions: Highlights for Children is an educational book for children ages 2 through 12. It is available by enrollment only. It is not sold on any newstand, contains no advertising and is created primarily for family use.
It is sold through authorized independent representatives directly to families, teachers, preschools, daycare centers, doctors' offices, etc. Exclusive territories are given so there may not be openings in some areas.
Requirements: Must be located where there exists an opening.
Provisions: Exclusive leads are provided. Hours are totally flexible. No investment is required. Training and ongoing support is provided. Pays commission, bonus plan, and incentive gifts.

HILLSTAD INTERNATIONAL, 1545 Berger Dr., San Jose, CA 95112.
Positions: Direct sales of nutritional supplements.

HOME INTERIORS & GIFTS, INC., 4550 Spring Valley Road, Dallas, TX 75244.
Positions: Direct sales of pictures, figurines, shelves, foliage, and other home accents. Reps set up exclusive shows that include about 35 pieces of merchandise. After the show, the rep offers individual service and decorating advice to the customers.
Requirements: Reps must order, deliver, and collect.
Provisions: Training is provided in the form of ongoing sales classes, weekly meetings and monthly decorating workshops. The average rep presents about three shows a week and works about 25 hours a week.

HOUSE OF LLOYD, 11901 Grandview Road, Grandview, MO 64030.
Positions: Home party sales reps and supervisors. Product line includes toys and gitfts.

Provisions: Training and start-up supplies are provided with no investment. Commission equals approximately $9 an hour. Can live anywhere.

HY CITE CORPORATION, ROYAL PRESTIGE, 340 Coyier Lane, Madison, WI 53713.
Positions: Home party sales of cookware, china, crystal, tableware, stoneware, and cutler.
Provisions: Training is provided. Pays commission. The company's marketing division provides all of the product literature, sales tools, and field assistance needed. All supplied are training manuals, presentation aids, and videotape and cassette training programs. Reps benefit from national advertising and customer promotion campaigns.

JAFRA COSMETICS, INC., P.O. Box 5026, Westlake Village, CA 91359.
Positions: Jafra makes high quality, "natural" cosmetics and skin care products. Reps sell the products through the party plan and by offering free facials to participants.
Provisions: Pays commission.

JEN DALE, P.O. Box 5604, Charlottesville, VA 22905.
Positions: Direct sales of personal care and vitamins.

KARLA JORDAN KOLLECTIONS, LTD., 10633 W. Oklahoma Ave., West Allis, WI 53227.
Positions: This company specializes in unique handcrafted jewelry and accessories. Independent sales consultants sell the jewelry in a variety of ways such as personal accessory consultations, in-home presentations, fashion shows, etc. Sales consultants purchase the jewelry and accessories at wholesale prices direct from the company, hand-picking their own inventory. Opportunities exist anywhere in the U.S.
Provisions: In addition to profiting from sales markups, the company offers special promotional programs and incentives. Commissions are paid to those consultants who develop an organization of reps.

JUST AMERICA, Oak Springs Rd., Rutherfordton, NC 28139.
Positions: Party-plan sales of skincare products.

THE KIRBY CORPORATON, 1920 W. 114 St., Cleveland, OH 44102.
Positions: Kirby has been selling its vacuum cleaners door-to-door for many years. Now, reps use telemarketing methods to prearrange demonstrations.
Provisions: Some write-in leads are provided. Pays commissions.

KITCHEN FAIR, 1090 Redmond Rd., P.O. Box 100, Jacksonville, AR 72076.
Positions: Kitchen Fair is a 60 year old maker of cookware, kitchen accessories, and home decorative items. All products are sold in home demonstrations. There is no ordering, packing, or shipping merchandise and no collection by the consultants.
Provisions: Training is provided. Regional advertising is provided by the company and the resulting inquires are passed along to the area consultants. The initial kit is free. Pays commission to consultants and up to 7% override to managers.

LADY FINNELLE COSMETICS, 1376 River St., P.O. Box 1726, Haverhill, MA 01831.
Positions: Home party sales of cosmetics and skin care products.
Provisions: Training is provided. Pays commission plus incentive bonuses.

LADY LOVE COSMETICS, INC., 1515 Champion Dr., Carrollton, TX 75006.
Positions: Direct sales of cosmetics and skin care products. Most reps conduct home parties, but they can use any methods they choose.
Provisions: Training is provided. Pays commission.

L'AROME, 456 Lakeshore Prkwy., Rock Hill, SC 29730.
Positions: Direct sales of fragrances, haircare and skincare products through party-plan methods.

LASTING IMPRESSIONS, 3683 Enochs St., Santa Clara, CA 95051
Positions: Lasting Impressions sells specialty chocolates via hotels, florists, card shops, gift shops, etc. The company is expanding nationwide and is looking for wholesale reps in every state.
Requirements: Send letter of interest.
Provisions: Training is provided along with necessary literature, samples, etc. Pays commission.

LAURA LYNN COSMETICS, INC., 5456 McConnell Ave., Suite 189, Los Angeles, CA 90066.
Positions: Direct sales of cosmetics and skin care products. Reps are trained in color by season consultation as a method of gaining a regular clientele.
Provisions: Training is provided. Pays commission.

L'ESSENCE, P.O. Box 1447, Friendswood, TX 77546.
Positions: Direct sales of perfumes and toiletries.

LITTLE BEAR ENTERPRISES, 3311 S. Saint Lucie Dr., Casselberry, FL 32707.
Positions: Little Bear sells unusual handcrafted home accessories with a country theme through home parties. Customers buy directly from inventory, not catalogs, and the inventory changes constantly to create a demand for additional parties.
Requirements: A minimum investment of $100 is required.
Provisions: A guaranteed return of a minimum $30 base pay for each party plus commissions of 20% are offered.

LONGABERGER MARKETING, INC., 2503 Maple Ave., Zanesville, OH 43701.
Positions: Longaberger markets maple wood baskets that are handmade in America. Each basket is signed by the weaver. Longaberger consultants sell the baskets though home parties.
Requirements: The initial investment of $300 covers the cost of sample baskets, catalogs, invitations, a handbook, and enough materials to hold several shows.
Provisions: Training is provided not only for sales techniques but for learning how to best decorate and display the baskets. Pays commissions starting at 25% plus overrides for managers. Three levels of management opportunities exist. Managers are provided with special management award baskets, mailings, meetings, training sessions, incentives, and other awards.

LUCKY HEART COSMETICS, INC., 138 Hurling Ave., Memphis, TN 38103.
Positions: Lucky Heart is a line of cosmetics for black women. The products are sold direct by independent distributors in any way they choose.
Requirements: A one-time $10 start-up fee is required.

Provision: Color catalogs, samples and testers are provided. Pays commission plus bonuses. Management opportunities exist.

JOE MARTHA TELEMARKETING, 1615 Republic St., Cincinnati, OH 45210.
Positions: Telemarketing of Catholic publications.
Provisions: Training is provided. Good repeat business. Can be located anywhere in the U.S. Pays good commission.

MARY KAY COSMETICS, INC., 8787 Stemmons Freeway, Dallas, TX 75247.
Positions: Beauty consultants and sales directors. Mary Kay started this cosmetics empire on her kitchen table in 1963. In 1984 there were 151,615 consultants and 4,500 sales directors producing over $300 million in sales. All of these people worked from their homes.
Requirements: An investment of $100 is required to start.
Provisions: Pays commission up to 12%. Offers incentives such as jewelry, furs, cars and trips through special promotions and contests. Consultants can earn over $30,000 annually, generally averaging over $10 an hour after taxes. Directors average over $100,000 a year. Can live anywhere.

MASON SHOE MANUFACTURING COMPANY, 1251 First Avenue, Chippewa Falls, WI 54729.
Positions: Mason is a 35-year-old family business with an extensive line of American made, quality shoes. All shoes are guarenteed for quality and fit and can be easily exchanged or refunded.
Provisions: Reps are provided with catalogs and all necessary supplies. Incentive bonus plans several times a year. Portion of the retail price is taken out by the rep before placing the order with the company.

MCCONNON & COMPANY, McConnon Drive, Winona, MN 55987.
Positions: Direct sales of household products, animal health products, and insecticides. McConnon & Company was founded in 1889 by a doctor and a druggist. The company manufactures flavoring extracts, spices, vitamins, food specialties, home medicines, household products, livestock pre-mixes, miscellaneous farm line products and insecticides. Some McConnon dealers have been with the company for over 30 years. Profit margins for dealers range from 40 to 50 percent. Items may be purchased in any quantity.
Requirements: McConnon dealers should have a good reputation in the community, the ability to meet people and a desire to serve them regularly, an interest in building a successful business, and a desire to improve their way of living.

MIRACLE MAID, P.O. Box C-50, Redmond, WA 98052.
Positions: Miracle Maid cookware is sold through pre-arranged product demonstrations in customers' homes.
Provisions: Training is provided. Pays commission.

MONITOR BUILDERS, 135 East 9th Ave., Homestead, PA 15120.
Positions: Telemarketers set appointments for outside sales force. Work is available within local calling area; no set territories.
Provisions: Method and rate of payment is worked out with individual workers.

Homeworker Profile
Linda Ragel, Commissioned Sales Manager

Reaching the magical sales mark of $1 million a year is the accomplishment of a lifetime. But for Linda Ragel, once was not enough. She reached that lofty goal twice.

After sixteen years in the cosmetics industry, Linda Ragel had progressed to a top management position with Jafra Cosmetics. Her annual sales figures had topped $2 million when a Swedish company, Oriflame International, came to her with an offer. The company had decided to enter the U.S. market and Linda was asked to help get things rolling.

"With Oriflame, it would be virtually starting a new company," she says. "There were no employees and no one had heard of the product even though it had been in Europe for twenty years. For me, it was going to be starting all over again from scratch. That seemed like an exciting opportunity, one that I couldn't resist."

That was in 1982, Linda went from managing 1,500 consultants to fifteen. Her job consists mainly of finding new people and training them as beauty consultants. "I just love working with people," she says. "It's what I do best. Many years ago, before I was in management, I thought it was really rewarding helping women feel better about themselves by showing them how to use my products as customers. But in management I can do much more. I am helping women become even more satisfied through their accomplishments in business. Being able to offer them the opportunity to become self-sufficient is very special."

Today, Linda is in charge of 700 independent contractors and fifteen key management people and has climbed back up to the million-dollar sales mark.

Linda doesn't take her success for granted. "I was fortunate to choose a good company with a lot of potential for upward movement, and the product was one I could believe in," she says. "You have to choose something that you can be committed to. Then balance that by developing the right qualities: self-discipline, organization, and being a good goal setter."

As for working at home, Linda says she's enjoyed it. "I love the environment of home, I gain a lot of strength being around things that I am familiar with."

MULTIWAY ASSOCIATES, 633 Lawrence Street P.O. Box 2796, Batesville, AR 72501.
Positions: Multiway sells its line of health products through independent contractors who are free to sell the products in any manner they wish. Although the company has suggested retail prices and the reps deduct the wholesale prices to deduct their commissions, the reps are free to set any prices they want.
Requirements: A one-time fee of $39 is required for a starter kit which includes all necessary instructions, paperwork and samples. No product inventory is required. No set territories.

NATIONAL MARKETING SERVICES, 451 E. Carson Plaza Dr., Ste. 205, Carson, CA 90746.
Positions: Work is available for various telemarketing projects; most involve selling tickets to charity events. Projects are available nationally as well as locally.
Requirements: Experience is required.
Provisions: Pays commission which varies with each project, but is typically in the $6 to $15 an hour range. Hours can be part-time or full-time, days or evenings. Scripts are provided.

NATIONAL PARTITIONS & INTERIORS, INC., 340, W. 78th Rd., Hialeah, FL 33014.
Positions: National Partitions is major manufacturer and exporter of modular in-plant and exterior building systems. The company is looking to expand its domestic and foreign sales and in having foreign firms license the their products.
Provisions: A 5% finder's fee is paid to anyone securing sales and a 10% finder's fee to anyone securing foreign licensing agreements for the company.

NATIONAL SAFETY ASSOCIATES, INC. 42600 E. Raines Road, Memphis, TN 38118.
Positions: Direct sales of water treatment systems. NSA offers a proven program for part-time sales opportunities wherein a person can work 8-12 hours per week and earn up of $10,000 a year.
Requirements: New distributors of NSA products must first be sponsored by someone who is already a distributor. If one cannot be located, then the interested person must attend a regional training class. A schedule will be provided upon request.
Provisions: Training is provided. NSA products are sold through a trial use approach. A customer is given the opportunity to try the product for a few days, and then make the decision whether or not to purchase. Because of this method of selling, NSA recommends that distributors have 4-5 units on hand for this purpose. NSA provides a credit line so that the new distributor has no purchase requirements to get started. Pays commission plus bonuses through the company-sponsored rebate program.

NATIONAL TELEMARKETING ASSOCIATION, 908 Palmer Rd., Walnut Creek, CA 94596.
Positions: Telemarketing on a variety of projects.
Requirements: Experience is preferred, but not required.
Provisions: Work is available anywhere in the country. Training is provided. Pay varies.

NATURAL ACCENTS BY PHILLIPINE IMPORTS, 8 B Street, Hyde Park, MA 02136.

Positions: Handcrafted decorative accents for the home are sold primarily through home party sales and also with the aid of catalgs.
Provisions: Catalogs are provided. Pays commission plus bonus plan.

NATURAL IMPRESSIONS CORP., 182 Liberty Street, Painesville, OH 44077.
Positions: Direct sales of jewelry.
Provisions: Pays commission. Catalogs are provided.

NATURE'S SUNSHINE PRODUCTS, INC., 1655 N. Main, P.O. Box 1000, Spanish Fort, UT 84660.
Positions: Direct sales of herbs, vitamins, and personal care products.
Requirements: New distributors must attend a one-week training session at company headquarters at their own expense. Reps are trained to sell the products through network marketing.
Provisions: Commissions start at 8% and go up to 30%. Managers receive generous override commissions. Participating managers receive health and dental insurance, new car allowance, and a retirement program. Sales aids and incentive programs are provided to everyone.

NATUS CORP., 4445 West 77, Ste. 230, Minneapolis, MN 55435.
Positions: Direct sales of haircare, skincare and health and fitness products.

NEO-LIFE COMPANY OF AMERICA, P.O. Box 5012, Fremont, CA 94537.
Positions: Direct sales of household products, vitamins, minerals, and some food products. Multilevel techniques are used.
Requirements: A small investment is required.
Provisions: Pays commission on a sliding scale.

NIMBUS INTERNATIONAL, 1313 A Simpson Way, P.O Box 270577, San Diego, CA 92128.
Positions: Direct sales of drinking water systems.

NOEVIR, INC., 1095 S.E. Main St., Irvine, CA 92714.
Positions: Direct sales of cosmetics manufactured by Noevir, all of which are completely natural and herbal. Noevir has over 15,000 operators currently serving the U.S. The company is an affiliate of a larger Japanese company, and also has an office in Canada. Noevir is a wholly-owned subsidiary of Noevir, Co., Ltd., the second largest direct selling company in Japan.
Requirements: The initial investment in Noevir is $30 for registration in addition to the purchase of one starter kit. These kits contain products, training information, and samples for the new operator. The kits, (choice of 2) are $150. There is also an option"C" which is a "build-your-own" kit. The minimum purchase for this kit is $50.
Provisions: Noevir offers a generous compensation package in addition to very high quality products.

NUSUS, 2300 Valley View Lane, Ste. 230 Farmers Branch, TX 75234.
Positions: Direct sales of skincare, health and fitness products through party-plan methods.

NUTRI-METRICS INTERNATIONAL, INC., 19501 East Walnut Drive, CIty of Industry, CA 91749.

Provisions: Direct sales of cosmetics, food supplements, and bras.

NUTRITIONAL EXPRESS, Houston, TX.
Positions: Nutritional Express (formerly Consumer Express) offers a wide variety of products including food, cleaning products, cosmetics, and health care. It also offers services such as the Legal Services Plan. Direct distributors are free to market these products and services any way they wish with no set territories or methods.
Requirements: Pays commission plus bonus plan. This is a multilevel marketing plan so extra bonus plans for enrollments are available, but it is not the primary thrust of the program. Complete training is available.

KENNETH OLSON & ASSOCIATES, 399 Main St., Los Altos, CA 94022.
Positions: Telemarketers for business-to-business insurance sales.
Requirements: Must be local resident. Prefers experience in business-to-business dealings.
Provisions: Specific training is provided. Leads are also provided. No high pressure selling involved. Part-time hours only. Pays salary plus "substantial" commission.

OMNI CREATIONS, 28651 Darrow Ave., Saugus, CA 91350.
Positions: Direct sales of extensive jewelry line. Reps sell through home parties, fashion shows, wholesale, and any other method they choose. Company is now 11 years old.
Requirements: No investment is required. The company is expanding nationwide, but for now it is mostly operating in New York, New Jersey, California, Illinois, and Florida.
Provisions: There is a start-up program available for anyone interested in management opportunities in states not mentioned above. Work is part-time and reps average $30,000 a year.

ORIFLAME INTERNATIONAL, 76 Treble Cove Road, North Billerica, MA 01862.
Positions: Direct sales reps for European cosmetics line. Oriflame International is a high-quality cosmetic line that has gained a reputation for being "the largest, most prestigious direct sales company in Europe." Company has been expanding throughout the U.S. for about five years. Advisors are trained as skin consultants. Business does not usually consist of door-to-door or party style sales. More often, advisors act as make-up artists and customers come to their home offices by appointment only. Opportunity also for part-time sales leadership positions. Significant "groundfloor" opportunity for Group Directors.
Provisions: Complete training is provided. Commissions are reportedly the highest in the U.S. for a direct sales company.

OZARK TREASURES, 1103 South Lafayette, Neosho, MO 64850.
Positions: This crafts company is looking for sub-wholesalers for rack merchandising, wholesaling to retail stores, wagon jobbing, customer retail sales, mall catalog shopping centers, wholesale customer buying clubs, and a home party hostess program
Requirements: The sub-wholesaler program requires a $25 fee for all books and information and a $25 or $50 deposit for display samples, order blanks, etc. The party hostess plan requires a $25 deposit for all books and information and a $100 deposit for party plan samples to start with.
Deposits are refundable.

PAMPERED CHEF, 9913 Kell Avenue South, Bloomington, MN 55437.
Positions: Consultants and their supervisors conduct gourmet cooking demonstrations

Homeworker Profile: Nancy Maynard

Nancy Maynard's work has changed in ways she never expected since graduating from Berkeley with two degrees. Her work life started in the corporate world of Xerox.

"If found there was pressure to slow down, to do just what you're supposed to do. There was no encouragement to do more to earn more. Raises were the same for everyone; they came along once a year no matter what. After six years, I asked myself why I should work hard for another $10 a week—especially since I'd get it regardless of my accomplishments."

Shortly before leaving Xerox, Nancy started working with Oriflame, selling their European skin care system. The initial intent was to make a little extra cash. Much to her surprise, she matched her corporate salary within six months. In another six months she became assistant manager and was well on her way to earning her present $40,000 a year salary, plus bonus gifts.

"My whole way of thinking has changed. The corporate atmosphere fosters short-term thinking. Back then, if I wanted a new car, I'd have to wait and see what kind of a raise I got to decide if I could afford it. In direct sales, a person is in control. I can say, 'I need a car. I'll buy it and work an extra four hours a week to pay for it.'" She adds, "Of course, I don't need to do that. I've earned a gold Mercedes through Oriflame's incentive bonus plan!"

Nancy believes direct sales is an ideal choice for women who want to combine working and homemaking. It gives them control over their earning power and greater flexibility in their daily schedules.

For Nancy, that means spending time with her husband, who also works at home, and with their five year old daughter. "We both like to take time out of the day when we want to go to the park, have lunch together, or maybe just go for a walk. It allows us to give our daughter a better sense of us as people. What could be better than that?"

in order to show the Pampered Chef line of kitchen tools.
Provisions: Training is provided. Pays commission plus override for supervisors.

PARENT & CHILD RESOURCE CENTER, INC., P.O. Box 269, Columbus, OH 43215.
Positions: Direct sales of educational publications and magazine.

PARTYLITE GIFTS, Building 16, Cordage Park, Plymouth, MA 02360.
Positions: Home party sales of decorative accessories and giftware for the home.
Provisions: Pays commission plus bonuses. Management opportunities available.

PERFUME ORIGINALS, INC., 45 West 34 Street, New York, NY 10001.
Positions: Perfumes, oils, and Ultramink skin care systems are marketed in the home by skin consultants.
Requirements: To become an independent product representative you must first place an order for yourself.
Provisions: Upon placing your personal order, all future orders are 30% off (your commission). After $145 in retail sales, a sales kit is forwarded free; the kits contains a sales manual, necessary order forms and paperwork, and a vial box containing samples of the complete line of fragrances. Commissions climb with volume and go as high as 50%.

PETRA FASHIONS, INC., 335 Cherry Hill Drive, Danvers, MA 01923.
Positions: Direct sales of lingerie and sleepwear. All items are under $30. Petra consultants demonstrate the lingerie collection in private home parties. Consultants test show guests' "romance ratings" and offer fashion advice on garment style and fit. They do not collect money, take inventory or make deliveries. Petra accepts Mastercard and VISA and all show orders are shipped C.O.D. by UPS directly to the party hostess.
Requirements: No investment or experience is necessary. Petra offers a free starter kit of sample garments and paperwork that is valued at more than $500. There are no quotas or sales territories.
Provisions: Petra provides free training, hostess incentives, profit per show in excess of $75, advancement opportunities, overrides, awards, and recognition.

DAVID PHELPS INSURANCE, 7844 Madison Avenue, Suite N111, Fair Oaks, CA 95628.
Positions: Insurance sales for special program offered by National Association of Self Employed (NASE).
Requirements: Must live in Northern California to work for this particular agency.
Provisions: All leads are supplied by the association. Pays commission. Training is provided.

PLANTMINDER, INC., 22582 Shanon Circle, Lake Forest, CA 92630.
Positions: Direct sales of self-watering plant containers. Reps sell the product in a variety of ways, usually starting by placing ads.
Provisions: Pays commission.

POINT OUT PUBLISHING, 26 Homestead St., San Francisco, CA 94114.
Positions: This European publisher of maps and guides uses home-baed telemarketers to make appointments for salespeople. Work is not permanent; it comes and goes all the

time.
Requirements: Good phone manner and experience is required.   San Francisco residents only.
Provisions: Pays $8 an hour.

POLA, U.S.A., INC., 250 East Victoria Avenue, Carson, CA 90746.
Positions: Home party sales of cosmetics.
Requirements: A start-up kit requires an investment.
Provisions: Pays commission.

PRIMA FACEY, 783 Park, Glen Ellyn, IL 60137.
Positions: Image consultants give personal and corporate workshops to men and women on how they can enhance their image. The consultants work on location, which can be in their own home or in someone else's home or office.

Requirements: There is a $500 initial investment to become certified as an image consultant and for the necesary tools to start. This investment can result in annual commissions of $40,000 or more.
Provisions: Training sessions are held throughout the country on a regular basis. Hours are extremely flexible.

PRINCESS HOUSE, INC., 455 Somerset Avenue, North Dighton, MA 02764.
Positions: Home party sales of crystal products.
Provisions: Pays commission plus override for managers. Training is provided.

PRO-AG, INC., 2072 E. Center Circle, Minneapolis, MN 55441.
Positions: Direct sales of Impro/NU-AG agricultural products.

PROFESSIONAL ACCOUNTANCY PRACTICE, 14111 Buckner Drive, San Jose, CA 95127.
Positions: Telemarketing of professional services to businesses only.
Requirements: Must be local resident. Experience is required.
Provisions: Specific training is provided. Pays commission weekly.

PRO-MA SYSTEMS, 976 Florida Central Pkwy., Ste. 136, Longwood, FL 32752.
Positions: Direct sales of autocare products, skincare, and cosmetics through party-plan method.

PURE LIFE SYSTEMS, 209 East William, Ste. 650, Wichita, KS 67202.
Positions: Direct sales of health and fitness products and nutritional supplements.

QUEEN'S WAY TO FASHION, INC., 43 W. Jackson Blvd. #1122, Chicago, IL 60604.

Positions: Direct sales of women's fashions mostly, but not necessarily, through home parties.
Requirements: There is a deposit required for the start-up kit.
Provisions: Training is provided. Pays commission "on a higher level than any other direct sales apparel company in the U.S." Management opportunities are available.

RACHAEL COSMETICS, 155 W. Highway 434, Winter Springs, FL 32708.
Positions: Direct sales of cosmetics through home parties.

RAMA ENTERPRISES, P.O. Box 976, New Philadelphia, OH 44663.
Positions: Rama is a Christian oriented direct sales company using multilevel techniques to market personal care products such as perfume, shampoo, bath oil, skin care products, and home cleaning items.
Requirements: A $35 fee is required to register with the company. There is a quota of $25 a month in sales to continue as a rep. Pays 7% commission. Matches your 10% tithing to the ministry of your choice out of company profits.

THE W. T. RAWLEIGH COMPANY, 1501 Northpoint Parkway, Suite 100, W. Palm Beach, FL 33407.
Positions: Direct sales of household products, food, cleaning products, medicine, and pet supplies. Reps use any sales methods they choose.
Provisions: Pays commissions.

REGAL WARE, INC., 1675 Reigle Dr., Kewaskum, WI 53040.
Positions: Direct sales of cookware, usually through home parties.
Provisions: Training is provided. Pays commission.

REMOTE CONTROL, 514 Via de la Valle, Suite 306, Solana Beach, CA 92075.
Positions: Over 50 telemarketers sell the company's software from their home phones.
Requirements: Sales experience and a background working with a computer are required.

RENA-WARE COSMETICS, INC., P.O. Box 97050, Redmond, WA 98073.
Positions: Cookware is sold by independent reps in any manner they choose.
Provisions: Pays commission.

REXAIR, INC., P.O. Box 3610, Troy, MI 48007.
Positions: Direct sales of rainbow vacuum cleaners, AquaMate, and related products.

RICH PLAN CORP., 4981 Commercial Dr., Yorkville, NY 13495.
Positions: Direct sales of food, beverage products, and home appliances.

RICKSHAW IMPORTS, 800 North Edgewood Ave., Wood Dale, IL 60191.
Positions: Direct sales of decorative wicker accessories.

RUBINO PUBLISHING, INC., (800)749-1333.
Positions: Publishers of business manuals seeks independent contractors to market secured credit cards. Work mostly involves taking incoming phone orders.
Requirements: Manual and instructions costs (one time fee) $59.95.
Provisions: Can live anywhere. Bank processing centers pay regardless of approval.

SALADMASTER, INC., 131 Howell St., Dallas, TX 75207.
Positions: Home party sales of cookware and tableware.
Provisions: Training is available. Pays commission plus bonus plan.

SALES PLUS, P.O. Box 28441, Baltimore, MD 21234.
Positions: Part-time telemarketers set appointments from home. Business to business calls only.

Requirements: Must be local resident. Experienced professionals only.

SAMANTHA JEWELS, INC., 162-27 99 Street, P.O. Box 477, Station B, Howard Beach, NY 11414.
Positions: A line of more than 2,000 kinds of jewelry (mostly gold and diamond) are sold direct with the aid of mail order catalogs.
Requirements: A $4 fee for a sales package including the catalog with wholesale price instructions, sales instructions and paperwork supplies.
Provisions: Pays commission of a minimum 55%.

SAN FRANCISCO CHRONICLE, Circulation Department, 925 Mission, San Francisco, CA 94103.
Positions: Telemarketers sell subscriptions. Work is part-time.
Requirements: Some previous telemarketing experience is required.
Provisions: Can live anywhere in Northern California. Training is provided. Some leads are supplied. Pays commission and bonuses.

SASCO COSMETICS, INC., 2151 Champion Drive, Carrollton, TX 75006.
Positions: Home party sales of cosmetics and personal care products, mostly based on aloe vera.
Provisions: Training is provided. Pays commissions. Management opportunities available in most areas.

SCHOOL CALENDAR, P.O. Box 280, Morristown, TN 37815.
Positions: Account executives sell advertising space. Company is a 30 year old publishing firm.
Requirements: Must be bondable.
Provisions: A protected territoty is assigned. Training and accounts are provided. Pays commission and bonuses.

SHAKLEE CORPORATON, Shaklee Terraces, 444 Market Street, San Francisco, CA 94111.
Positions: Shaklee's line of products includes "natural" cosmetics, health care products, household products, and now some services as well. All of Shaklee's products are sold by independent distributors.
Requirements: Distributors must stock inventory in all basic products which does require a cash investment.
Provisions: Pays commission.

SILVAN EVE, 560 Oakbrook Parkway, Suite 170, Norcross, GA 30093.
Positions: High quality silver and gold jewelry is sold by independent reps through a variety of methods.
Requirements: A refundable deposit is required for start-up sample case.
Provisions: Provides new catalogs as they come out. Training is provided. Pays substantial commission.

SOCIETY CORPORATION, 1609 Kilgore Ave., Muncie, IN 47304.
Positions: This is a manufacturer of cookware, china and crystal. The product line is sold through independent reps with assigned exclusive territories.

THE SOUTHWESTERN COMPANY, P.O. Box 305140, Nashville, TN 37230.
Positions: Southwestern is a well established publisher of educational books and cassettes. Independent reps sell the products, mostly with the aid of company provided leads. Exclusive territoties are assigned and many are taken by long-time reps so there may not be anything available in your area.
Provisions: Pays commission plus bonus plan.

STANHOME, INC., 333 Western Avenue, Westfield, MA 01085.
Positions: Direct sales of household cleaning products and personal grooming aids. Reps can used any method for marketing the products.
Provisions: Pays commission.

STEINHAUS AUTO ELECTRIC SERVICE, 3717 2nd Avenue, Sacramento, CA 95816.
Positions: Telemarketers set appointments for alarm systems salespeople.
Requirements: Must live in Sacramento. Experience preferred.
Provisions: Training provided. Pays guaranteed hourly rate.

THE STUART MCGUIRE COMPANY, INC., 115 Brand Road, Salem, VA 24156.
Positions: Direct sales of shoes and clothing for both men and women through the use of catalogs.
Provisions: Catalogs are provided. Pays commission on a sliding scale.

SUBSCRIPTION PLUS, 228-35 Edgewood Avenue, Rosedale, NY 11422.
Positions: Subscription agents for several hundred major consumer magazines.
Provisions: Some training is provided. Can be located anywhere in U.S. Pays commission up to 50%.

SUITCASE BOUTIQUE, 12228 Spring Place Court, Maryland Heights, MO, 63043.
Positions: Suitcase Boutique is a home party business. Home party demonstrators sell hand crafted items like stuffed animals, wood crafts, toys, soft sculpture, framed pictures, and cross-stitch.
Requirements: Investment is required for start-up kit, but kit will be bought back upon request.
Provisions: Pays commission. Training is provided. Work is part-time; average income for demonstrators is $9,000 a year. Can live anywhere.

THE SUNRIDER CORPORATION, 452 West 1260 North, Orem, UT 84057.
Positions: Direct sales of food products and personal care items using the multilevel techniques.
Requirements: A small investment in inventory is required.
Provisions: Pays commission on a sliding scale plus bonus incentives.

SYBIL'S, 9034 Natural Bridge Road, St. Louis, MO 63121.
Positions: Direct sales of jewelry and fragrances. Reps mostly use home parties, but it is not required.
Requirements: A refundable investment in start-up kit is required.
Provisions: Pays commission plus bonuses.

TECHPROSE, 370 Central Park West, Suite 210, New York, NY 10025.
Positions: This is an unusual company that does electronic marketing for clients using electronic databases, modems, and fax machines to conduct its business. Market researchers and their support staff handle the various telecommunications tasks and prepare reports from their home offices.
Requirements: A solid background in marketing plus experience with electronic networking are required. Send resume.

TELEMARKETING ASSOCIATES, 2924 North River Rd., River Grove, IL 60171.
Positions: Telemarketing in various fund raising projects. Some projects are nationwide so home workers can live anywhere. Most projects, however, are in Illinois only.
Provisions: Training is provided. Pays hourly wage or high commission.
"One of our projects pays $500 and up per week in commission."

TIARA EXCLUSIVES, 717 E St., Dunkirk, IN 47336.
Positions: Home party sales of decorative home accessories mostly consisting of glassware.
Provisions: Training is provided. Pays commission plus override for managers.

TIME-LIFE BOOKS, 777 Duke St., Alexandria, VA 22314.
Positions: Direct sales of educational publications.

TOMORROW'S TREASURES, INC., 111 North Glassboro Road, Woodbury Heights, NJ 08097.
Positions: Direct sales of photo albums, cameras, and other photographic equipment. Reps mostly use direct mail.
Provisions: Pays commission.

TOWN & COUNTRY, 5060 Gardenville Road, Pittsburgh, PA 15236.
Positions: Telemarketing for carpet cleaning company.
Requirements: Must live in the greater Pittsburgh area.
Provisions: Training is provided. Each telemarketer is assigned a territory. Pays commission.

TRI-CHEM, INC., One Cape May Street, Harrison, NJ 07029.
Positions: Tri-Chem has manufactured craft products since 1948 and the complete line is now sold in more than 40 countries around the world. The leading product in their line is a liquid embroidery paint. Reps conduct craft classes to show potential customers how to use the products.
Requirements: To become a Tri-Chem instructor, you must hostess an introductory class, book at least 4 more classes for your first two weeks, and pay a small registration fee.
Provisions: Training is provided. Pays commission starting at 25% and going up to 50% with volume. Tri-Chem offers new instructors a consultant kit worth up to $260 and bonus coupons for free products worth up to $234. Bonus programs provide additional earnings, vacation trips plus special seminars and conventions to enhance training. Management opportunities are available.

TUPPERWARE HOME PARTIES, P.O. Box 2353, Orlando, FL 32802.
Positions: Direct sales of plastic food storage containers, cookware, and children's toys.

TYNDALE HOUSE PUBLISHERS, INC., 336 Gundersen Dr., Wheaton, IL 60189.
Positions: Home-based telemarketers.
Requirements: Must be local resident. Experience required.

U.N.I., 1600 Quail Run, Charlottesville, VA 22901.
Positions: A wide variety of products including pet care, personal care, vitamins, and home cleaning products are sold direct using catalogs. All items are sold at distributor prices.
Provisions: Pays commission.

UNITED CONSUMERS CLUB, 8450 South Broadway, Merrillville, IN 46410.
Positions: This is a consumer group buying system that solicits new members through home parties.

U.S. SAFETY & ENGINEERING CORPORATION, 2365 El Camino Avenue, Sacramento, CA 95821.
Positions: Direct sales of security systems including fire and burgular alarms. Reps have exclusive territories and are free to use any sales methods they choose. Most use telemarketing to set appointments for personal consultations.
Provisions: Pays commission.

UNDERCOVERWEAR, INC., 331 New Boston St., Wilmington, MA 01887.
Positions: Home party sales of clothing, mostly lingerie.
Requirements: Rep is required to host a home party first.
Provisions: Pays commission. Training is provided.

UNION TRIBUNE, 4069 - 30th Street, Suite 9, San Diego, CA 92104-2631.
Positions: Telemarketers sell subscriptions.
Requirements: Must live in the San Diego area. Self-discipline is important.
Provisions: Training is provided. Some leads are supplied. Pays commission plus bonus.

UNIQUE DECOR, P.O. Box 491, Mansfield, MA 02048.
Positions: Decorative home accessories are sold by independent reps in exclusive showings.
Provisions: Training in both sales and some interior decorating techniques is provided. Pays commissions.

UNITED LABORATORIES OF AMERICA, INC., 1526 Fort Worth Avenue, P.O. Box 4499, Station A, Dallas, TX 75208.
Positions: Direct sales of photo albums, photo enlargements, books and Bibles.
Provisions: Pays commission.

UNITED MARKETING GROUPS, 1950 Clay #203, San Francisco, CA 94109.
Positions: Telemarketers work on a variety of projects throughout the Bay area.
Requirements: Experience is required in some kind of phone work. Must live in the Bay area.
Provisions: Training is provided. Leads are supplied. Pays commisison.

USA TODAY, P.O. Box 500, Sixth Floor Circulation, Washington D.C. 20044.
Positions: Telemarketers solicit subscriptions. Work is distributed to home workers on

a local basis only through USA Today's distributors. Distributors can be found in the phone book, or you can contact the main office to locate the distributor in your area.

VITA CRAFT CORPORATION, 11100 West 58 Street, Shawnee, KS 66203.
Positions: Home party sales of cookware, china, crystal, tableware and cutlery.
Provisions: Pays commission and bonuses. Training is provided.

VIVA AMERICA MARKETING, 946 West 17 St., Costa Mesa, CA 92627.
Positions: Direct sales of cleaning products, cosmetics, and nutritional supplements through home parties.

VORWERK USA, INC., 222 Westmonte Dr. S., Altmonte Springs, FL 32714.
Positions: Independent sales advisors (over 11,000 of them) sell products directly to consumers for the maintenance and cleaning of floor textiles.
Provisions: Complete training is provided.

WATER RESOURCES INTERNATIONAL, INC., 2800 East Chambers St., Phoenix, AZ 85040.
Positions: Direct sales of water conditioning and purification systems.

WATKINS INCORPORATED, 150 Liberty St., Winona, MN 55987.
Positions: Watkins is a well established company that uses independent reps to sell its extensive line of household goods including food, health products, and cleaning items.
Requirements: A small start-up investment is required.
Provisions: Pays commission.

WEBWAY, INC., 2815 Clearwater Road, P.O. Box 767, St. Cloud, MN 56302.
Positions: Direct sales of photo albums.

WECARE DISTRIBUTORS, INC., 7415 Pineville Matthews Rd., Suite 400, Charlotte, NC, 28226.
Positions: Direct sales of skin care products and cosmetics.

WELCOME WAGON, Welcome Wagon Bldg., 145 Court Ave., Memphis, TN 38103.
Positions: Welcome Wagon is a personalized advertising service. Individuals in all areas work from home to represent local businesses in the homes of brides-to-be, new parents, and newcomers.
Requirements: Outgoing personality, articulate, past-business or community experience. Car is a necessity.
Provisions: Training is provided. Flexible scheduling, part-time or full-time. Pays commission.

THE WEST BEND CO., Premiere Cookware Division, 400 Washington St., West Bend, WI 53095.
Positions: Direct sales of cookware and electrical appliances. The company started in 1911 and has been a member of the Direct Selling Association since 1927. West Bend has a deep respect for the direct selling industry because of the success of their other company, Tupperware.
Provisions: Training is provided through the use of Zig Ziglar training programs. In addition to commission, reps earn bonuses and can advance to management.

WINNING EDGE, P.O. Box 305140, Nashville, TN 37230.
Positions: Direct sales of home safety products including fire extinguishers, water purifiers, and fire alarms.

WORLD BOOK, INC., 510 Merchandise Mart Plaza, Chicago, IL 60654.
Positions: World Book, the encyclopedia publisher, sells its products through the use of direct sales reps.
Provisions: Training is provided. Some leads are provided. Pays commission. Sales kit is provided without cost. Managment opportunities are available

YANBAL LABORATORIES, 1441 S.W. 33 Pl., Ft. Lauderdale, FL 33315.
Positions: Direct sales of cosmetics and skincare products through home parties.

ZONDERVAN BOOK OF LIFE, P.O. Box 6130, Grand Rapids, MI 49506.
Positions: The Book of Life is a set of boks based on the parables of the Bible. The company was established in 1923 and has always used direct salespeople to market the product.
Requirements: A refundable $20 deposit is required.
Provisions: The deposit buys a sales kit which includes all necessary training materials. Pays commission on a sliding scale which increases with volume. Cash bonuses and promotions are available. Also available are credit union membership, company-paid insurance, and a deferred retirement compensation plan.

TELECOMMUTING AND OTHER EMPLOYEE OPTIONS

If you are like most people, you think that if you want a job working at home, you will have to give up your present job and start from scratch, and look for a new job that could be done at home. The fact is, however, that for 13 million Americans, taking their work home at least one day a week is routine. These home workers are commonly referred to as "telecommuters."

Telecommuting is an often misused term. It means transporting work to the worker rather than the worker to the workplace. This can be accomplished in a number of ways, but most often it involves the use of telephones, computers and modems, and facimile (FAX) machines.

In this book, telecommuting will be defined as an option open to employees who are currently working for a company and have an express need to take their work home. A temporary need might be illness, temporary disability, pregnancy, or the need to take care of family members. Some workers desire to move home in order to work more productively on long projects, cut down on commuting, or spend more time with family.

Some telecommuting is done temporarily, some is part-time, and some is permanent. It is becoming a very common option in the corporate world with as many as 500 corporations reporting some kind of work-at-home option available to employees on an informal basis. A few of those have formal programs with the rules for working at home laid out in very specific detail.

If you are already working and you want to work at home, look in your own back yard first. Many employees have the opportunity to work at home and just don't know it. Before looking elsewhere for a new job that can be done at home, why not start by discussing with your manager the possibility of moving your present job home? You might be surprised by the answer.

The listings in this section should be considered as examples of successful telecommuting programs only. None of them are open to inquiries from anyone who is not currently an employee.

Moving Your Work Home

Moving your present job from its current location to your home is an option that you should explore before looking for a new employer.

Large corporations are most likely to accept the telecommuting arrangement. Of the several hundred major corporations in the U.S. that have home workers on the payroll, very few hire home workers from the outside. As a rule, they want to develop confidence in their employees before allowing them to take their work home. Therefore, the very first thing to do is make sure you are known for being a valuable and trustworthy employee.

Next, develop a plan of action. Define the job tasks which are feasible for home work. Don't ignore problems that could arise later and undermine your position. Consider all of the possible problems and devise a "worst case" scenario and alternative solutions for dealing with each of them. That way, you will be prepared and can confidently assure your company there will be no unpleasant surprises.

You will need to sell your home work idea to your employer, focusing on the ways moving your work home will benefit the company. Remember, your employer is in business to make a profit, and while he/she probably prefers happy employees, the bottom line is ultimately the highest priority. You can take comfort in the fact that the benefits employers gain from work-at-home arrangements are well documented. If you want to refer to some success stories, see the company profiles scattered throughout this book. In addition, the following information is likely to grab your employer's attention.

The number one benefit to employers is increased productivity. The best documented cases are from Blue Cross/Blue Shield of South Carolina, which reported productivity gains of 50%, and from Control Data Corp., which showed gains of 35%. Employees at home tend to work at their individual peak hours, don't get paid for long luch hours and time spent at the water cooler, and often continue to work while feeling slightly under the weather rather than take time off.

The second greatest benefit to employers is the cost savings from not spending money on additional office space, utilities, parking space, etc. This is especially helpful for growing companies and also for home-based businesses that need to expand, but want to limit the costs of doing so. Some companies have even sent employees home and rented out the unoccupied space to compatible firms. As a direct result of its home work program, Pacific Bell closed three offices last year, saving $40,000 in rent alone.

Another advantage to employers is a far lower turnover rate among employees allowed to work at home. In some industries, rapid turnover is a serious problem. The insurance industry, for instance, has a turnover rate between 30% and 45%. As you would expect, recruiting and training costs are very high in such industries.

Even governments have come to view telecommuting as a viable solution to some of society's most pressing problems–air pollution, traffic conjestion, and energy consumption. It has been estimated that a 20% reduction in commuting nationwide could save 110,000 barrels of gasoline a day! For these reasons, several states–including California, Washington, and North Dakota–have formally endorsed telecommuting. California is even considering offering tax incentives to companies that will send some of its employees home to work. And, in a speech on energy conservation, George Bush came out in favor of the idea.

All of this should give you ample ammunition to convince your manager(s) to let you try working at home. It's usually best not to try for an immediate move to full-time home work, though. Start slowly, asking to take your work home a couple of times in the afternoon, and then proposing a two-day project. While you're testing the waters, make sure you check in by phone to see if anything has come up at the office that you need to take care of. After a few months of occasional home work, you'll be ready to go to your manager and point out that you get a more accomplished when you're not distracted by office routines and don't have to waste valuable time commuting. Remember, you're not asking for favors. You are simply offering what every employer wants—a motivated, efficient worker interested in increasing productivity.

COMPANIES WITH TELECOMMUTING PROGRAMS

ALLERGAN, INC., California.
Allergan is a well-known manufacturer of eye care products. For the last decade, company programmers have been working at home due to lack of space at company headquarters. The policy has saved the company considerable money (from not having to expand) and given employees freedom and flexibility.

ALLSTATE INSURANCE COMPANY, Illinois.
Allstate's telecommuting program originally started as an option for disabled employees, all of whom were programmers. The first was a systems programmer who was injured in a car accident. Then came some entries placed by Lift, Inc. Now, Allstate is open to the telecommuting option for any current employee with a job suitable to be taken home on an alternating schedule.

AMF BOWLING PRODUCTS GROUP, INC., New York.
Office-based employees are provided with computer terminals and telecommunications equipment for after-hours telecommuting. Most telecommuting is done by company programmers.

AMTRAK, Washington, DC.
Amtrak's Customer Relations Group has increased its productivity and employee morale by implementing telecommuting on a small scale. Nine writers in the group work at home on a rotating schedule, with one writer working one day at home, then the next taking one day, and so on.

ANASAZI, INC., Arizona.
Programmers, engineers, and other high level technical personnel work at home. Company is very careful who is selected for telecommuting. Only persons who have proven to be self-managing, have some experience working at home, and have proper technical equipment can participate. Employee status remains intact.

ANDREWS GLASS COMPANY, INC., New Jersey.
Glass lampwork and tool work on laboratory glass products is dispensed as an option for extra income for after-hours work for established employees only.

APPLE COMPUTER, INC., California.
Telecommuting at Apple is a natural. All employees receive an Apple computer for their home use and are part of the company's electronic network automatically. Couple that with the company's liberal attitude toward its employees in general and you have a lot of people worrking at home whenever it seems appropriate.

AT&T, California.
AT&T, like most of the "Baby Bells," is not only a participant in the telecommuting trend, but a leader as well. It's own formal telecommuting program involves almost a hundred employees in various job categories. These people sign contracts that specifically lay out the rules of the arrangement and they then attend orientation training.
But more widespread is the compnany's informal consent to literally thousands of employees who find it efficient to spend at least part of their work week at home. The

policy is so liberal even newly hired employees can arrange to telecommute right from the start if that is the custom of the group they will be working with.

In addition, AT&T helps set up telecommuting programs for other companies in the Southern California area.

BALTIMORE EVENING SUN, Maryland.

The work-at-home option, used by writers of all kinds, is available to any employee with the necessary equipment.

BANKERS TRUST COMPANY, New York.

Bankers Trust recently conducted its initial telecommuting pilot program with the help of Electronic Services Unlimited. 20 employees worked at home for six months on a part-time basis only. The usual time spent at home working was two days a week unless the particular project allowed for longer periods of time. Employees were supplied with IBM PCs tied into the mainframe in Manhattan. The work was done in the local mode using and transferring floppies. The pilot was successful so the program has been expanded to include 10 more people.

BATTERYMARCH FINANCIAL MANAGEMENT COMPANY, Massachusetts.

Batterymarch is an international investment counseling firm with $12 billion worth of funds, mostly corporate pensions, to manage. Operation requires a 24-hour vigilence in order to keep up with world markets. Most employees, 30 out of 35, have terminals at home connected to the company's mainframe. 20 professional brokers are also "on-line" with their own PCs. If a broker has a problem with the system, he/she can call one of the others at home for help. Throughout the night, the company's "Phantom Program" monitors the system automatically and transmits wake-up calls if something goes wrong.

"We've been using this system for over 10 years. Since starting the work-at-home routine, our productivity has increased tremendously. The owner had a vision that at some time everyone would work at home unless they absolutely could not."

BELL COMMUNICATIONS, New Jersey.

Experienced employees in the Research Department can make arrangements with their managers to take their work home on a project-by-project basis. There have been some full-time telecommuters, but the situation is not the rule.

BELL SOUTH, Arizona.

Bell South is conducting an experimental two-year telecommuting program. Tele-commuters are all regular employees of Bell South and include both high-tech and low-tech personnel, mostly middle managers and marketers.

BENEFICIAL CORPORATION, New Jersey.

Data processors and the top brass share the telecommuting option at Beneficial.

BEST WESTERN HOTELS INTERNATIONAL, Arizona.

This is an interesting project where the home workers telecommute from their home in prison. About 10 women prisoners in the Arizona State Prison handle telephone reservations for the hotel chain. They are provided with computer terminals, telecom-munications hookups, extra phone lines, and complete training.

BLUE CROSS/BLUE SHIELD OF MARYLAND, Maryland.

This particular branch of Blue Cross/Blue Shield is still in the beginning stages of telecommuting. Only a handful of experienced employees are working as cottage keyers. They are part-time employees with part-time benefits.

BLUE CROSS/BLUE SHIELD OF THE NATIONAL CAPITOL AREA, Washington, DC.

This program was fashioned after the similar program at Blue Cross/Blue Shield of South Carolina's data entry program. Basically, cottage keyers key in data from insurance claims. The main difference is that here, all cottage keyers are former employees. Also, instead of keying onto tape, these workers key directly into the company's mainframe.

Each worker has a quota of at least 400 claims per day. IBM terminals with modems are leased to the home workers. Pays so much per claim on a biweekly basis.

BORG-WARNER CHEMICAL COMPANY, West Virginia.

Sales personnel are equipped with PCs at home which are hooked up to company's mainframe. Telecomunications capabilities include E-mail. Sales people can now do analysis and forecasting without going into the office.   Other professionals on staff are similarly equipped and can work at home as the need arises.

BRONNER MANUFACTURING AND TOOL COMPANY, New Jersey.

Work to take home is assigned only to regular in-house employees that wish to earn extra money at home. Work involves milling, turning, deburring, drilling, and lathe work. Pays piece rates.

BROWN WILLIAMSON TOBACCO COMPANY, Kentucky.

Systems programmers work on a contract basis and divide their time between home and office. Only programmers that were previously employed in-house are chosen.

CALIFORNIA STATE DEPARTMENT OF GENERAL SERVICES, California.

After two years of planning, The California State Telecommuting Project is finally underway. State workers from 14 different state agencies can volunteer to participate. Anyone who thinks his/her job can be done at home can volunteer. A minimum of 200 will participate with job titles ranging from clerk typists to managers. Locations have been scaled back to include the greater Los Angeles area, San Francisco, and (primarily) Sacramento.

Those chosen will be outfitted with PCs and ergonomically correct furniture. An electronic bulletin board will replace the "water cooler" as the center of internal communications. All workers are required to return to the office of origin at least once a week.

Jack Nilles, sometimes known as the "father of telecommuting" wrote the 150-page "Plan For Success" and has been selected to direct the project. David Fleming, who initiated the idea, hopes the experiment will serve as an example of successful telecommuting and thereby open up telecommuting opportunities elsewhere in government and private industry. To that end, many aspects will be monitored and evaluated to conclude how much fuel was saved, effects on traffic flow, possible effects on air quality, etc.

CHATAS GLASS COMPANY, New Jersey.

Glassblowing and grinding of laboratory glassware can be done as a secondary income opportunity by established employees. Only part-time work is allowed at home. Pick up and delivery of supplies and finished work is provided. This is handwork, so no machinery is needed. Pays piece rates.

CHILTON CREDIT REPORTING, Massachusetts.
In-house employees must be thoroughly experienced before moving work home. About 14 workers have taken advantage of the option. They proof computer sheets and analyze the "decisions" made by the computers. Pays piece rates equalling approximately the same as in-house workers doing similar work.

CITIBANK, New York.
Citibank offers telecommuting as an option to regular employees on an informal basis as the need arises. Employees most often work at home during temporarily disability or pregnancy.

COLORADO NATIONAL BANK, Colorado.
This major Colorado bank is currently conducting a pilot telecommuting program within the MIS department only. The purpose of the project is to determine whether telecommuting can help cut costs as it has in so many other organizations. The telecommuters write systems documentation four days a week. The PCs are provided by the workers. Colorado National expects to expand the program to perhaps two dozen telecommuters at the end of the pilot phase.

THE COMPUCARE COMPANY, Virginia.
Several high level employees have found working at home necessary for various personal reasons.

COMPUTERLAND, California.
Computerland is conducting a two-year telecommuting experiment for current company marketing personnel and their managers. All necessary equipment is provided.

CURTIS 1000, Connecticut.
Company offers home work arrangement as option to in-house employees with proven need. For example, one disabled worker does hand inserting and other mail processing work at home.

DATA GENERAL CORPORATION, Massachusetts.
Data General manufactures, designs, and sells business systems. One product is the "Comprehensive Electronic Office" system which includes E-mail, spreadsheet analysis and more. Working at home is an option to in-house employees on a departmental level. Those taking advantage of the option are most often programmers, engineers, and word processors involved in software development.

Employee's department is responsible for providing necessary equipment, generally a PC and modem which will be logged onto the company mainframe. This is usually older equipment that has already been costed out. "Working at home has proven to be a convenient and useful tool. The key benefits are convenience and being close to family."

DECORATED PRODUCTS COMPANY, Massachusetts.
About 8 employees here make extra money by taking extra work home. They inspect nameplates manufactured at the plant. They are required to pick up and deliver the work themselves. Pays piece rates.

DETROIT FREE PRESS, Michigan.
Reporters, columnists, and editors telecommute. PCs (IBM, AT&T #6300, or

Leading Edge) are supplied. Work is transmitted to mainframe via telecommunications network. Examples of telecommuters include one-person bureaus in Los Angeles and Toronto, and a columnist who lives 40 minutes away fom the office and has no reason to commute anyway for that type of work. Telecommuting was implemented as a company policy in 1984. Detroit Free Press also has several home-based freelance photographers who work on an assignment basis. Currently has about 20 home workers. All telecommuters are staff members and are paid the same salary and benefits they could receive if they were in-house. Freelancers are paid by the job.

DIGITAL EQUIPMENT CORPORATION, Massachusetts.

Digital, like Apple, has a very progressive attitude about its employees. Most of the technical workers have computers in their home offices and are allowed to work at home at their own discretion. Informally, the number of telecommuters (who work at home only part of the time) may run into the thousands.

EQUITABLE LIFE ASSURANCE, New Jersey.

Several programmers and managers are participating in a pilot telecommuting program. Work involves database development, technical support, troubleshooting, budgeting, project monitoring and progress reporting. All equipment is supplied. Home terminals are connected to the large mainframe IMS. There is also a $400 allowance for furniture. Employees are salaried with employee status intact. After final review of pilot, Equitable will decide whether to expand telecommuting option to other departments. So far, it is reported to be successful.

COMPANY PROFILE

Success is a word that is rapidly becoming synonymous with telecommuting pilot programs. Equitable Life Assurance is no exception.

Last year Equitable relocated some of its departments from corporate headquarters in midtown Manhattan to Secaucus, New Jersey. For most employees involved, this was merely a matter of traveling in a different direction; some even lived in New Jersey and it meant less traveling. But, for those who lived on Long Island, travel time would double and it was feared that that would be too much for some.

It was clear that something had to be done to avoid the costs of replacing valuable personnel. Telecommuting was offered to key people as an incentive to stay with Equitable. Six people, programmers, analysts, and one administrative assistant, were encouraged to stay home two or three days a week. They were each given all necessary equipment, a $400 furniture allowance, and retained their salary levels and employment status.

Telecommuting project coordinator, Jack Tyniec, credits Electronic Services Unlimited with providing the necessary training and guidance. ESU worked closely with Equitable's legal department, personnel manager, and prospective telecommuting managers to avoid problems in advance.

"We had no idea how many things could just creep out of the woodwork. ESU helped us spell out the issues and deal with them in advance — things like local zoning restrictions, labor laws, insurance liability both for company provided medical coverage and Workmen's Compensation, and even seemingly innocent wordings in our company personnel policy."

Words like"...work to be performed in company office...," found in standard employment contracts, may not have been intended to restrict working at home, but that is the legal effect, Tyniec points out. To rectify that situation, a supplementary contract was drawn up to specifically allow work at home.

The first formal review of the Equitable telecommuting program indicates that all is going well. The telecommuters love it, Tyniec says, and their managers are equally enthusiastic. "Not only have we kept good people, but productivity has increased as well. We've measured productivity in terms of quality, not quantity, from a managerial point of view. The managers are unanimously in favor of continuing the program. The consensus is that these people (telecommuters) were good anyway, but now they're even better."

It is expected that telecommuting will be formally integrated into Equitable's overall personnel policy. In the meantime, though, "It will spread now of its own accord," says Tyniec. "Our personnel manager gave a presentation to other company PMs at their urging. It seems that somebody has to slay the dragons first, but once that's been done and it's been clearly demonstrated that it works, others will follow. At least for corporations, someone has to champion the effort to get telecommuting started."

FEDERAL RESERVE BANK, Georgia.

Federal Reserve Bank offers a work-at-home option to its regular professional staff. First started as an experiment in the early 80's with more than 65 employees in the research department participating, working at home is now an option incorporated into departmental policy for anyone who performs tasks such as writing or editing either full-time or part-tme. Computers, when used, are usually PCs owned by the employees. "Reports of our home work program have been greatly exaggerated by the media. When they (employees) can work better at home, they do. It's a simple as that."

FIRST NATIONAL BANK OF CHICAGO, Illinois.

Company has a formal home work program intended especially for data processing and other non-technical personnel. Program guidelines are designed to insure success. "It basically uses a foundation of trust and it's up to the managers to make it work. There is support from top management in the company." There are no number goals or monitoring of employees. Working at home is considered a careeer option which managers can use as a possible solution to employees' problems as they arise. "We've had some good experiences. In the case of some clericals, there has been a 30% increase in productivity." Any necessary equipment is paid for by the business unit budget. This is a program for experienced current employees only.

FT. COLLINS, Colorado

Working at home is a city-wide option open to all city employees. If work can be done at home, it will be permitted. Several hundred city employees are currently working at home in Ft. Collins. Any necessary equipment, furniture, or supplies will be provided. Employees retain full status, pay and benefits.

GANNETT, Virginia.

Newspaper reporters and editors who are currently employed by Gannett can work at home with manager approval.

GE PLASTICS, West Virginia.

Although the bulk of GE Plastics 100 telecommuters are sales and sales support staff, anyone here may telecommute as long as there is manager approval. Most employees have their own computers at home, but the company will sometimes supply the necessary equipment for telecommuting.

GENERAL TELEPHONE, California.

GTE first experimented with telecommuting during the '84 Summer Olympics as part of a citywide call for people to reduce commuting as much as possible. The pilot program involved technical and programming personnel and systems analysts. All were provided with PCs, modems,
printers, and pagers and all were kept on straight salary. The experiment was considered a complete success and now GTE is broadening the scope of telecommuting across departmental lines. Planners of the program feel management skills should improve after telecommuting employees are trained in self-management skills and managers learn to gauge productivity rather than count heads. GTE is also participating in telecommuting as part of the Southern California Association of Governments' plan to reduce traffic congestion and pollution. "We think telecommuting over a period of time will have a substantial impact on traffic in Southern California. There is a lot of potential here."

HARRIS TRUST AND SAVINGS BANK, Illinois.

Harris Trust has an informal agreement that allows certain experienced employees to work at home on computer terminals to complete paperwork.

HARTFORD INSURANCE GROUP, Connecticut.

Data processors and programmer analysts. Hartford has conducted a telecommuting pilot project with guidelines developed by a special committee. Employees, all volunteers, were required to have a good performance record with the company, be highly productive, not be working on "sensitive projects", and have a manager's approval. Each worked four days a week at home and one day a week at the office. Hartford supplied computer equipment hooked up to the company's mainframe plus extra phone lines. Employee status and salary remained unchanged. Although some problems were reported, telecommuting was integrated into Hartford's overall personnel policy, mostly as a reward for highly
productive, experienced employees.

HEWLETT PACKARD LABORATORIES, California.

Working at home as an option is offered department-wide. Home workers are usually programmers, hardware and software engineers, applications engineers, research scientists, speech writers, and managers. Most work at home part of the time during the week; some do so in addition to in-house work. Equipment is provided as necessary. Individuals are responsible for their own phone bills, but can avoid toll charges by calling the company mainframe and requesting a callback - made at company expense.

HIGHLAND SUPPLY CORPORATION, Illinois.

Highland Supply is in the business of converting aluminum foil and films. Employees perform packaging tasks for extra income.

HOLT, RINEHART, & WINSTON, New York.

In-house copy editors and proofreaders can get permission to work at home if they have a need for any personal reason. Employees must have editor's approval.

HOMEQUITY, INC. Connecticut.

Telecommuters do programming, evaluating, systems analysis, and software development. Homequity is a leading relocation service company. Its primary business consists of finding new housing for transferred corporate employees. Phase One of the telecommuting pilot project lasted about four months and gave the comnpany a chance

A Closer Look: Fort Collins, CO

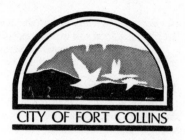

CITY OF FORT COLLINS

Ft. Collins, Colorado, a city of 85,000 located 60 miles north of Denver, is the first municipality to institute routine telecommuting.

The foundation for the project is a large electronic mail network set up by Peter Dallow, Information and Communications Systems Director. The system was originally designed as a good means of communications between city employees and city council members. Each user had to be supplied with a computer, of course, and once several hundred of them were linked together by the system, telecommuting was simply the next logical step.

Asked about surveys or other scientific bases for the project, Dallow shrugs off any such notion. "It was no big deal once the equipment was in place."

As a matter of fact, the program's policies and procedures are found on a one-page sheet outlining blanket acquisition procedures for necessary hardware and software. Any other issues that may arise will be handled on a case-by-case basis. Thus far, no problems have been reported.

"Normally, you don't tell an employee to be sure and take home some supplies—that would be called pilfering. But, now we encourage them to take home the whole office," says Dallow.

It would take a lot of software, disk drives and other equipment and supplies to equal the cost of building more office space. The personal computers had to be purchased regardless of where they would be used, and telecommuting has proven to be an excellent way to deal with Ft. Collins' office space crunch.

Several hundred city workers on many different levels are now participating in the project, which includes council members, accountants, data processors, rate analysts for the utility department and secretaries. Most work at home part of the time with a small percentage doing so full-time. Prime candidates for telecommuting, says Dallow, are top level professionals such as programmers and systems engineer. Just about everybody is eligible for part-time participation except the police and fire fighters.

Dallow cites benefits for both the workers and the city. For the workers, there is flexibility, job enrichment, a way to retain employee status during maternity leave, and new opportunities for Ft. Collins' handicapped citizens. For the city, there is increased productivity, a partial solution to the office space problem, lower costs, greater employee retention and the ability to attract employees in otherwise hard-to-fill jobs.

to evaluate cost savings and productivity. The initial findings were excellent and Phase Two, "continuation and expansion," is now in progress. Since most of the participants in Phase One were computer personnel, they were supplied with PCs and modems. "Telecommuting only makes sense because the future of this business is in computer."

HONEYWELL, INC., Minnesota.

Working at home is an informal option for Honeywell employees on a departmental level. One example of its use involves handicapped phone operators. The operators have dedicated phone lines in their homes which route long distance calls on weekend and nights. Calls are relayed from Honeywell employees on the road who don't have access to touch-tone phones. Home operators patch through the calls, using a network. Pays salary plus benefits.

THE H.W. WILSON COMPANY, New York.

Like Information Access Company (see below), this company is in the abstracting and indexing field. Although the number is smaller than its competitor, H.W. Wilson's indexers also work at home utilizing the company's electronic network and Federal Express.

IBM, New York.

Home work is a company option for IBM employees only. IBM has provided over 8,000 PCs for its employees to use at home, either part-time during regular business hours or after hours. Home work is allowed during regular hours on a project basis as a convenience to employees. Company recently participated in a formal two-year telecommuting experiment conducted by The Center for Futures Research at U.S.C.

INDUSTRIAL INDEMNITY INSURANCE, California.

Approximately 125 insurance auditors in the company have been outfitted with Visual Commuter Portable Computers, Hayes modems, HP printers, and Super Audit software at the expense of the company. The purpose was to reduce commuting time to and from the office and to increase overall productivity. Both goals have been achieved.

INFORMATION ACCESS COMPANY, California.

This company collects information from magazines and trade journals to maintain databases, including Magazine Index, Management Contents, and Trade and Industry Index; all of which are found in most libraries. At one time, Information Access had a fairly large home work operation with over 150 home-based indexers. Upon moving the operation to California, however, the home work program was scaled back severely. Now home-based indexers work only on weekly or monthly publications so deadlines can be met comfortably.

Workers come in once or twice a week to get supplies, materials, and any special instructions and to meet with their supervisor.

Company provides Apple PCs and special software. (Indexes are written on diskettes which are returned to the office.) Workers are full employees with benefits and promotional opportunities equal to those of their in-house counterparts. Home indexers are used because they are more productive and have fewer errors.

JET PROPULSION LABORATORY, California.

Telecommuting is an employee option to be used only for health reasons.

KEATING OF CHICAGO, INC., Illinois.
Keating is in the business of commercial kitchen equipment. Typing for its sales department is performed at home by employees who are either previous in-house employees or referrals.

LANIER BUSINESS PRODUCTS, INC, Georgia.
Lanier makes "Telestaf," a product used in telecommuting which was used in American Express' initial homebound training program. It includes features such as voice mail and is transcription-facilitated. Within Lanier, home work is allowed as a necessary option. Usually home workers are word processors and secretaries working at home part ot the time as the need arises.

LENCO ELECTRONIC, INC., 1Ilinois.
Lenco is an electronic manufacturing company. Experienced employees perform a small part of the job at home, connecting and soldering wires onto transformers.

ARTHUR D. LITTLE, INC., Massachusetts.
Telecommuting is an informal option offered to staff members. Most telecommuting is done by information systems consultants. Equipment is provided as necessary.

LOS ANGELES COUNTY, California.
In 1989, Los Angeles County joined a small, but growing, number of government entities who have decided to combat the problems associated with heavy work-related traffic with a telecommuting program. About 150 county employees started working at home as part of the initial pilot program. As many as 2,000 of the county's 17,000 employees could be telecommuting within the next 5 years. All departments have been instructed to identify and select potential telecommuters within their employee pools.

MARINE MIDLAND BANK, New York.
Regular employees of Marine Midland have the option of working at home as the need arises. The option is most often taken by professionals on staff in cases of temporary disability or pregnancy. The company is planning to develop more definitive guidelines for telecommuting in the future after current reorganization is completed.

MCDONALD DOUGLAS, California.
At one time (before company went through reorganization) there were 200 full-time telecommuters, plus another 2,000 employees that worked at home part of the time. These were mostly consultants, project managers, sales and marketing personnel, programmers, and engineers. Home work is not nearly so prevalent now, but it is still possible on an informal basis. Any experienced worker whose job can be done at home can require permission from the manager in charge of their department.

MELLON BANK, Pennsylvania.
Mellon Bank has made personal computers available to its programmers and other personnel for several years. Mostly the PCs are used at home for after-hours work, but some employees, programmers in particular, can work at home full-time on a project-by-project basis. Working at home is also used as a perk to boost the morale of management level employees.

METROPOLITAN LIFE INSURANCE COMPANY, New York.
Metropolitan has several handicapped computer programmers trained by Lift, Inc. (see listing). Agents are also home-based. Necessary equipment and phone lines are provided. All home workers are paid full benefits.

MONTGOMERY WARD & COMPANY. INC., Illinois.
Montgomery Ward uses home-based workers to handle mail opening and other jobs involved in the direct mail operation for insurance companies and other financial service clients. Only current employees or people referred by employees are considered. All are local residents.

MULTILINK INCORPORATED, Massachusetts.
MultiLink is in the telecomferencing business, so telecommuting comes naturally. About a dozen employees involved is setting up teleconferences do so from home.

NEW YORK LIFE INSURANCE COMPANY, New York.
About two dozen home workers are insurance claims processors and contract programmers. Equipment is provided as necessary. Employees retain in-house status and benefits.

NORTH CAROLINA NATIONAL BANK, North Carolina.
Telecommuting is being offered on a limited basis, along with other work options, as part of this company's personnel policy. The purpose of offering options is to answer some of the family issues raised in an employee survey. Currently, three women are taking advantage of the telecommuting option by dividing their work equally between home and office.

NORTHWESTERN BELL INFORMATION TECHNOLOGIES, Nebraska.
Northwestern Bell is involved in a two-year telecommuting experiment involving middle managers, marketing personnel, and data processing personnel. The guidelines for the program were developed by the Center for Futures Research at USC. After conclusion of the experiment, telecommuting will be evaluated and considered as a permanent overall company policy.

ORTHO PHARMACEUTICAL CORPORATION, New Jersey.
Although telecommuting started small here with just a handful of computer programmers and data processors, it is an option that is being offered to any employee who deems it appropriate. Supervisors have reported increased productivity, therefore many more employees will likely be working at home in the future with management's blessing.

PACIFIC BELL, California.
Engineers, marketing planners, project managers, forecasters, programmers, analysts, and some technicians and service reps work for Pacific Bell at home. Currently has over 200 telecommuters in both Northern California and Southern California. Though not all positions require computers, PCs are supplied as necessary. Pagers and extra phone lines are also provided as necessary.

PEAT, MARWICK, MITCHELL & COMPANY, New York.
Throughout its 100 offices nationwide, this major accounting firm has provided its field auditors with MacIntosh computers in order to increase productivity. The auditors

Linda Anapol, Director of Teleservices Applications for Pacific Bell, at work in her home office. (Photo curtesy of Pacific Bell.)

are now able to work for several days without actually returning to the office.

Like most major accounting firms, this one also has a "stable" of on-call accountants that handle assignments on a freelance basis during peak periods. These independent accountants are mostly former employees or are highly recommended by current employees.

J.C. PENNEY COMPANY, INC., New York.

Telemarketers take catalog orders in Milwaukee, Columbus, Sacramento, Richmond, Buffalo Grove (Illinois) and Atlanta, where the company catalog distribution centers are located. This program has increased from about 18 home workers in 1981 to 60 in 1987. The number rose again in 1988 to 206, making it one of the largest and technologically advanced telecommuting programs in the country. Computer terminals (hooked up to the company mainframe) are supplied, along with two phone lines - one for data and one for voice contact with the customer. Supervisors visit home workers to make sure the home work space is adequate. They expect a minimum of 35 square feet of work space that is isolated from family activities (noise).

Home workers are paid the same as in-house workers. In order to qualify to participate in the telecommuting program, a worker must have worked in a Penneys phone center for at least a year. The program is expected to grow even more, since it will save the company a lot of money by not having to build new facilities.

PRIME COMPUTER, INC., Massachusetts.

At any given time, about 100 of Prime's 12,000 employees are working at home on company provided computers. Most are in the customer service area, but others are in

Rick Higgins, Pacific Bell Marketing Manager

A Corporate Profile
Pacific Bell

Pacific Bell has a work-at-home program that, after only five months, was hailed as a complete success. While most telecommuting programs to date have been designed specifically for data processing personnel only, from the start Pac Bell wanted to prove that any job could be done at home. And, they have done just that.

75 employees went home in the program's first year, and 100 more are expected to make the move shortly. All are volunteers and no re-

strictions have been placed on job titles. The range of job classifications is broad—everything from marketing personnel to engineers.

Computers are used only by those who needed them before moving their work home. Second phone lines and pagers are the most often added equipment. The home workers are spread out geographically all over the state of California.

Being closer to clients was the first noticeable benefit. "This made us much more effective in servicing our clients," says Leslie Crawford, Marketing Manager for the Pacific Bell Telecommuting Department. "We soon realized how much 'windshield time' (time wasted behind the wheel commuting) was actually being spent on driving to the office first, then to the client."

The company was naturally pleased to improve service to clients, but there have been other benefits as well. For one thing, moving the work home has resulted in closing three offices with savings on space leases totaling $40,000 annually. There were no deliberate plans to close the first office; all the employees went home and there simply was no one left to mind the store. Two other offices then closed down and several more are expected to close soon.

But the biggest advantage to the program, according to Crawford, is flexibility for everyone concerned—for the company, for the employees, and for the clients. Increased flexibility has meant many jobs have been redefined with a new look at what they are, what they should accomplish, and how.

The program is working so well that Pac Bell's account executives have been looking at telecommuting as a possible solution to client's problems. Pointing to themselves as a prime example is often the best way to sell the idea. "To some, however, the very word 'telecommuting' sounds foreign. To them, we point out that their own salespeople have been doing it for years. Telecommuting is just a new word to describe it. When they realize that, it doesn't seem like such a weird idea after all."

This may all sound unrealistically positive, but when asked about disadvantages, Crawford said she couldn't think of any. "Maybe it's because everyone in the program volunteered," she said. "They knew their jobs, their managers knew them, and they knew from the advance planning what to expect. No one has voiced a problem and no one has left the program."

If there is a problem, she added, it would be not enough people. "More bodies in more homes around the state would be good for us," she laughs. "We are very, very pleased with the success of our telecommuting program and the enthusiasm with which it has been received. It has already been established that telecommuting works for data processing professionals. Now we have proved it is possible for all fields."

management and marketing. To take advantage of the telecommuting alternative, employees must first demonstrate the need.

PUBLIC SERVICE COMPANY OF NEW MEXICO, New Mexico .
Working at home is an option offered to permanent employees who need it. PCs are provided as necessary.

SOUTHERN CALIFORNIA ASSOCIATION OF GOVERNMENTS, California.
SCAG started its telecommuting program two years ago with 20 staff members, including accountants, legal staff members, planners and writers. The purpose of the program is to find a way to reduce work-related driving in Southern California by 12% by the year 2000. This project is one of several being conducted under the umbrella of the Central City Association. During the initial project, the home workers kept a log of transportation charges, telecommunications usage and utilities usage. Each was periodically interviewed to determine the best methods for expanding the program. Workers have their choice of part-time or full-time telecommuting. There is no change in salary, benefits, or employee status for anyone who chooses to work at home.

SOUTHERN NEW ENGLAND TELEPHONE, Connecticut.
Working at home is an option open to all Southern New England Telephone employees. If the option is needed for any reason, working at home will be okayed as long as the job can be done at home.

STATE OF SOUTH DAKOTA, South Dakota.
Working at home is facilitated on a statewide level by several electronic networks and PCs that are provided to all professional personnel in all state agencies. Working at home is considered informal, but is clearly acceptable; especially since it is donated time.

TRAVELER'S LIFE INSURANCE, Connecticut.
Resident claims operations adjusters are provided with briefcase computers so they don't have to return to the office from the field to finish work. Data processors are also provided with home terminals, E-Mail, formal training in telecommuting procedures, and a telecommuting handbook. Telecommuting is a formal program for established DP employees only.

UNION MUTUAL LIFE INSURANCE COMPANY, Maine.
Union Mutual's "Flex-Program" is an option offered to employees as needed. Examples of need include, but are not limited to, pregnancy or temporary disability. "Currently, the program is driven solely by managers/employees' interests. After expressing a desire to work at home, employees must demonstrate a legitimate need for an alternative work arrangement to their managers."

UNITED PRESS INTERNATIONAL, Washington, DC.
Most of UPI's news bureaus are small operations scattered around the country and abroad. It only makes sense to allow the news correspondents and sales reps to work from home if they choose. Since home-based correspondents and reps are regular salaried employees of UPI, normal hiring procedures and requirements apply.

UNITED SERVICES AUTOMOBILE ASSOCIATION, Texas.
Programmers for this insurance company are provided with PCs, both for after-hours work and also on a project-by-project basis.

Homeworker Profile
Carol D'Agostino

In 1976, Carol D'Agostino's life was on a downhill track as she joined the ranks of divorced mothers. Reentering the workforce can be tough, and for Carol—who is physically disabled—it was near impossible.

Taking in borders in her Long Island home provided some income, but it was a difficult way to make a living. "It was eroding my health even further. I needed something else, something better."

She heard about the External Education Program for the Homebound at Queensborough Community College and enrolled with the hope of upgrading her rusty office skills.

The college provided an Apple computer on loan and lessons were sent to Carol's home via telephone hookups to the classroom. Before long, she had the word processing skills necessary to enter an intern program requiring 90 hours of work for an employer. Her internship was with Electronic Services Unlimited, a New York based research and consulting firm that plans, advises, and implements telecommuting programs for major corporate clients. The internship later became a permanent, full-time job.

Carol receives work assignments electronically. She handles database management, miscellaneous word processing, mailings and research, and is responsible for production of the company newsletter, *Telecommuting Report*. "The work changes every day. In a small company you have to be able to do a lot of different things."

While Carol originally intended only to upgrade her skills to improve her job prospects, she is now continuing in computer education with a good shot at an AS degree.

"Thanks to the Homebound program, I have new skills and new confidence. I went from no opportunities to unlimited opportunities. I'll never be unemployed again!"

UNIVERSITY OF WISCONSIN HOSPITAL AND CLINIC, Wisconsin.

Medical transcribers handle physicians' notes for 50 clinics. To qualify for working at home, employees must first gain experience by spending six months in the office doing the same work that will be done at home. Work is to completed on 24 to 48 hour turnaround schedule; same as for in-house workers.

Dictaphones and word processors are provided. Home workers are regular employees with salaries and benefits identical to that of in-house workers. Performance is measured by characters typed (home workers are found to be 40-50% more productive than in-house workers). Home workers are represented by Local 2412 of the Wisconsin State Employees' Union. "There is an interest here in expanding the program. We can add one home worker for every one-and-a-half in-house workers."

US WEST, Colorado.

Nearly 500 engineers, writers, computer programmers, and their supervisors work at home. Telecommuting has become a fully-accepted way of working at US West because it has proven to be very economical for the company. Equipment is supplied as necessary. Home workers are represented on the project planning team by The Communications Workers of America. Employee status remains unchanged.

WENDY'S INTERNATIONAL, INC., Ohio.

A couple dozen employees in a wide variety of administrative positions work at home as needed. Wendy's has supported telecommuting for a number of years and now provides laptop and portable computers to those who need them at home.

WEYERHAUSER COMPANY, Washington.

Marketing personnel can work out of their homes full-time. In-house employees in Washington have the option to work at home part-time on an informal basis. The option is usually used on a project-by-project basis. Weyerhauser has a very flexible time policy in general. The work-at-home option is most common among systems developers, technical professionals and sales personnel in the Research & Development and Data Processing departments.

HOME BUSINESS OPPORTUNITIES

BUSINESS OWNERSHIP:
THE FINAL STEP TO INDEPENDENCE

It wasn't long ago that starting a new business was beyond the reach of many. Starting a business from scratch required a large investment, usually over $100,000 for a storefront operation. Keeping the business going with the high overhead took a great deal of time and effort. For those of us interested in adding more freedom and flexibility to our lives, business ownership was a fate worse than a job.

Times change. There are now a growing number of ways to go into business without the heavy burdens of the past. You can start a business at home without the huge investment and with much of the risk removed. By buying into a proven business system, you can take advantage of the knowledge and experience of a successful business. For as little as a few hundred dollars, you can have independence and security — an unbeatable combination.

This section is not about starting a business on your own. Instead, it contains over 150 opportunities to buy into a proven business system. Some are franchises, some are not. All offer some level of training and support and all give you a better chance of success than going it alone.

A franchise is a successful business formula that essentially sells a clone of itself to a franchisee for a license fee, and then collects royalties on the revenues. Franchising is a preferred way for a business to expand its operations. The franchisee gets a business plan, financial planning and marketing strategies, a trademark, advertising help, training and ongoing technical and business support. The franchisee has the satisfaction of running his or her own business, but still has the security and support of being associated with a large organization. There is a price to be paid for the security–in the form of royalties and also in being obligated to do things according to the company's policies and guidelines.

For those with more independent leanings, there are many stand-alone business systems that offer a basic package similar to a franchise, but without the ongoing obligations. You can buy a turnkey system that provides you with everything you need to get started - from a business plan to paper clips. But an independent turnkey business system is generally less expensive that a franchise because they don't offer ongoing support, use of the company name, or national advertising. And, while franchises often grant territorial exclusivity, independent business opportunities generally offer no such protection against local competition. But - in addition to lower upfront costs - they don't charge ongoing royalties or advertising fees. Some independent business systems do offer ongoing support or consultation services for a set period of time, usually a year, so there is plenty of time to get valuable answers to questions about your new business.

Not all independent business systems are turnkey. You'll see, as you read through some of the listings, that there is a wide range of services offered. With many, you can decide for yourself how complete your package should be. You may want, for example, to obtain training at home through the use of video tapes if you can't afford to get away for a week to attend training classes at company headquarters. With many companies, you have that choice. Other options might include office equipment, a computer system and/or software, a start-up tool kit, advertising materials, or consulting services.

No matter which type of business opportunity you opt for, you are to be congratulated for having the courage to take the final step to independence. In addition to having more control over your life, business ownership is a great way to insure yourself of optimal income potential. For anyone who is serious about making money at home, the listings in this section offer the best chance for success.

AUTOMOTIVE

AMERICAN AUTO FINDERS, P.O. Box 2694, Colorado Springs, CO 80901. (800)395-FIND.
Franchise: No.
Description: A unique computer-based locating network that allows vehicles to be found quickly on a local and national level. Can be used for wholesale or retail buying.
Requirements: $12,000 for complete start-up package plus $200 annual licensing fee.
Provisions: The Autofinders system includes hardware (based on a 386 computer), software (the heart of the system), training, and printed office supplies. The training covers both computer set up and operation as well as marketing.
Profit Potential: Varies widely, but can go as high as $100,000 a year.
Comments: This business makes excellent use of computer networking for profit; however, experience in auto sales is necessary to understand the business and its potential.

CLOSEUP: AMERICAN AUTOFINDERS

Frequent buyers of cars such as rental car agencies or tax companies have alway used networking as a tool to get what they need. Now American Autofinders offers a unique computer-based locating network that allows vehicles to be found quickly on a local and national level.

"I was working on this idea myself last year when I came across American Autofinders by pure accident," says John Zambreski, a veteran data processing professional of Dallas, Texas. "It actually made me kind of mad at first, but then I realized to get the business off the ground myself would have taken at least three years and maybe as much as $100,000 to develop."

For $12,000 you can buy the complete Autofinders system of hardware (based on a 386 computer), software, training, and printed office supplies. The training covers both computer set up and operation as well as marketing.

The core of the system is the custom locating program with fully automated daily listing updates. With this program, vehicles can be located by many different characteristics and combinations throughout the country. Updated information is shared by everyone on the network each day by uploading and down-loading through the main computer data bank. Essentially what the customer is buying is access to the network and to the information that will give him a leg up on the competition. "The network is the heart of the concept," says Zambreski, "and its a good one."

AUTOMOTIVE REFERRAL SERVICES, Crozer Mills Enterprise Center, 600 Upland Ave., Suite 101, Upland, PA 19015. (215)499-7484.
Franchise: No.
Description: Auto buying service. You act as an independent buying agent for your customer, saving them up to $2,000 and earning you a broker fee of between $250 and $300 per vehicle. The customer takes delivery of the vehicle at a dealership and gets a full warranty as usual.
Requirements: $695 total fee.

Provisions: Manual emphasizing low cost ways to acquire customers, how to establish working relationship with dealers, how to negotiate, getting paid, and adding potential profit centers.
Profit Potential: Four sales per week should amount to $1,000 profit.
Comments: Can be started part-time.

CAR CHECKERS OF AMERICA, 1031 Route 22W, Suite 302, Bridgewater, NJ 08807. (800)242-CHEX
Franchise: Yes.
Description: The only international on-site (mobile) vehicle inspection, appraisal, and diagnostic franchise. The service starts with a full structual analysis. The car's body and frame are examined for signs of damage or previous collisions, then the interior of the vehicle is checked to make sure all accessories are working properly and the odometer reading is verified. A test drive is performed. In all, 3,500 mechanical and electrical components of the automobile are analyzed. Upon completion of the inspection, a computerized report is immediately issued. Included is an appraisal of the vehicle's exact dollar value. Appraisals are based on the average wholesale and retail book values, the vehicle's mileage and condition. Antique and exotic appraisals are rated on a scale of one to six.
Requirements: Franchise fee of $17,500 plus additional start-up needs totaling $32,550 to $39,550. This includes a van lease deposit.
Provisions: Training in sales, management, and service production techniques. Computerized diagnostic equipment is mounted into your van. Help in securing accounts in your area is provided.
Profit Potential: The service, which takes less then an hour, costs the customer a flat fee of $75 to $100.
Comments: This company has sold 25 franchises and considering the popularity of the idea, growth is certain. When going to buy a used car, $75 is a small price to pay for avoiding a lemon.

THE CURTIS SYSTEM, Mountain Road, Box 250, Stowe, VT 05672 (800)334-3395.
Franchise: No.
Description: Auto detailing, which is the ultimate car cleaning and polishing service.
Requirements: Package costs $1,500 complete. No experience is necessary.
Provisions: Learn at home with an illustrated manual and 95 minute training video. Also included are tools, sales and business techniques, supplies, and ongoing support with a toll-free hotline and newsletter. In addition to learning how to detail cars, you will learn how to build and run a business, how to advertise, how to get and keep customers, and how to build repeat business. The sales promotion kit provides ads, brochures, etc.
Profit Potential: Some detailers report earning $100 to $200 per car and up for about 3 - 4 hours of work.
Comments: Gross sales from auto detailing is expected to reach $2.5 billion by 1995. This business can be run part-time while staying at your present job or you can run it as an absentee owner by hiring a crew to do the work for you.

EXPRESS WASH, INC., 908 Niagara Falls Blvd., N. Tonawanda, NY 14120-2060; (716)692-4681.
Franchise: No.
Description: Mobile car wash. With this system, it takes only 4 gallons of clean water and a few drops of soap concentrate to clean each vehicle. The system has been designed for use in high density parking facilities where hundreds of cars park every day such as

office buildings, industrial parks and shopping centers.
Provisions: Equipment plus complete instructional and marketing program. Manual inclludes a marketing plan, scheduling, sample presentation letters, business start-up information, pricing, professionnal cleaning methods (including shortcuts), employee hiring tips, promotional materials and other printed formms. Free telephone advice and consultation is always available.
Profit Potential: Prices range from $10 to $20 and it takes less then 20 minutes. Current Express Wash owners are earning an averrage of $30 to $40 per hour.

FITZGERALD'S, 2221 East Miner Ave., Stockton, CA 95205. (209)463-1483.
Franchise: No.
Description:Repair and recoloring of car interiors. The typical job takes less then an hour and the work is done on-site right out of the licensee's vehicle.
Requirements: From $500 to $5,000.
Provisions: All licensees receive all of the necessary equipment and chemicals. The $5,000 fee includes repair materials for car seats, automotive moldings and striping, a three-day training session, a manual, a bi-monthly newsletter and unlimited follow-up assistance.
Profit Potential: Not available.
Comments: Fitzgerald's has over 700 homebased licensees.

GEO SYSTEMS, P.O. Box 8163, Clearwater, FL 34618-8163; (800)237-0363.
Franchise: No.
Description: Professional auto detailing. Optional add-ons services include teflon protective coating, building and fleet power washing, steam cleaning, window tinting, alarm systems, and windshield repair.
Requirements: Several options are available starting with a "Level I" start-up package costing $1,595. Total cost for a top-of-the-line, self-contained van unit is $17,950 plus a van lease.
Provisions: The systems include training and all equipment, tools, and supplies necessary to go into business full-time. Training includes physical hands-on training at corporate headquarters, manuals, videos, newsletters, marketing seminars, and toll-free phone consultation. Training and support covers technical and product training, management training, marketing and sales training, and financial training.
Profit Potential: Working part time, detailing three cars per week, your yearly profit would be about $18,000. Working full-time, detailing three cars per day, your profit would be over $90,000 per year.
Comments: The potential looks real good for someone without experience and little start-up capital.

GLASS TECHNOLOGY, INC., 434 Turner Drive, Druango, CO 81301; (303)247-9374.
Franchise: No.
Description: Windshield repair.
Requirements: Total cost is $2,455.
Provisions: Glass Technology offers a complete windshield repair business including everything needed to get started: equipment, supplies, training, and ongoing support. Training covers not only the technical aspects of the business, but business management as well.
Profit Potential: Profit per repair is about $34 for 15 minutes of work. Performing nine repairs per day would yield $80,000 per year.

Comments: This can be a good business if you take advantage of the market by approaching insurance companies, fleet accounts, and car dealers. How to get these accounts is included in the training.

THE LUBE WAGON, 9430 Mission Blvd., Riverside CA 92509; (714)685-8570.
Franchise: No.
Description: Mobile lube service.
Requirements: Cost for exclusive rights to a city is $12,000; for a state $24,000. A Lube Wagon operator must build one of the company's patented trailers which takes about 100 hours and costs $2,000. The cost of the two-week training is $500.
Provisions: Names of suppliers are provided (company does not sell supplies.)
Profit Potential: The profit from one oil change is $19.50.

MOBILE AUTO SYSTEMS, 11883 Dublin Blvd., Suite A245, Dublin, CA 94568; (415)828-2131.
Franchise: Yes.
Description: Mobile Auto Systems sells on-site automotive engine tune-ups. Optional profit centers are minor engine repairs, regular fleet maintenance, and inspection services. The services are performed from a computerized diagnostic van and the business is run from an office (which can be in the home). Services are performed by appointment only.
Requirements: The initial investment is $5,000 and set-up costs run about $10,000 (including a deposit on the van). Royalty fees are $325 per month and advertising fees are $43 per month.
Provisions: The training program, which takes one week, combines classroom and hands-on training to cover both technical and business issues. Manuals are also provided along with advertising materials and marketing support. The marketing and advertising plan is the basis for most sales. Some referrals are provided by the company.
Profit Potential: No information is available.

OIL CAN VAN, INC., One Flagler Ave., Stuart, FL 34994, (800)545-9626.
Franchise: No.
Description: Mobil oil change service.
Requirements: $39,900 including van or $14,900 without.
Provisions: Turn-key package includes equipment, computer, custom designed software for tracking and billing, media kit, and two weeks of training at your home location.
Profit Potential: Based on the average service of ten vehicles per day, five days per week, and a per vehicle service cost of $21.95, the gross annual sales would be $57,070 with a profit of $30,570. After gaining experience and efficiency that profit can go up to $74,640.

PERSONALIZED AUTOART PRODUCTS, INC., 2046 W. Park Place, Suite D, Stone Mountain, GA 30087, (800)237-8510.
Franchise: No.
Description: Personalized license plate dealerships plus automobile-related novelty items such as a line of Route 66 sings, guide books and tee-shirts.
Requirements: $2,995 for dealership package start can gross $9,975 in business.
Provisions: Initial inventory package, equipment, supplies, and training video. Also provided are support services, toll-free consultation, national advertising to pre-sell the product and optional factory training.
Profit Potential: Information not available.

BUSINESS SERVICES

ADVANTAGE PAYROLL SERVICES, 800 Center St., Auburn, ME 04210; (207)783-2068.
Franchise: Yes.
Description: Complete payroll and payroll tax reporting services for small businesses.
Requirements: The franchise fee is $10,000 with no royalties. Another $5,000 will be needed for start-up expenses. Sales experience is also required.
Provisions: The franchise fee buys a territory with a minimum of 5,000 businesses plus software to connect with the company. Financing for half of the fee is available at 10% interest over four years.
Profit Potential: Not available.
Comments: The company has about two dozen franchisees.

AFTE BUSINESS ANALYST, 13831 Northwest Freeway, #335, Houston, TX 77040; (713)462-7855.
Franchise: Yes.
Description: Standardized bookkeeping and tax services to small businesses.
Requirements: The franchise fee is $4,000. You will also need $500 for initial supplies, $990 for the customized software package, and an IBM-compatable computer system. No experience is required. Royalties are 7% of gross receipts.
Provisions: Complete training is provided starting with two weeks of marketing at corporate headqquarters. There is financing available from the company.
Profit Potential: Not available.
Comments: This is a well established company offering an inexpensive way to get into a computer based business.

AIR BROOK LIMOUSINE, P.O. Box 123, Rochelle Park, NJ 07662; (201)843-6100.
Franchise: Yes.
Description: Limousine service to transport business owners and managers between office and airport.
Requirements: The franchise fee ranges from $7,500 to $12,500. A refundable deposit of $2,000 is required for start-up. Royalties range from 35% to 40%.
Provisions: The fee buys a 10-year franchise license and training. Financing is available from the company with no interest.
Profit Potential: Not available.
Comments: This company has been around since 1969 and has over 125 franchise operators.

ALPHA LASER CARTRIDGE, INC., P.O. Box 1178, Ormond Beach, FL 32175; (800)627-ALPHA.
Franchise: No.
Description: Basic service is laser cartridge recharging. Optional services include repair, cleaning, and maintenance of laser printers and copiers.
Requirements: The basic cost of becoming a "trainee" is $2,295.
Provisions: The fee covers two days of one-on-one instruction at company headquarters in Florida including hotel accomodations, all tools and supplies necessary to start

recycling laser and copier cartridges, a business start-up seminar, a technical manual, and toll-free technical support. To help get you started, the company also provides training on how to acquire new accounts, a list of the most recent laser owners in your area, and samples of ads.
Profit Potential: Gross profit from recharging four cartridges per day amount to $1,000 per week.
Comments: Can be part-time.

ALU, INC., 17717 Vail St., #524, Dallas, TX 75252; (800)752-7370.
Franchise: No.
Description: Laser recharging service.
Requirements: The cost of repair class is $1,295 and includes enough inventory and equipment to perform 60 recharges. There are no ongoing royyyalties, however, there is a $1 per cartridge royalty only for accounts that ALU acquires for you.
Provisions: In addition to technical training, ALU offers a marketing program and addresses of laser printer and copier owners in your zip code areas (free), and co-op advertising. Training is conducted for two days in Dallas and hotel accomodations are included. A training manual and ongoing consulting service are also provided.
Profit Potential: For no more than 15 minutes of work, your profit will be about $32.
Comments: ALU claims to have a unique process that sets them apart from the numerous other recharging systems. Their cartridges print at least 25% longer than a new one because they put in more toner than the original manufacturer.

AM MARKETING, 694 Center St., Chicopee, MA 01013; (413)733-7659.
Franchise: No.
Description: Full color printing of photo business cards as well as brochures, sell sheets, and related materials.
Requirements: $325.
Provisions: The fee includes a distributors training manual, a full color catalog, 300 samples, order forms, flyers and other promotional material, and toll-free on-going support. The initial fee will be refunded after your orders total $10,000 gross.
Profit Potential: Up to $1,000 per week.

AMERICAN ADVERTISING DISTRIBUTORS, INC., 234 South Extension, P.O. Box AAD16964, Mesa, AZ 85211; (602)964-9393.
Franchise: Yes.
Description: Cooperative direct mail advertising for small businesses.
Requirements: The franchise fee ranges from $23,500 to $41,500 depending on the territory. An additional investment of $10,000 will be needed for start-up costs. The company prefers someone with sales or marketing experience, but it is not absolutely necessary.
Provisions: The fee covers four weeks of training, ongoing support, regional meetings, start-up materials (letters, business cards, etc.) and ad tracking services.
Profit Potential: Not available.
Comments: Although this company has been around since 1979 and has over 110 franchisees, the investment is very high and there is no financing available. This is an industry with big profit potential, but there are cheaper ways to get into it.

AMERICAN BUSINESS ASSOCIATES, 475 Park Ave. S., 16th Floor, New York, NY 10016; (212)689-2834.
Franchise: Yes.

Description: A formalized networking organization intended to generate sales leads and marketing information for business owners.
Requirements: The franchise fee is $25,000. You'll also need about $10,000 for home office equipment and start-up costs. Royalties are 10% of gross receipts and the advertising fee is 2%.
Provisions: The fee buys two weeks of training - one at company headquarters and one in the field, business forms, a newsletter, and ongoing support.
Profit Potential: With a good territory, you should be able to gross over $100,000 by your second year with less than 25% expenses. No-interest financing is available with $10,000 down.
Comments: This is a great franchise opportunity, particularly for women.

BASCO, 9351 De Soto Ave., Chattsworth, CA 91311-4948; (818)718-1506.
Franchise: No.
Description: Business advertising specialties based on the BASCO imprinting machine.
Requirements: $1,000 if machine is included; $50 minimum order if not.
Provisions: The BASCO pad printing machine, training manuals for learning how to use the machine and sell the products, and on-going consultation.
Profit Potential: Up to $75 per hour.

BINEX-AUTOMATED BUSINESS SYSTEMS, INC., 4441 Auburn Blvd., Suite E, Sacramento, CA 95841; (916)483-8080.
Franchise: Yes.
Description: Financial management consulting, including a broad range of computerized services (financial statements, payroll, taxes, accounting, accounts receivable) for small businesses.
Requirements: The ability to use computers and some knowledge of business managmement is required. Although this is technically a franchise, there is no franchise fee, only a license renewal fee of $1,000 per year after five years. Start-up costs are around $8,500.
Provisions: The start-up costs include the license fee for the first five years, training, advertising and promotion, software and software training.
Profit Potential: Not available.

BLUEJAY SYSTEMS, 41 Driscoll St., Peabody, MA 01960; (508)531-5256.
Franchise: No.
Description: Professional billing service that provides small businesses with invoice preparation and receivables management.
Requirements: $289 complete.
Provisions: Included are software, detailed marketing plans, various forms, and ongoing support.
Profit Potential: $1100-$2000 per month working part-time only 8 hours per week; $5,000 full time. The typical account is worth $100 per month which makes average income range from $25 to $65 per hour.
Comments: This is a very good buy for anyone starting out in this business.

COMPREHENSIVE BUSINESS SERVICES, 1925 Palomar Oaks Way, Suite 105, Carlsbad, CA 92008; (619)431-2150.
Franchise: Yes.
Description: Comprehensive provides monthly accounting, bookkeeping, business

206 The Work-at-Home Sourcebook

consultation, and tax services to business owners.

Requirements: The franchise fee is $17,500. Start-up costs will require $10,000, office equipment will be about $12,000, and working capital of at least $5,000 will also be needed. Royalties for the first year are 4% of gross paid monthly and the advertising fee is 1% of gross. To be considered, you need a four-year degree in accounting or its equivalent in experience, good credit, and a net worth of $100,000.

Provisions: Franchisees receive two weeks of training at coorporate headquarters, a variety of continuing training programs, software, field support, and a professional direct mail program designed to provide you with prospects and appointments from the first week you are in business.

Profit Potential:

Comments: This is a well-established company that started in 1965.

GENERAL BUSINESS SERVICES, 20271 Goldenrod Lane, Germantown, MD 20874; (301)428-1040.

Franchise: Yes.

Description: Full service financial planning (including tax planning) and financial management for small businesses.

Requirements: The franchise fee is $15,000 or $25,000 and start-up costs are about $5,000. Royalties are 7%.

Provisions: The investment covers manuals, ongoing support, field-support training, and initial inventory.

Profit Potential: Not available.

Comments: This is one of the oldest franchises around. It was started in 1962 and now has over 500 franchise operators.

E.K. WILLIAMS & CO., 8774 Yates Dr., Suite 210, Westminster, CO 80030; (303)427-4989.

Franchise: Yes.

Description: Information and management consulting services for small business. The company is also a software services company and is one of the largest publisher of business recordkeeping systems in the world.

Provisions: Once in business, franchisees attend mandatory training courses at least once a year.

Profit Potential: Not available.

Comments: This company has been in business since 1935 and was named the number one business service franchise by Entrepreneur Magazine in 1990.

ENERGY AUTOMATION SYSTEMS, INC., 114 Canfield, Bldg. A-8, Hendersonville, TN 37075; (615)822-7250.

Franchise: No.

Description: Dealers sell energy automations systems to businesses. Customers receive a detailed energy survey and comprehensive analysis of electrical usage, a set of recommendations to reduce the electrical bill, a projection and a guarantee of savings, and a return on investment higher then 50% a year. Products include occupancy sensors, fluorescent light controllers, transient surge protectors, etc. The company produces the actual report for you and local contractors of your choice perform installations.

Requirements: An entry level dealership costs $12,500. There are no ongoing fees. You can attend a free, one day orientation in Nashville with no obligation.

Provisions: Complete training.

Profit Potential: The average gross profit for each sale is between $15,000 and $20,000.

FIESTA CARTOON MAPS, P.O. Box 3137, Tempe, AZ 85281; (800)541-4963.
Franchise: No.
Description: Dealers sell cartoon maps of area, usually as a fund raising project for local organizations.
Requirements: One time licensing fee of $9,495 includes enough territory to accomodate three separate maps.
Provisions: The fee covers hotel and round trip airfare to Phoenix for three days of training, operations manual, sales manual, 100 maps for samples, invoices, business cards, reference letters, in-house production, ongoing support, and promotional materials.
Profit Potential: Net profit for the first should be close to $70,000.
Comments: This can be run part-time or as an absentee ownership. Part of the training course is devoted to hiring, training, and managing sales teams.

GREETINGS, P.O. Box 25623, Lexington, KY 40524; (606)272-5624.
Franchise: Yes.
Description: Advertising business utilizing hot air balloons.
Requirements: The franchise fee is $15,000. In addition to the franchise fee, you will need approximately $11,950 for supplies, equipment, working capital, etc. All franchisees are required to attend training in Lexington at their own expense. There is a 5% royalty based on gross sales.
Provisions: The fee covers training, operating system, promotional programs, a recordkeeping system, customer references, and ongoing support.

HEALTHTEK, INC., 95 White Bridge Road, Suite 303, Nashville, TN 37205; (615)352-4200.
Franchise: No.
Description: Operators screen for factors the American Heart Association has recognized as being modifiable in the control of heart disease. The equipment used is completley portable and individual screenings can be performed in about 20 minutes. The data obtained from the screenings, in conjunction with a lifestyle profile, are used to generate a printed risk assessment. The goal is to help corporate clients solve health care cost problems by providing effective employee wellness assessments and wellness programs.
Requirements: Costs start at $12,000.
Provisions: Turn-key system
Profit Potential: Providing assessments for 120 people would take a staff of two, one week to complete and could potentailly generate a gross income of about $3,750 to $6,570, based on 20 minutes per person.

IMPACT, 205-8475 Ontario St., Vancouver, B.C. Canada V5X 3E8; (604)324-6600.
Franchise: No.
Description: Impact's basic service is an advertising display called Tel-Ad. It is a case that holds as many as 100 professionsl advertising photos. The photos are identified with stick-on numbers that coincide with a push button pad located in the counter top for direct access to the advertiser's business premises. The heart of the display is a programmable logic board that is capable of storing up to 100 numbers in its memory. Once a patron has selected a service to contact, they would simply pick up the handset and press the number of the advertiser shown on the photo. The Tel-Ad displays are placed by independent business operators wherever tourists traffic such as hotel lobbies.
Requirements: The purchase price is $5,000.

Provisions: The price covers the price of a complete display plus supplies and four manuals. The manuals include installation instructions, business start-up procedures, complete instructions on how to work with hotels, signs, contracts, ads, phone scripts, and everything needed to make this a viable business.
Profit Potential: One system should generate from $20,000 to $45,000 a year.
Comments: Impact has more than 75 operators.

INFORM BUSINESS, INC., 233 East 86th St., Suite 21B, New York, NY 10028; (212)831-7337.
Franchise: Yes.
Description: Business forms and printing. Franchisees are connected electronically to Inform's main office and works closely with headquarters.
Provisions: Fee includes training, ongoing support services, and an industry and marketing manual. Also provided are a computer with modem along with Inform software to hook up with headquarters.
Profit Potential: Not available, however, this is a huge industry that is growing at 11% annually.

INKY DEW, 405 West Washington St., Suite 22, San Diego, CA 92103; (619)266-8872.
Franchise: No.
Description: Service that re-inks fabric computer ribbons.
Requirements: The initial license package costs $1,500. There are no royalties.
Provisions: Fee covers a turn-key system with equipment and supplies and 24 hour help line.
Profit Potential: About $23.40 per hour.

LASERFAX, INC., 2020 124th N.E., Suite C-207, Bellevue, WA 98005; (206)883-9398.
Franchise: No.
Description: Laser cartridge recycling.
Provisions: Two days of training in office set-up, marketing, remanufacturing toner cartridges for laser printers, and servicing of laser printers.
Profit Potential: Not available.
Comments: This company was started in 1987 in the president's garage, but now is housed in a 2,000 square foot warehouse and office. That is some indication of how this industry is growing.

LASER PRODUCT CONSULTANTS, 1075 Bellevue Way N.E., Suite 501, Bellevue, WA 98004; (800)878-7008.
Franchise: No.
Description: Laser cartridge recharging.
Requirements: Prices start at $495 and go up to $5,995.
Provisions: All packages include home study training materials and supplies. All training packages have a marketing and advertising package, which includes sample advertisements and flyers as well as proven marketing strategies. Technical training includes correct gapping methods, drum care and lubrication, cleaning and inspection, proper toner refilling and sealing procedures, worn parts replacement, troubleshooting, and cartridge testing.
Profit Potential: Not available.
Comments: This company has over 800 dealers in the U.S., Canada, Europe, Asia,

Africa, Australia, Central America, and the Middle East. Their training program appeared in a book entitled "100 Best Spare Time Businesses in America" published by John Wiley & Sons.

LASERCHARGE, 1113 Metric Blvd., Austin, TX 78758; (800)999-8134.
Franchise: No.
Description: Laser Cartridge recharging.
Requirements: Total investment for renewable 10-year license, training, and supplies is $4,900. Optional third day repair and maintenance class is another $2,000.
Provisions: Fee includes enough supplies to generate up to $3,500 in revenue, all necessary tools and equipment, two days training class covering marketing and all other business topics, hotel and air fare to Austin for training, ongoing toll-free support, and a newsletter.
Profit Potential: Not available.

LCR TECHNOLOGIES, INC., P.O. Box 871237, Dallas, TX 75287-1237; (214)418-6658.
Franchise: No.
Description: Toner remanufacturing and repair/service maintenance business for laser printers and PC copiers. The company offers a variety of different programs, from home study instruction manuals and videos to comprehensive onsite training.
Requirements: A complete turn-key system costs $4,900. The cost for the home training program is $1,695; with technical training is $3,390. Add $1,400 for a laser printer.
Provisions: See above.
Profit Potential: About $60 per hour.
Comments: Can be run part-time.

MONEY MAILER, 15472 Chemical Lane, Huntington Beach, CA 96249; (714)898-9111.
Franchise: Yes.
Description: Cooperative direct mail advertising for small businesses.
Requirements: The franchise fee is $17,000 and up depending on the territory. You will need another $10,000 for living and operating expenses plus the cost of a Macintosh computer and customized software. Royalties are 10%.
Provisions: The investment buys training and start-up materials (first mailing is free). Money Mailer helps find outside financing.
Profit Potential: Not available.

NAMECO SYSTEMS, INC., 7 Strathmore Rd., Natick, MA 01760; (508)655-0510.
Franchise: Yes.
Description: Target advertising for local small businesses through the sale of exclusive space on plastic phonebook covers called Tel-A-Covers.
Requirements: The franchise fee is $28,500 and other start-up costs are around $5,000.
Provisions: The fee includes a defined geographic area of rated households with effective buying income of $10,000 or more, four days of classroom training, two weeks of field training, ongoing telephone support, and a weekly newsletter.
Profit Potential: Not available.
Comments: Namco started with this simple idea back in 1953 and has around 45 franchisees.

O2 EMERGENCY MEDICAL CARE SERVICE, 5829 W. Maple Rd., Suite 123, West Bloomfield, MI 48322; (800)777-4535.
Franchise: Yes.
Description: In this business you would provide an emergency first aid program (including emergency oxygen unit, first aid kit and first aid training) to businesses.
Requirements: The franchise fee is $12,500 and the estimated total investment is around $50,000. The royalty fee is based on oxygen units only and it is $5.75 per unit. There is also a 3% advertising fee.
Provisions: The investment covers initial training program expenses, three operations manuals, initial inventory, office equipment and supplies, insurance, an exclusive territory, and toll-free support. The extensive training covers all aspects of business including sales, marketing, office set-up, and business record keeping. A field representative will be assigned to you and will periodically visit your location to help provide any information you require.
Profit Potential: Not available.

THE OFFICE ANSWER, 8445 Keystone Crossing, Suite 165, Indianapolis, IN 46240; (800)678-2336.
Franchise: Yes.
Description: Telephone answering service. During the franchise operator's day, incoming calls are answered with the appropriate company's name and chosen greeting. The message taker sees the vital statistics of the company of a computer display monitor. They can then speak intelligently as company representatives and take accurate messages. Callers may never realize they've reached an answering service.
Requirements: Licience fee with training costs $8,500. The answering system which includes a computer, telephone answering electronics, and work station is leased at a cost of $225 a month.
Provisions: The license fee covers telephone answering computer software with customer billing functions, on-the-job training programs and resource materials, business set-up guidance, operational and accounting systems, professionally prepared advertising material and marketing strategies, all necessary supplies, and ongoing support.
Profit Potential: Not available.

PDP, INC., 400 West Highway 24, Suite 201, Box 5289, Woodland Park, CO 80866; (719)687-6074.
Franchise: Yes.
Description: Business consulting service matching jobs to people and people to jobs using an array of software programs to aid in the analysis.
Requirements: The licensing fee is $14,900.
Provisions: The fee covers five days of formal training at corporate headquarters, a coordinator/technical manual, software user's guide, the software operating system, and ongoing support services.
Profit Potential: Not available.
Comments: PDP is a 13 year old company with 30 franchises as far-flung as Brazil.

PRICECHECK, 2970 Lakeshore Blvd. WWest, Suite 205, Toronto, Ontario, Canada, M8V 1J6; (416)255-9385.
Franchise: Yes.
Description: Hands-on marketing service for local businesses. Examples of the service include checking prices; gathering market information; distributing coupons, pamphlets,

products; making local advertising and promotional copy changes; in store merchandising; shelf-stock counts; arranging local ti-in promotions, etc. The head office does bookkeeping of interoffice payments and all billing and collecting work.

Requirements: The franchise fee is $12,900. About $1,500 working capital plus three months income will also be necessary.

Provisions: The fee covers four days of field training and other business start-up activity in your market, office equipment and furniture, operating manual, artwork for office forms, referrals from the head office, and ongoing support.

Profit Potential: Not available.

Comments: Opportunities exist throughout the U.S. and Canada. No experience is necessary.

PROFORMA, INC., 4705 Van Epps Rd., Cleveland, OH 44131; (216)741-0400.

Franchise: Yes.

Description: Sales of business products including forms, commercial printing, and computer and office supplies.

Requirements: The franchise fee is $39,500. You will need $5,000 for living expenses while you get started. The royalty is 8% and the advertising royalty is 1%. Marketing or executive management experience is required.

Provisions: The fee buys marketing systems, license agreement, ongoing support, trademarks, vendor relations, and lines of credit.

Profit Potential: Not available, but this is a huge industry.

Comments: This is a highly rated company with about 100 franchise operators.

PROVE, 4806 Shelly Drive, Wilmington, NC 28405; (919)392-2550.

Franchise: Yes.

Description: Mystery shopping service for merchants that want to know what level of salesmanship and/or customer service is being provided by employees.

Provisions: The fee covers the use of the company's trademark and logo, all forms to start operations, an initial supply of office materials and efficiency reports, 10 days of initial training followed by training updates at national conventions, optional group insurance, and ongoing support.

Profit Potential: Not available.

Comments: Prove began operating in 1977 and franchising in 1987.

RESEARCH MARKETING, 2561-C Nursery Road, Clearwater, FL 34624; (813)530-4330.

Franchise: No.

Description: Dealers sell a point-of-purchase communications device called the "Magic Message" as an interactive marketing tool. It is a device that can allow a department store display, for instance, and when the customer touches it as instructed, it will immediately begin talking, explaining the product or service.

Requirements: Minimum dealership costs $285.

Provisions: Sales tools including a domonstration case, printed materials such as brochures, and pre-recorded audio demonstration tapes.

Profit Potential: Not available.

SERVING BY IRVING, Woolworth Building, 233 Broadway, Suite 1036, New York, NY 10279; (212)233-3346.

Franchise: Yes.

Description: Serving by Irving is a franchised, nationwide network of process servers.

Law firms use Serving by Irving to serve the papers that notify people when they are required to appear in a court of law, or that a legal action has begun. The company has an extraordinary success rate of 98%.

Requirements: The franchise fee is $85,000. The company's tongue-in-cheek motto is "If they're alive, we'll serve them, if they're dead, we'll tell you where they're buried."

Provisions: This is a turn-key franchise. The fee covers a complete equipment package that includes a fax machine, personal computer, photocopier, typewriter, electronic beeper, paperwork and forms, bookkeeping supplies, and inventory supplies. All of the above will be installed for you and you will be trained how to use them. Your fee also includes an exclusive territory, an operations manual, a proven grand opening advertising program, continual promotion by the company, and training. Training is conducted in the classroom and in the field and covers managmement, administrative, and marketing techniques as well as successful investigative techniques and the rules and methods for proper and efficient service of process.

Profit Potential: Although a franchise by law cannot make income claims, this is clearly a sophisticated business with high income potential.

Comments: Company started in 1977.

SPECIALTY MERCHANDISE CORPORATION (SMC), 9401 Desoto Ave., Chatsworth, CA 91311-4991; (818)998-3300.
Franchise: No.
Description: Dealership of specialty merchandise.
Requirements: Minimum start-up package costs $24.95.
Provisions: Fee covers merchandise catalogs; a sub-wholesaling program with supplies, price lists, and instruction; instruction manuals for business procedures, and numerous types of marketing programs and techniques for succeeding in each; supplies including order forms, brochures and advertising circulars; and free business advisory service.
Profit Potential: Not available.

SUNSTATE LASER PRODUCTS, 8812 N.W. 76th St., Tamarac, FL 33321; (800)366-2512.
Franchise: No.
Description: Sunstate is a toner cartridge recycler on contract.
Requirements: The Basic program costs $3,995.
Provisions: The cost includes materials, supplies, equipment, and training. Training consists of two and a half days of intensive hands-on training on how to recharge toner cartridges plus two manuals covering both technical and marketing aspects of the business, and video tapes to be used with the technical manual. There are enough initial supplies to recharge 101 toner cartridges.
Profit Potential: Not available.
Comments: The company points out that this industry is expected to exceep $1 billion by 1993.

THE TAYLOR REVIEW, 4806 Shelly Dr., Wilmington, NC 28405; (919)392-2550.
Franchise: Yes.
Description: Pre-employment screening and credit check.
Requirements: The franchise fee is $7,500 and you will also need about $5,000 for training, promotional materials, and special forms. The company prefers someone with a background in human resources management, but it is not required. The royalty is 8%.

Provisions: The fee buys access to the company network, support, and use of logo and trademark.
Profit Potential: Not available.

TP BUSINESS SERVICES, P.O. Box 399, Sunny Lane, Beach Lake, PA 18405; (800)255-4583.
Franchise: No.
Description: A TP Business Service Center uses different computer programs to provide 25 different services such as voice mail and the "Arts, Entertainment, & Travelers Guide".
Requirements: The standard system costs $9,980.
Provisions: The cost covers a 386 computer with a telecommunications system, operational software, pre-recorded sales tapes and sales presentation kit, a manual of sales programs and procedures, and a manual of standard business operating procedures.
Profit Potential: Not available.
Comments: The idea is similar to CBC (see above).

TREASURE PAK, INC., 2228 28th St. North, St. Petersburg, FL 33713; (800)237-8896.
Franchise: No.
Description: Direct mail coupon business.
Requirements: A distributorship costs $19,600. (The company will waive the start-up cost provided that you have the necessary background.) **Provisions:** The fee covers training, sales materials, sales tools, production services, and ongoing support.
Profit Potential: One mailing a month should net $71,352 a year.

TRIMARK, INC., 184 Quigley Blvd., P.O. Box 10530, Wilmington, DE 19850-0530.
Franchise: Yes.
Description: Direct mail coupon advertising for the local small businesses.
Requirements: The franchise fee is $5,000 and up depending on the territory. Start-up costs are about $5,000. There are no royalties. Sales experience is preferred, but not required.
Provisions: The fee buys two weeks of training (one week at corporate headquarters and one week in the field), ongoing support, and the first six months of supplies (presentation packet, stationery, and contracts.)
Profit Potential: Not available.
Comments: TriMark, a company that has been in business since 1969, offers the best deal in the industry to potential franchisees.

VIDEO/AD, P.O. Box 111, Willows, CA 95988, (916)934-8827.
Franchise: NO.
Description: This is an advertising business that places ads inside rental video cassette cases.
Requirements: $769 for the basic system.
Provisions: The fee covers a turn-key system including business manuals, protected territory, presentation materials and samples, a discount printing source, forms and contracts, promotional materials, and continuing support.
Profit Potential: Video/Ad says that just three video stores can earn you over $7,200 per month.

HOME/COMMERCIAL IMPROVEMENTS AND MAINTENANCE

AMERIBRITE SYSTEMS, INC., 170-180 E. Hillsboro Blvd., Deerfield Beach, FL 33441; (305)481-2929.
Franchise: No
Description: Ceramic tile restoration that is better than new. With the Ameribrite system you can restore any age ceramic tile to its original color, brightness, and shine with sharp, clean, leakproof, and mildew resistant grout.
Requirements: The complete start-up package is $9,975.
Provisions: Fee covers tools, supplies, and training (five training videos with a manual. A TV commercial is also supplied.
Profit Potential: Material costs are only 10, so the profit from any given project is 90%.

BASEMENT DE-WATERING SYSTEMS, INC., 162 East Chestnut St., Canton, IL 61520; (800)331-2943.
Franchise: No
Requirements: $15,900 for the business system. An additional $2,000 will be needed for tools (some of which you may already have.)
Provisions: Fee covers enough baseboard material and epoxy to recoup the entire investment. You will allso receive an inventory of sales forms, business cards, presentation materials, advertising slicks, prepared radio commercials and television commercials. The three-day training workshop covers the proper method of installing the system through hands-on-training. Ongoing support is provided.
Profit Potential: Most dealers average from $15 to $22 per installed foot of baseboard. The company founders generated over $100,000 in their first year of business working from home.
Comments: The company has over 110 dealers in 35 states with a success rate of 86%.

BATH GENIE, 69 River St., Marlboro, MA 01752; (800)255-8827.
Franchise: Yes
Description: Porcelain resurfacing service.
Requirements: $24,500.
Provisions: Fee includes protected territory, $1,000 of initial advertising paid by the company, expense-paid training at company headquarters, all necessary porcelain resurfacing equipment, all advertising and marketing materials, office supplies, ongoing support, and enough resurfacing supplies to completely recoup your investment.
Profit Potential: Performing five jobs a week (10 hours time) you would earn $54,875 per year.

BLACK MAGIC, Box 250, Mountain Road, Stowe, VT 05672-0250; (800)334-3395.
Franchise: No
Description: The Black Magic commercial kitchen vent cleaning system is a specialized cleaning techniique that removes cooking grease from exhaust hoods, ducts, and fans. A self-contained pressure washer forms on a special cleaner, then blasts away stubborn grease.
Requirements: The system costs $7,480 plus $445 for the training seminar.
Provisions: This is a turn-key system.
Profit Potential: $65 per hour.
Comments: Can be run part time.

CARPET SCULPTURE GALLERY, 510A W. Central Ave., Brea, CA 92621; (800)348-6934.
Franchise: No.
Description: A unique art form in which the operator actually changes the shape and texture of carpets using special tools and dyes.
Requirements: One time fee of $9,900 covers all training and followup support. (Company will supply tools at their cost (approximately $3,000)
Provisions: During three days at the company's "Gallery," you will receive one-on-one training in every aspect of the business, from carving and bas-relief techniques to bidding a job through to acquiring materials and delivering in the finished product. The market package includes proven marketing and promotional materials, six months of back-up support, exclusive area rights, and a portfolio of sample carpets.
Profit Potential: This is clearly a product for the rich and profits are going to be high. One designer reported earnings of $2,250 for three days work.
Comments: The results of carpet sculpting are quite spectacular; send for information to see beautiful photos of examples. This can be run part-time, full-time, or as an add-on to an existing business such as interior design.

CEILTECH, 825 Gatepark Drive, #3, Daytona Beach, FL 32114; (800)662-9299.
Franchise: No
Description: Ceiling cleaning service.
Requirements: The system sells for $3,495 complete with leasing plans available.
Provisions: The system includes all necessary equipment, supplies, and accessories to generate over $4,000 in gross income. Also included are marketing materials and a training manual.
Profit Potential: You can net in excess of $150 per hour.

CLASSY MAIDS, P.O. Box 160879, Altamonte Springs, FL 32716-0879; (407)862-6868.
Franchise: Yes.
Description: Residential and commercial cleaning service, specializing in single family homes and offices.
Requirements: The franchise fee ranges from $5,900 to $9,500 depending on population of territory. Start-up costs run about $4,000. There is a 6% royalty.
Provisions: The fee buys training, ongoing assistance, and a starter kit of cleaning equipment and supplies. The company will finance half of the fee over four years.
Profit Potential: Not available.

COASTAL MAINTENANCE, INC., 139 Ledge St., Providence, RI 02904-1532. (800)753-3177.
Franchise: No
Description: Window cleaning service.
Requirements: Complete system is under $1,000.
Provisions: Turn-key system includes equipment, supplies, training, and resources. To appreciate the equipment and supplies, you really have to send for their borchure. The training includes a video on window washing techniques and manual that includes instructions on how to estimate jobs, how to acquire federal and state government contracts, how to promote your business with no money, 10 sure-fire ways to acquire accounts, how to make your own professional strength glass cleaner for pennies a gallon, sample contracts, and a lot more.
Profit Potential: $60 per hour and up.

Comments: There are some great stories that surface from time to time about enterprising individuals who started with nothing more than a squeegee and pail and went on to make piles of money. Best of all, the stories are all true. The owner of Coastal Maintenance grossed $250,000 last year. This company offers a way to get started in this highly underrated business opportunity in a very professional way for an unbeatable price.

COLOR/MATCH, 1872 Del Amo Blvd., #C, Torrance, CA 90501; (800)228-3240.
Franchise: No
Description: On-location carpet and upholstery dyeing.
Requirements: Training is at company headquarters in Los Angeles and is $300 for the first person for the first day; it is $250 a day thereafter.
Provisions: The company offers marketing assistance and technical training.
Profit Potential: Not available.

COVERALL NORTH AMERICA, INC., 3111 Camino Del Rio North, Suite 1200, San Diego, CA 92108; (800)537-3371.
Franchise: Yes
Description: Commercial cleaning service.
Requirements: Many of the company's basic franchise programs are unavailable, therefore you must buy a master franchise owner. The requirements are business an/or sales management experience, liquid assets of $100,000, reside in or be willing to move to an available metropolitan area of 750,000+ population.
Provisions: Complete business set-up including training, customers, equipment packages, and ongoing support.
Profit Potential: Not available.
Comments: Franchises are located throughout the U.S., Canada , and England.

DECORATING DEN, 4630 Montgomery Avenue, Bethesda, MD 20814; (301)652-6393.
Franchise: Yes
Description: Decorating Den is a shop-at-home decorating service. The franchisee goes by appointment to a customer's home in a "ColorVan" containing over 5,000 samples of fabrics, wall coverings, carpets, draperies, furniture, and accessories. There is no charge for the decorating service because the profit comes from the difference between the wholesale and retail prices on the products sold to the customer. There are over 1,100 franchises operating throughout the U.S., Canada, United Kingdom, Japan, Europe and Australia.
Requirements: The franchise fee is $6,900 for an Associate franchise or $18,900 for a Senior franchise.
Provisions: The franchise fee covers complete training which takes about six months, national advertising, promotional materials, business and record keeping systems, access to quality products at wholesale discounted prices, a selection of product samples, and all the necessary paperwork down to printed checks and business cards.
Profit Potential: Not available.

DELCO CLEANING SYSTEMS, 2513 Warfield St., Fort Worth, TX 76106; (800)433-2113.
Franchise: No
Description: Power wash system.
Requirements: Equipment, supplies, and training are all sold separately. Training

videos and manuals start at $100 and can go as high as $2,000 for "Mobile Power Wash School".
Provisions: See above.
Profit Potential: Not available.

FABRIZONE, 315 Bering Ave., Toronto, Ontario, Canada M8Z 3A5; (416)231-1155.
Franchise: Yes
Description: Drycleaning and purification process for carpets and upholstery, ceiling cleaning, and insurance damage restoration.
Requirements: Total investment requires $8,000. There is financing available from the company.
Provisions: Training and ongoing technical and promotional support.
Profit Potential: Not available.
Comments: Franchise opportunities exist in both the U.S. and Canada.

CLOSEUP: FLOOR COVERINGS INTERNATIONAL

When Mary Noble of Little Rock, Arkansas, went looking for a franchise opportunity last year, she had already been running her own part-time window covering business for more than four years. She was looking for a compatible product. "I wanted to increase my revenues without increasing my hours," she explains. "But I also needed to continue operating from my home office and stay flexible with scheduling."

Floor Coverings International not only allows franchisees to work part-time; it boasts that a majority of its franchisees are home-based operations. Mary paid $9,500, which went toward training, a down payment on a van (full of floor covering samples), and advertising materials.

Mary now spends four to five hours each day showing customers floor coverings and window blinds in their homes–by appointment only. The business doesn't require a computer, but Mary uses one for bookkeeping and to prepare marketing materials. Mary's husband Scott, a management consultant by day, helps out by doing the books at night. "I really feel satisfied working part-time," says Mary. "It allows me to do other things besides just working."

JANITIZE AMERICA, INC., 20300 Superior, Suite 190, Taylor, MI 48180; (800)456-9182.
Franchise: Yes
Description: Commercial cleaning service.
Requirements: The franchise fee is $8,500 and the initial start-up package (computer system, equipment, supplies, etc.) is another $4,000. You can lower that cost by using the company's computer service instead which reduces the cost by $2,500. Monthly royalties are 8% of gross sales and the advertising fee is %1 of gross.
Provisions: In addition to the provisions stated above, Janitize provides all business forms, a supply of uniforms, and ongoing support.
Profit Potential: Not available.

KOTT KOATINGS, 23281 Vista Grande Dr., Suite B, Laguna Hills, CA 92653; (714)770-5055.

Franchise: No
Description: Porcelain and fiberglass refinishing.
Provisions: A dealer package includes 5 days of training at company headquarters, a complete custom "factory on wheels" trailer unit with generator, a complete equipment package of all necessary tools and supplies, a protected territory, and manuals.
Profit Potential: Not available.

MAID BRIGADE, 850 Indian Trail, Lilburn, GA 30247; (404)564-2400.
Franchise: Yes
Description: Supervised team cleaning services for single family homes.
Requirements: The franchise fee is $16,900. Operating expenses will require an additional $15,000+. The royalty is 7% and the advertising royalty is 2%. A business background is perferred.
Provisions: The fee buys the right to use the name, a one-week training class, operations manual, and a start-up kit that includes janitorial supplies, printed materials, training videos, and marketing materials.
Profit Potential: Not available.

MAID EASY, 33 Pratt St.., Glastonbury, CT 06033; (800)395-MAID.
Franchise: Yes
Description: Residential maid service.
Requirements: Total investment is about $22,000.
Provisions: Fee includes an advertising program, sales training, operational manual, motivational training, employee training video and manuals, protected territory, and ongoing support. Equipment and supplies are purchased seperately.
Profit Potential: Not available.
Comments: Can be operated part-time, without any office employees. The company boasts of having a system that allows you to pay maids almost twice the going rate.

THE MAIDS INTERNATIONAL, 4820 Dodge St., Omaha, NE 68132; (402)558-8797.
Franchise: Yes.
Description: Completely computerized residential cleaning service.
Requirements: The franchise fee is $16,900. Another $25,000 will be needed for operating capital including leases for cars and computers, labor and advertising. The royalty ranges from 5% to 7% and the advertising royalty is 2%.
Provisions: The fee buys the use of the company name, the exclusive system, pretraining, corporate training, posttraining, and a complete equipment and advertising package. Financing is available only for expanding territories.
Profit Potential: Not available.

MCMAID, INC., 10 W. Kinzie, Chicago, IL 60610; (312)321-6250.
Franchise: Yes
Description: Residential cleaning service utilizing team cleaning methods.
Requirements: A business background is preferred. The franchise fee ranges from $15,000 to $30,000 based on numbers of households in the population. You will also need $22,400 for cleaning equipment, supplies, office space, insurance, office furniture, advertising, car leasing, and operational expenses. Royalties are 6% and advertising royalties are 2%.
Provisions: The fee includes the use of the name, two weeks of training, ongoing support, and supplies at cost. Financing is available with a $15,000 minimum down payment.

Profit Potential: Not available.
Comments: The costs for this particular maid service franchise are out of line and there are much better deals available.

MIRACLE METHOD, 3732 West Century Blvd., Suite 6, Inglewood, CA 90303; (213)671-4995.
Franchise: Yes
Description: Bathroom restoration.
Provisions: Start-up training takes two to three weeks of intense on-the-job work. Training covers the use of the Miracle Method bonding agent and all aspects of restoring tubs, tile, fiberglass, and cultured marble. The fee includes equipment and enough supplies to restore 20 tubs. Marketing assistance is also provided with company representatives actually accompanying you on sales calls to hotels, construction sites, and private homes.
Profit Potential: Not available.
Comments: Opportunities exist throughout the U.S., Europe, and Australia.

MOBILE SERVICES, INC., 5020 Ritter Road, Suite 201, Mechanicsburg, PA (800)444-CLEAN.
Franchise: No
Description: Mobile power wash and restoration.
Requirements: The economy starter unit system costs $6,995.
Provisions: The above package includes complete training in every aspect of the business, equipment, and supplies as well as ongoing support.
Profit Potential: Not available.

MOLLY MAID, INC., 3001 S. State St., #707, Ann Arbor, MI 48108; (313)996-1555.
Franchise: Yes.
Description: Regularly scheduled cleaning services.
Requirements: No experience is necessary, but a business background is considered a plus. The franchise fee is $16,900. You will need another $8,000 for working capital including leased cars, insurance, and bonding of the employees. The royalty decreases from 6% to 3% as sales increase. The advertising royalty is 2%.
Provisions: The fee buys exclusive rights to the territory, equipment and supplies, training, and start-up business documents.
Profit Potential: Not available, however, franchisees said that they were earning well into the six figures and grew so fast it was hard to keep the business at home.
Comments: This is the largest maid service franchise with over 400 operators. The compnay believes in projecting a quality image and it works.

NATIONAL INSTALLATION SYSTEMS, INC., 400 Hawthorne Ave., Athens, GA 30606; (404)548-6437.
Franchise: No
Description: Selling and installing window treatments.
Requirements: The entire cost of a distributorship is $1,995.
Provisions: In addition to a five-day training seminar, the fee inclues custom installation equipment, window covering samples, and advertising and management assistance.
Profit Potential: An average installer can easily do three or four installations a day and make at least $250 to $300 a day.

PRIME SHINE AMERICA, INC., 2525 Hospital Road, Saginaw, MI 48603; (800)456-8588.

Franchise: No
Description: Residential maid service.
Requirements: The complete start-up package costs $1,295.
Provisions: Included in the complete package are supplies and equipment for your first maid team, a maid training video, an operations manual, and two days of training at company headquarters. Any of the above may be purchased seperately.
Profit Potential: The company claims that following their procedures, you sould be able to gross over $80,000 a year within two years.

THE PROFESSIONALS, INC., Family Acres Estates, Rt 1 Box 2400, Ranger, GA 30734; (800)289-8642.
Franchise: No
Description: Residential maid service.
Requirements: Turn-key system costs $5,990.
Provisions: Package includes manual, master copies of 22 different forms needed for all aspects of the business, a market format package, two bookkeeping manuals with a "fill in the blanks" accounting system, desk organizer, five training videos, eight audio cassettes, and one full year of consultation and support.
Profit Potential: The company claims anyone following their system should be able to gross $250,000 annually by the end of the second year.
Comments: The company has an exceptional record. Of its 700+ operators, none have failed.

CLOSEUP: THE PROFESSIONALS

"You would think," says Joyce Pierson, of Montgomery, Alabama, "that running a maid service would be easy. It isn't. I seriously considered starting one myself, but I'm glad I didn't."

Instead Pierson bought an independent maid service system from The Professionals, Inc., just over a year ago. There are many franchised maid services in the $9.2 billion industry, but The Professionals offers a complete system with no royalty payments and no territorial restriction.

The professionnals system leaves nothing to chance. Included in the base fee ($5,990) are training manuals, master copies of every form needed to run an efficient maid service, a marketing format package, a customized accounting system, a desk organizer, five video and eight audio training cassettes, and one full year of consultation. Customized software and a computer system are separate options. The price is much lower than that of any franchised maid service.

The add-on business plans — an option unique to the industry — are particularly impressive. For $3,000, you can buy six more business plans designed to bring additional profits. Pierson is especially excited about the Post-Partum Services (for new mothers).

The Professionals maid service has 730 clients (operators). None have failed in the company's 13 year history. Only five have not grossed $80,000 in the first year and $250,000 in the second, according to the company. The average net profit is 41% of revenues.

"A tried and true business system is the only way to go," says Pierson, who is likely to gross $250,000 in her second business year. "It took me less than a month to start making money."

REPAIR-IT INDUSTRIES, INC., 440 West Hopocan, Barberton, OH 44203; (800)772-0155.
Franchise: No
Description: Repair and recoloring of vinyl, leather, windshield glass, fabric, velour, formica, and laminate.
Requirements: There are three plans. The first costs $100, the second costs $400, and the most expensive is $1,395.
Provisions: All plans have complete financing available. The most expensive plan inclues three days of factory training, a complete video training program, manual, and toll-free assistance.
Profit Potential: Not available.

SCREEN MACHINE, P.O. Box 1207, Sonoma, CA 95476; (707)996-5551.
Franchise: Yes
Description: A mobile service business specializing in the custom fabrication, replacement, and repair of window and door screens as well as other related services.
Requirements: The franchise fee is $13,500. An equipment and supplies package costs at least $11,350 and general business expenses are $5,500 minimum. The total initial investment ranges from $30,350 to $49,500.
Provisions: Your investment buys training in marketing strategies, advertising techniques, business management, basic accounting methods, operational procedures, and "hands-on" technical instruction on how to custom fabricate screens and perform screen repair and related work. Also provided are advertising materials, audio visual training, ongoing support, and all of the materials, supplies, and equipment necessary for the basic operation of the business. A custom built mobile workship with a generator and power miter-box saw are all part of the equipment package.
Profit Potential: Not available.

SERVICEMASTER, 2300 Warrenville Rd., Downers Grove, IL 60515; (708)964-1300.
Franchise: Yes
Description: Professional residential and commercial cleaning and lawn-care services with more than two million customers worldwide.
Requirements: The franchise fee ranges from $6,000 to $18,000 depending on the type of franchise. You will need up to $10,000 for training, equipment, and supplies. The royalty is 10% and the advertising is 1%.
Provisions: The fee buys one week of training at headquarters and ongoing support. Financing is offered to up to 65% of total investment.
Profit Potential: Not available.
Comments: This is a franchise that everyone knows. It has been around since 1947 and now has over 4,200 franchise operators!

SHADE SHOWER, INC., 7360 E. Acoma Drive, Suite 15, Scottsdale, AZ 85260; (602)443-0432.
Franchise: No
Description: Mobile windows and blinds washing service.
Requirements: $7,995.
Provisions: A custom built mobile wash wagon including a complete equipment package and operations manual.
Profit Potential: Up to $75 - $100 an hour.
Comments: Can be run part-time or full-time or as an absentee ownership.

SHINE A BLIND, 31201 Chicago Road South, Suite A303, Warren, MI 48093; (800)446-0411.
Franchise: No
Description: Ultrasonic window blind cleaning.
Requirements: The initial investment is between $14,000 and $55,000 (the latter includes a fully equipped truck mounted machine).
Provisions: The basic business start-up package includes marketing materials, business forms, a marketing guide, and supplies.
Profit Potential: One job is work about $325.
Comments: The initial investment can be financed through the company.

SPARKLE WASH, 26851 Richmond Rd., Cleveland, OH 44146; (800)321-0770.
Franchise: Yes
Description: Mobile power cleaning and restoration services for truck fleets, industrial plants and equipment, oil/gas production and storage facilities, railroad cars, commercial and industrial buildings, historic structures, statues, signs, roofs, residential and mobile homes, pools, and boats.
Requirements: Total basic entry cost is $13,120. Royalties are 5% of gross.
Provisions: The cost covers home office and field training with continuing support, protected territory, start-up business package and supplies, equipment, accessories, and spare parts.
Profit Potential: Not available.
Comments: This company has been in business since 1965 and now has over 180 franchisees. Excellent financing is available to help people get started without investing a fortune.

SPR INTERNATIONAL, INC., 3398 Sanford Dr., Marietta GA 30066.
Franchise: No
Description: Bathtub restoration.
Requirements: The complete start-up package costs $1,995.
Provisions: Provided are business supplies and printed materials, all equipment and supplies to perform the work, a proven marketing plan, and training.
Profit Potential: $150 an hour minimum.

STAINED GLASS OVERLAY, INC., 2392 Morse Ave., Irvine, CA 92714; (800)654-7666.
Franchise: Yes
Description: The Stained Glass Overlay business is a patented process used to manufacture solid, seamless, one-piece stained glass in any design or pattern. It turns everyday glass into designer glass.
Requirements: The minimum investment is about $50,000. The franchise fee is $34,000, the franchise package that provides training, support materials, a business start-up package, and show quality display materials is $8,000, and other materials cost an additional $3,000. Royalties run 5% of gross sales plus another 2% for the advertising fee.
Provisions: Training starts with 40 hours of classroom and hands-on instruction and includes manuals.
Profit Potential: Not available.
Comments: This franchise is available in the U.S., Australia, the United Kingdom, Israel, Japan, Norway, Thailand, and has locations in 13 other foreign countries.

ULTRASONIC BLIND CLEANING SYSTEMS, 4464 Industrial St., Simi Valley, CA 93063; (800)669-8227.
Franchise: No
Description: Mini-blind cleaning service.
Requirements: The total investment is under $20,000.
Provisions: All necessary equipment and a training video.
Profit Potential: About $100 an hour.

___

CLOSEUP: JANI-KING

There are more than 2,000 janitorial franchises available, but Jani - King is the world's largest. Jani-King franchisees manage light office-cleaning and janitorial services for commercial and industrial buildings on a long-term contract basis. Jani-King supplies the franchisee with training and equipment (as you would expect), but also offers to drum up contracts.

For $6,500, a franchisee receives training but no initial business contracts. A $9,500 fee buys $1,000 in monthly business.; $12,000 buys $2,000 worth; and $14,000 buys $3,000 worth of business contracts. Financing for all fees is available. However, the franchisee pays a commission to the franchisor for the first year of the contract.

Josie Wheeler, of Dallas, Texas, has been running her franchise, Wheeler Services Group, for nearly two years now. During the day she is an accountant, but at night she is a part-time business operator. Wheeler hopes to build it into a full-time business eventually. However, she has some advice about accepting the Janii-King contract deals. "It took me about six months to figure out that letting the company get my accounts for me was costing more than I wanted to give up. On a $2,000 contract, for instance, I'd have to pay $400 a month for a year to pay off the commission."

Josie went back to Jani-King for sales training. "The training was great," she says. "Now I enjoy going out and getting my own accounts. It'll take me longer to build the business, but I still prefer keeping the commissions for myself."

___

UNICLEAN SYSTEMS, INC., 642 West 29th St., North Vancouver, British Columbia, Canada V7N 2K2; (604)986-4750.
Franchise: Yes
Description: Commercial cleaning service.
Requirements: The franchise fee is $19,500. Royalties start at $50 per $10,000 gross revenue.
Provisions: The franchise package includes training, office materials, equipment and supplies, an initial customer base, and ongoing support.
Profit Potential: Not available.

THE UNWALLPAPER CO., P.O. Box 757, Silver Spring, MD 20901; (301)680-2512.
Franchise: No
Description: Design wallprinting with paint rather than wallpaper.
Provisions: Training and supplies.
Profit Potential: High net profit is $60,000 annually.

Could you manage a crew like this? Photo courtesy The Maids International.

URO-TILE, INC., 139 West Royal Palm Road, Boca Raton, FL 33432; (407)394-6701.
Franchise: Yes
Description: Uro-Tile is a patented system which enables on-site manufacturing of tile, stone, and wood. There are no limitations to the designs, colors, textures, or finishes that can be created with the system. It is an interior-exterior system that can be used on floors and walls or on the facings of home or roof-tops.
Requirements: A non-exclusive contractor's license costs $5,000; an exclusive 100,000 population area costs $20,000.
Provisions: Training and supplies.
Profit Potential: Not available.
Comments: There are currently over 20 franchisees in the U.S. and in foreign countries.

WASH AMERICA, 943 Taft Vineland Road, Orlando, FL 32824; (407)855-2215.
Franchise: No
Description: Mobile power wash and restoration.
Requirements: The mini start-up package costs $4,995.
Provisions: The package mentioned above includes the company's HydroJet unit; essential equipment, accesories, and chemical start-up package; training packaging including factory training and a manual; and an upgrade guarantee.
Profit Potential: Not available.

WINCO, 1414 W. Larson, Knoxville, IA 50138; (515)828-8836.
Franchise: No
Description: Residential and commercial window cleaning.
Requirements: The one-time fee is $3,900.
Provisions: The package includes three days of training in the buyer's area, an exclusive area, two business and operations manuals, and marketing assistance.
Profit Potential: Winco has shown profits over $100,000 per year.
Comments: This can be a part-time business.

COMPUTER RELATED

COMPU-FRESH, 2512 Caledonia Ave., North Vancouver, B.C., Canada V7G 1T9; (604)929-7187.

Franchise: Yes

Description: Business service that cleans the external surfaces of computer equipment and related accessories, like printers, plotters and computer furniture. The cleaning procedures protect equipment from static and the transmission of bacteria and viruses.

Requirements: Area distributorship costs $15,000 plus $2,000 training fee. There are no royalties, however, there is currently an annual registration fee of $4,000. Additional start-up costs average $2,000 minimum.

Provisions: Fee includes a total equipment package with two full field kits and enough cleaning fluids to last for the first year in business. Also included are an area business plan, a marketing plan, five days of classroom and field training in Vancouver, exclusive territory, initial set-up of business procedures, training manual, training video that demonstrates every marketing, operational and administrative step of the business. The annual registration fee covers the use of the company's trademarks, continuing field training and promotional assistance, emergency consultation, and updating seminars.

Profit Potential: Following the system, you should be able to net $17,000 working part-time, two days a week or over $65,000 working full-time.

Comments: This franchise is available in both Canada and the U.S.

COMPUTER BUSINESS SERVICES, CBC Plaza, Sheridan, IN 46069; (317)758-4415.

Franchise: No

Description: This is a turn-key system based on the company's own 286 computers. The package includes hardware, software, and training (with videos and manuals) for 18 different computer-based businesses. The businesses are computer telemarketing, bi-weekly mortgage escrow, property tax reduction, voice mail, voice message center, help alert, "how are you today?", latch key kid assist, personalized children's books, computer credit network, manufacture-sell/rent computers, small business video service, long distance discount, phone at your table, Santa call, community alert, computer appointment verifier, and the time-weather-lottery result telephone number.

Requirements: $9,678.

Provisions: See above.

Profit Potential: The company claims profits of $4,000 to $10,000 per month are common with their system.

Comments: There has been no evidence to support income claims and this looks like a glorified attempt to sell overpriced computer systems.

COMPUTER RESEARCH, INC., 4504 Twin Oaks Drive, Suite 103-B, Pensacola, FL 32506.

Franchise:

Description: Document preparation service. Operators learn to prepare, using a computer, documents such as bankruptcy, articles of incorporation, personal will, premarital agreements, power of attorney, living trust, partnership agreement, and legal seperation. Typically, clients for these services are soliciated through advertising in local newspapers, on TV, and other media.

Requirements: The cost is $495. There are no continuing fees.

Provisions: For the initial fee you will receive a business start-up and marketing manual, an initial supply of legal supplies, seven document-producing computer programs, and two business computer programs. You also have the option of paying an additional $1,500 and getting an IBM compatible computer with a 20MB hard drive. Telephone support is available as long as you need it.

Profit Potential: The company claims that with minimal advertising, you can expect to generate at least $100,000 per year.

Comments: There is a growing interest in this type of business, and Computer Research offers an inexpensive way to enter the field. The profit potential is probably a little high, but there is definitely profit to be made. This can be a part-time business started with no experience.

CYGNUS SYSTEMS, INC., 1719 W. Zartman Rd., Kokomo, IN 46902; (317)453-7077.

Franchise: No

Description: Computer protrait system.

Requirements: $3,650 for the black/white video system and $24,410 for the color photography system complete with a 386 computer with digitizing hardware.

Provisions: See above.

Profit Potential: Not available.

PYRAVISION, 3810 Wilshire Blvd,. Suite 1216, Los Angeles, CA 90010; (800)244-0415.

Franchise: Yes

Description: Company offers four complete business systems: automated voice mail/messaging/paging service, 900 "pay-per-call" business, telephone answering service, and Pyravision's dealership.

Requirements: $15,000 to $20,000.

Provisions: Fee includes all necessary equipment and operational materials plus training. Training covers equipment, operations of the voice-mail system, marketing and advertising techniques, programming, and public relations service. Field support and cooperative advertising are also provided. Financing is available for entire fee.

Profit Potential: Not available.

REAL ESTATE AND FINANCIAL SERVICES

AMERICAN ACCENT HOMES, 300 North Cannon Blvd., P.O. Box 131, Kannapolis, NC 28082-0131.
Franchise: No.
Description: Sales of contemporary "kit" homes.
Requirements: Representative must have a company-approved model home erected within their sales area. A $4,000 nonn-refundable deposit, which applies fully toward the purchase of an approved models, is sufficient to secure a representative agreement. No real estate license is required.
Profit Potential: A representative earns 20% of the retail price on the sale of a kit; gross profits of $8 t0 $12 per sq. ft. are generally expected on completed homes; therefore gross profits of $16,000 to $20,000 can be realized on a 2,000 sq. ft. house.

AUDITEL MARKETING SYSTEMS, 12033 Gailcrest, St. Louis, MO 63131; (800)622-2940.
Franchise: No
Description: As a consultant, you would find where companies have been overcharged on their telephone and utility bills. You would then get refunds or credits for your clients and receive a percentage of the savings.
Requirements: The one-time affiliation fee is $9,900. There are no royalties or additional percentages paid to the company.
Provisions: The fee includes two days of training at company headquarters, four manuals, over 100 different forms to be used in your business, a copy of the monthly newsletter, and six months of unlimited training and consultation.
Profit Potential: The president of the company consistently netted over $100,000 a year working at this part-time.

CORRECT CREDIT COMPANY, 228 Highway 9, Howell, NJ 07731; (800)922-0508.
Franchise: Yes
Description: Credit creation, restoration, and referral service.
Requirements: The franchise fee is $20,000. Royalties start at $50 per credit repair contract and $25 per credit creation contract; the national advertising and promotion fund contribution is $350 per month.
Provisions: The fee includes an eight-week training program, exclusive territory, and ongoing support. The company advertises and generates high quality leads for the franchisees.
Profit Potential: Not available.

NATIONAL MORTGAGE PROCESSING CENTER, INC., 5530 Chattahoochee Industrial Park, Cumming, GA 30130; (404)889-7929.
Franchise: No
Description: Morgage loan broker.
Requirements: $1,995.
Provisions: The fee covers all training and support. Training includes a two-day seminar. After helping the applicant complete the forms, they are sent to headquarters and the company does the rest.

Profit Potential: Not available.
Comments: Can be run part-time.

NATIONAL TELE-CONSULTANTS, P.O. Box 4203, 39 S. Fullerton Ave., Montclair, NJ 07042; (201)783-6731.
Franchise: Yes
Description: As a "tele-consultant" for NTC, you will audit local telephone bills for overcharges on a no-risk contingency basis. The company says five out of ten local BellCo invoices are inaccurate. NTC franchisees use special tariff loopholes to return Bell refund checks to their clients on a 50/50 split basis. A secondary profit center comes from showing clients how to save up to 40% without changing carriers. By taking 15% of that in commission, residuals are paid to franchisees as long as the customer stays on the deeply discounted service. Target clients include small to medium size businesses that spend between $250 and $10,000 per month on long distance phone calls. There are more than 16 million such businesses in the U.S.
Requirements: The one-time fee is $6,500.
Provisions: The fee covers a complete training program and ongoing support. Everything you need to know about this business is covered in three days of intensive training. Unlimited consultation is available from headquarters throughout the franchise relationship.
Profit Potential: Not available.
Comments: This can be an absentee ownership.

RESIDENTIAL BUILDING INSPECTORS, 701 Fairway Drive, Clayton, NC 07520. (919)486-3429.
Franchise: Yes.
Description: Building inspection service.
Requirements: The franchise fee is $6,875 with start-up costs amounting to an additional $1,600 to $4,000. Royalties are 10% of gross monthly income.
Provisions: The fee covers marketing materials, camera-ready artwork for all kinds of ads, an operations and procedures manual, territorial protection, office supplies and forms, and ongoing support. The company provides a very comprehensive training program that includes a temporary certification process taking about six weeks to complete, on-site training in your area, and an inspection review process that results in final certification upon satisfactory completion.
Profit Potential: Performing only one inspection per week (2.5 hours of work) will result in $7,920 a year.
Comments: The company offers a great deal for anyone who doesn't have a lot of cash to get started. They will waive the franchise fee and instead charge a 20% royalty. All you have to come up with is the start-up capital.

U.S. MORTGAGE REDUCTION, 7272 E. Broadway Blvd., Suite 260, Tucson, AZ 85710. (800)456-8982.
Franchise: No
Description: Through a national network of sales agents, U.S. Mortgage Reduction offers its Equity Acceleration Program to homeowners. As an agent for the firm, you will be demonstrating to homeowners why paying for their home with a long term mortgage is a waste of many thousands of dollars in mortgage interest.
Requirements: $295.
Provisions: The fee covers a presentation binder/flip kit, training manual, computer software, brochures, contracts, cassette training tapes, and client presentation video.

Profit Potential: Not available.
Comments: There are also opportunities in regional management.

WES-STATE MORTGAGE, INC., 834 Pearl St., Eugene, OR 97401-2727; (503)485-4741.
Franchise: No
Description: Loan broker.
Requirements: $70.
Provisions: The program includes all documents, forms, step-by-step instructions, samples of brochures and advertising, source of lenders, and basically everything needed to run the business.
Profit Potential: Up to $100,000 a year.
Comments: Can be run part-time.

PERSONAL SERVICES

ACADEMIC GUIDANCE SERVICES, INC., 15000R Commerce Parkway, Mt. Laurel, NJ 08054; (609)727-1700.
Franchise: No
Description: Scholarship matching service. The company provides a computer-assisted financial aid finder program which matches students to financial aid sources, loans, scholarships, etc. Client students are sought out by mail marketing methods and you need never actually meet with them face to face.
Requirements: Total investment of $495.
Provisions: The investment covers home study training tapes, suggested ad copy, optional brochures and mailers, and access to names of students with address labels.
Profit Potential: Not available.
Comments: Can be run part-time or full-time with no personal selling involved.

ALBERT ANDREWS LTD., 111 Speen St., Suite 510, Framingham, MA 01701; (508)879-9510.
Franchise: Yes.
Description: Albert Andrews is in the business of custom menswear. From your home office you would prospect for clients, telephone, send information, and keep records. All measuring and fitting is done at your client's home or office using a special computerized fitting system. The computerized system allows the suit to be custom-made at company headquarters using corresponding computerized machinery. You act strictly as a person clothier offering service and convenience, not as a tailor.
Requirements: The start-up costs amount to about $34,550. There is an ongoing royalty of 10% of gross sales plus a 2% advertising fee. The minimum royalty is $400 per month.
Provisions: The initial investment covers a complete computer fitting system, training, manuals, office improvements, and working capital. Training includes self-study, classroom lessons, and actual field training. How to use the computer fitting system, proven marketing techniques for maximizing sales, customer service methods, hiring guidelines, and day-to-day support, professionally designed ad slicks and radio copy, advice on buying media, and follow-up customer service letters provided by headquarters.
Profit Potential: Actual numbers are not available, however this is a high-class business with very impressive materials.

BRIGHT BEGINNINGS, 18271 McDurmott West, Suite D, Irvine, CA 92714; (714)752-2772.
Franchise: Yes
Description: Neighborhood welcoming service. Franchisees visit new homeowners and tell them about products and services that are available in their new neighborhood. Local businesses pay fronchisees for advertising their products or services.
Requirements: The franchise fee is $11,000. You will also need a computer and laser printer. Royalties are 10% and advertising fees are 2%.
Provisions: The fee covers all the materials needed to start the business, as well as

marketing rights, software, ongoing support, an exclusive territory and five days of training.
Profit Potential: Not available.

CRADLE GRAM, P.O. Box 16-4135, Miami, FL 33116; (305)595-6050.
Franchise: No
Description: Personalized birth and baptismal announcements.
Requirements: One-time fee of $65.
Provisions: The fee covers the cost of a kit which includes everything from actual samples to a supply of four-color brochures. There is no inventory to be carried by you. You will be paid a 40% commission of gram sales up to $300 in one month and 50% on gram sales of $301 and up. Sales can be make in a variety of ways from in-home direct sales to fund raisering for organizations. The Cradle Gram marketing department is especially good at assisting with any type of in-store promotion campaign.
Profit Potential: Not available.

ENTREES ON TRAYS, INC., 3 Lombardy Terrace, Fort Worth, TX 76132; (817)735-8558.
Franchise: No
Description: A dinner delivery service. You would work with 20-50 local restaurants within a six mile radius, acting as a home delivery service, not a caterer. The business is run from home from 5:00 to 9:00 p.m.
Requirements: The one-time license agreement fee is $8,750.
Provisions: You will receive two days of training, working hands-on in Fort Worth. Also included with your fee is all equipment and materials necessary to initiate business (except radios negotiated on a local basis).
Profit Potential: See below.
Comments: This is a great business idea that has been perfected by this company. Entrees on Trays has delivered 100,000 dinners amounting to over $1 million annually in the Fort Worth metroplex while 11 out of 11 competing companies have gone out of business.

HOME CALL MOBILE VIDEO LIBRARIES, 8233-10 Gator Lane, West Palm Beach, FL 33411; (407)798-VANS.
Franchise: No
Description: The "Movie Man II" system utilizes your personal car which can be outfitted in approximately 10 minutes with a mobile video delivery system.
Requirements: The turn-key system costs $8,950.
Provisions: Licensees receive exclusive territory rights. The turn-key package includes 100 movies including the top 40, two VCRs, strobe light, musical chimes and lighted sign for top of the car, custom shelving, magnetic signs, catalog with movie titles, use of trademarks, and all start-up supplies. The advertising kit includes marketing flyers, Movie Man t-shirts, caps and business cards. Also included are membership kit and filing system with applications and necessary forms. Mapping, timing, and marketing strategies are all included with two days free training.
Profit Potential: Not available.

HOMEWATCH, 2865 South Colorado Blvd., Denver, CO 80222; (303)758-7290.
Franchise: Yes
Description: Full service housesitting by trained, bonded, and insured adults for people

who are away from home on business or vacation; companion sitting (nonmedical); and handyman services.

Requirements: The franchise fee is $6,000 and up depending on territory. Other start-up costs amount to about $10,000. Some managment background or previous business ownership is preferred.

Provisions: The fee buys a geographic area with a population of 200,000, four days of training including software training, logo, manual, and advertising materials. Financing is available, but only when buying multiple territories.

Profit Potential: Not available.

Comments: This is a good part-time business for retired or semi-retired people.

THE HOUSESITTERS, 530 Queen Street East, Toronto, Ontario M5A 1V2 Canada; (416)947-1295.

Franchise: Yes

Description: Services include live-in housesitting, periodic visit housesitting, and live-in family care. Ongoing service include dog walking, hourly family care, and residential cleaning.

Provisions: The franchise fee includes two weeks of training, customized computer software that not only handles all administrative tasks but runs a customized voice information system as well, the operations manual, and marketing support. The Housesitters head office prepares and mails announcements of your new operation to appropriate businesses while you are in training. The advance publicity usually generates enough sales leads to get you off to a running start.

Profit Potential: A population territory of 100,000 should yield a net profit of $29,200. Naturally, profits go up with the populations density.

MAIN EVENT LAWN SIGN, INC., 911 E. Brookwood Drive, Arlington Hgts., IL 60005; (708)677-7777.

Franchise: No.

Description: Special event signs are ordered to announce the many special occasions in a family's life throughout the year.

Requirements: The price of the basic business package is $2,295. Space requirements are about four feet by six feet against a wall to store the signs waiting to be rented.

Provisions: Included are 6 signs, 12 announcement inserts, two letter kits, an operations manual, camera ready advertising proofs, 20 store window posters, 5 store counter displays, and flyers.

Profit Potential: About $35 an hour.

MONEY FOR COLLEGE, 11846 Balboa Blvd., Granada Hills, CA 91344; (818)993-9031.

Franchise: No

Description: College financial planning service.

Requirements: $495.

Provisions: The fee includes a marketing and advertising manual, the business start-up manual, the manual for student aid counselors, and the names and addresses of students who are most likely to use the services.

Profit Potential: Not available.

PARAGRAVE, 1455 West Center, Orem, UT 84057-5104; (800)624-7415.

Franchise: No

Description: Ultra high-speed custom engraving to personalize valuables for decoration and anti-theft purposes.
Requirements: The complete "Parapak" system costs $2,399.
Provisions: The fee covers dealership privileges, an ongoing support program, all equipment necessary to perform the service, training videos, and illustrated manuals.
Profit Potential: Not available.

PET-TENDERS, P.O. Box 23622, San Diego, CA 92193; (619)283-3033.
Franchise: Yes
Description: Pet sitting service.
Requirements: The total investment is between $11,500 and $18,000. The royalty fee is 5% of gross sales per month and the advertising fee is 2%.
Provisions: The costs include the franchise fee for which you are given an exclusive territory, training, and a complete operation and training manual for your business. The training package includes up to five days of lectures, hands-on training, telephone techniques, voice training, and on-the-job training with a working pet-sitter.
Profit Potential: Not available.

R & J SERVICES, P.O. Box 1017, Murphy, NC 28906; (704)837-7432.
Franchise: No
Description: A neighborhood welcome service structured for smaller towns and communities.
Requirements: A complete business package costs $109.95.
Provisions: Included in the plan is a business manual that explains how to get started, how to find new residents, how to find good business prospects, a sample directory, printing templates for contracts and forms, an initial supply of personalized contracts and flyers, business cards, and sales tools.
Profit Potential: Not available.

SCM ENTERPRISE, W188 N11758 Maple Rd., Germantown, WI 53022 (800)755-0261.
Franchise: No
Description: Professional engraving system.
Requirements: Complete system is $1,995.
Provisions: The system includes all necessary equipment, training video, and toll-free technical support.
Profit Potential: Not available.

SITTERS UNLIMITED, 17941 Skypark Circle, Suite J, Irvine, CA 92714; (714)752-2366.
Franchise: Yes
Description: A coast to coast sitting service for children, the elderly, homes, and pets, on both a temporary and permanent basis. In addition to quality in-home care, traveling families can rely on hotel and convention care services.
Requirements: The franchise fee for an exclusive territory is $13,000.
Provisions: The fee includes five days of corporate training, ongoing training and support, and one month's free supply of required materials. Literature, business cards, and all required forms are designed for you. No purchasing of products except an answering machine and forms is necessary.
Profit Potential: Not available.

Comments: The company has been in business since 1979.

SPECIAL SELECTIONS, P.O. Box 3243, Boise, ID 83703; (208)343-3629.
Franchise: No
Description: Licensees offer personal and business gift shopping services to busy corporate executives, physicians, attorneys, professionals, and wealthy individuals and community leaders.
Requirements: The licensing fee is $495.
Provisions: The complete licensing package includes the right to use an internationally recognized trademark and a training manual. Instruction covers how to write a business plan, how to target and approach clients, a complete marketing plan, how to shop profitably without ever paying full retail, and how to price your services.
Profit Potential: You earn income two ways: first by charging an hourly fee, and second by obtaining commissions on the gifts you purchase. It is possible to earn thousands of dollars for a single situation.

TGIF PEOPLEWORKS, P.O. Box 828, Old Lyme, CT 06371; (203)434-1262.
Franchise: No
Description: Domestic and special help search-and -referral service for in-home help such as child care, elder care, and housekeeping.
Requirements: There is an initial cost of $350 to receive the complete and comprehensive Operations Manual which is used in your training. This manual includes camera-ready artwork for printing of materials to be used in the business. Set-up costs to get started should not exceed $800.
Provisions: You will be working as an independent business owner, but instead of paying royalties like a franchisee would, you will be paid a commission from the company.
Profit Potential: Not available.
Comments: This is a great business for women, especially those who are people-oriented.

PHOTO AND VIDEO

BIRD'S EYE VIEW PHOTOGRAPHY, INC., P.O. Box 394, Station A, Burlington, Ontario, Canada L7R 9Z9.
Franchise: No
Description: Aerial photography. The "Hi-shots" system consists of a thethered balloon which carries either a 35mm or Medium Format camera that can be rotated through 360 degrees. Both systems have a tilt feature which allows the camera to be adjusted vertically. A video picture is relayed to the operator on the ground. The monitor allows you to choose the perfect shot.
Requirements: The total investment is $22,900 for a 35mm system or $24,900 for the Medium Format system.
Provisions: The investment covers complete training and start-up assistance as well as all equipment.
Profit Potential: The photos sell for $250 and up and cost between $235 and $40 to produce. Each location takes only 20 minutes to photograph.
Comments: This can be a part-time, full-time, or absentee ownership business.

COLORFAST, 9522 Topanga Canyon Blvd,. Chatsworth, CA 91311; (818)407-1881.
Franchise: No
Description: Photographic business cards.
Requirements: A distributorship costs $200.
Provisions: The fee covers a home training video tape, advertising tools, and support.
Profit Potential: Not available.

IDENT-A-KID Services of America, Inc., 8430 Sixth Street, North, St. Petersburg, FL 33702; (813)577-4646.
Franchise: Yes
Description: Identification cards for children.
Requirements: Franchise Fee is $12,500
Provisions: Fee covers an exclusive territory, complete training, an IBM PC and custom designed software to produce the printed cards and forms, automatic identification camera, video presentation deck, laminator, marketing materials, and other supplies and equipment necessary to perform the service.
Profit Potential: Not available.

IMAGE MAKERS UNLIMITED, 1018 W. El Norte Parkway, Suite 200, Escondido, CA 92026.
Franchise: No
Description: Photographic business cards.
Requirements: $3,000.
Provisions: The fee includes six video training tapes, toll-free support, a professionally prepared sales presentation video tape that makes sales for you, and a complete set of all business forms needed to run this business.
Profit Potential: Not available.

PHOTO CARD SPECIALISTS, INC., 1726 Westgate Road, Eau Claire, WI 54703; (800)727-4488.
Franchise: No
Description: Photographic business cards and other high quality business products such as greeting cards, calendars, post cards, and video jackets.
Requirements: $150.
Provisions: The fee covers a sales kit and training manual. The kit includes a catalog, marketing information, order forms, and 100 sample formats.
Profit Potential: Not available.

UNIVERSAL ART, 1525 Hardeman Lane, N.E., Cleveland, TN 37311; (615)479-5481.
Franchise: Yes
Description: Photo processing and graphic communication specializing in photo protraits.
Requirements: The franchise fee is $9,000, photographic equipment is $6,000, and the company recommends you have access to around $10,000 to $12,000 in working capital. Some finanncing is available from the company.
Provisions: Comprehensive training and a guarantee of 2,000 to 3,000 customers per year.
Profit Potential: Not available.

VIDEO DATA SERVICES, 24 Grove St., Pittsford, NY 14534; (716)385-4773.
Franchise: Yes
Description: Videotaping service.
Requirements: $15,900 for a turn-key system.
Provisions: The price includes a complete equipment package based on the Amiga computer, training, marketing materials, and ongoing support.
Profit Potential: Over $100,000 annually.

VISUAL IMAGES, 300 Richfield St., Suite 201, Pittsburgh, PA 15234; (800)648-2105.
Franchise: No
Description: Marketing of full color, lithographed photo business cards.
Requirements: Total investment is $199.
Provisions: The initial investment includes samples of all products, templates, layout forms and other production materials, and toll-free support. You will also need a 35mm camera. The $199 is refunded with your 52nd order.
Profit Potential: Not available.

PUBLISHING

THE COUPON TABLOID, 4050 Calle Real #207, Santa Barbara, CA 93110; (800)888-8575.
Franchise: No
Description: The Coupon Tabloid is an advertising publication. All graphics are done through the company's production department.
Requirements: The one-time investment is $3,500.
Provisions: The fee covers an exclusive territory, one week of intensive training in your area, marketing materials, printed business supplies and other support materials, and ongoing support.
Profit Potential: Not available.

CREATE-A-BOOK, 310 SE Caroline St., Milton, FL 32570; (904)623-9833.
Franchise: No
Description: Personalized children's books.
Requirements: The cost of a dealership is $3,995 and the operator needs a computer. The annual software renewal fee of $200 is also required.
Provisions: The price includes the software, a training video that shows how to make the books and a list of available supplies, The company manufactures the books' pages and covers and then supplies the materials to the dealers. Also included in the price is a manual with instructions, tips, and camera ready ads.
Profit Potential: The books sell for about $12.95 and take about 15 minutes to put together. High-end earnings can be as much as $1,000 a day.
Comments: This 11-year old company has over 350 dealers in the U.S., 40 in Canada and three in Australia.

D & K ENTERPRISES, 2953 Ladybird Lane, Dallas, TX 75220; (214)353-9999.
Franchise: No
Description: Personalized children's books. With the D & K system, you can produce full color, hard cover, laser printed books in less than four minutes.
Requirements: The dealership fee is $2,495; other supplies bring that cost up to $2,990, and you will need a computer and laser printer.
Provisions: Included in the dealership package is the software to produce the books, a dealer manual with step-by-step instructions, a marketing manual and support, practice books, and location assistance with Sears concessions.
Profit Potential: A part-time dealer operating on week-ends only should profit over $10,000 a year.

FINDERBINDER and SOURCE BOOK DIRECTORIES, 4679 Vista St., San Diego, CA 92116; (619)284-1145.
Franchise: Yes
Description: Publishing of media directories for businesses in public relations, communications, advertising, consulting, or business management fields. This is designed as an add-on small business for consulting firms and community relations institutions.
Requirements: The franchise fee is only $1,000, but you will need at least $8,000 more for printing costs, supplies, and a research staff. You must have an established compatible business. Royalties run 5% to 15% (decreasing as sales increase).

Provisions: The fee buys a detailed operations manual, camera-ready art for advertising and promotion, software, and ongoing operational support.
Profit Potential: Not available.
Comments: Entepreneur Magazine declared this one of the best low-cost franchises several years in a row.

NETWORK PUBLICATIONS, INC., P.O. Box 100001, 2 Pamplin Dr., Lawrenceville, GA 30245; (404)962-7220.
Franchise: No
Description: Newtork Publications publishes "The Real Estate Books" which is the nation's largest full color real estate magazine network. Distributors act as "associate publishers" and handle the photography, set up distribution, and make contact with real estate brokers and builders who become advertising customers. The company provides the logo, graphic, and printing.
Requirements: The initial investment is about $15,000.
Provisions: Training starts at company headquarters and is followed by a field visit to your market.
Profit Potential: Not available.
Comments: This is a full-time business only.

PERSONAL INVESTING NEWS, 420 S. Orlando Ave., Winter Park, FL 32789; (407)629-9229.
Franchise: Yes.
Description: Personal Investing News offers territorial distributorships which operate as independently owned publications.
Provisions: The investment includes everything from advertising literature to hardware. Training starts at headquarters and continues with two weeks of onsite training in the local market. Distributors receive a complete support program that includes articles written by nationally recognized writers, a support staff capable in layout and artwork and a fully-equipped productions department. The support staff also includes legal and accounting assistance. Franchisees concentrate the majority of their efforts on earning advertising revenues.
Profit Potential: Not available.

PREMIER PERSONALIZED PUBLISHING, INC., 670 International Pkwy., #120, Richardson, TX 75081; (214)231-3598.
Franchise: No
Description: Personalized children's books (formerly known as About Me! Books).
Requirements: The initial licensing fee is $2,995 and is renewable each year for $195. Your initial inventory order should be about $525. You will also need an IBM compatable computer and printer.
Provisions: The start-up package will include complete training with a manual and video, software, and sample books.
Profit Potential: Not available.

REGAL PUBLISHING CORP., P.O. Box 5013, Cherry Hill, NJ 08034; (609)778-8900.
Franchise: No
Description: Distribution of the company's publication, Lottery Player's Magazine. Lottery sales totaled $18.8 billion in 1989. Lottery Player's Magazine is the consumer's window to the industry. The magazine acts as a clearinghouse of information for the

recreational gaming public. Independent dealers distribute the magazine to retail outlets and other distributors and wholesalers.

Requirements: A contract must be signed, there is no fee involved.

Provisions: Order forms, samples, and limited instructions.

Profit Potential: Commissions are paid on subscriptions sales equal to 60% of the base rate.

SMALL BUSINESS MEDIA NETWORK, 1858-C Independence Square, Dunwoody, GA 30338; (404)394-3268.

Franchise: Yes

Description: The Small Business Media Network, Inc., is the publisher of Small Business Digests. The purpose of the publication is to provide comprehensive and useful business information to small and medium-sized business owners helping them to make their businesses more profitable. A secondary goal is to provide an effective means of advertising for one business to reach another business. A franchisee's basic responsibility is to sell advertising space in his or her publication. The corporate office actually composes the editorial pages, prints and mails the publication to the local markets.

Requirements: The franchise fee is $23,500 for one publication. There are no royalties to pay.

Provisions: Included in the franchise fee is an exclusive territory, three days of classroom training, field training in your territory, an operations manual, initial supplies and sales support material, and ongoing support. Some advertising accounts are available from the national account program.

Profit Potential: Not available.

WEDDING INFORMATION NETWORK, 11128 John Galt Blvd., Suite 512, Omaha, NE 68137; (402)331-7755.

Franchise: Yes

Description: Publishing of "The Wedding Pages", a 250-page wedding planner, workbook, and local advertising directory offered free to newly engaged couples. Advertisers in "The Wedding Pages: are supplied with a market database compiled from reply cards that gives them a competitive edge in thie $33 billion industry.

Requirements: Experience is required in marketing, sales, media and advertising. The franchise fee ranges from $7,500 to $40,000 depending on the territory. Additional start-up costs range from $1,000 to $10,000 depending on the size of the territory. The royalty is 10%.

Provisions: The fee buys products and rights to be the local publisher of "The Wedding Pages".

Profit Potential: Not available.

TRAVEL

COMPUTERIZED TRAVEL NETWORK, INC., 4388 Civic Center Plaza, Ste. 200, Scottsdale, AZ 85251; (800)735-0541.
Franchise: No
Description: Travel Service.
Requirements: The fee for a turn-key system is $7,995. The monthly service fee is 3% of gross sales.
Provisions: Included in the fee are a computer, airline reservation software, nine days of in-depth training, stationery starter package, travel agency forms, manuals, agency books, and continuous support.
Profit Potential: Not available.
Comments: This is a unique travel service opportunity. The key is in the soiftware that makes it all possible.

CLOSEUP: COMPUTERIZED TRAVEL SERVICES NETWORK

Two years ago, Computerized Travel Services Network (CTSN), a 17 year old family business, became the first company to offer a home-based business opportunity in the travel industry. It is a classic example of a turnkey business system, one that provides you with everything you need to get started - from a computer to a business plan. Most franchises are turnkey businesses, but independent turnkey business systems are relatively new.

For $7,995, you can buy a business package including training, marketing, and IBM compatible computer (Packard Bell Force 4), software, and access to industry discounts through the company's licence. Buyers who already own a computer can subtract $1,000.

Since most travel bookings are sold over the phone, there's no real reason for a storefront, except to attract traffic. Using the CTSN software, a home-based operater can access all airlines, cruise lines, hotels, tour companies, and car-rental companies for reservations and send the ticket request and creditcard information to CTSN. CTSN prints out the tickets and sends them overnight to the customer. The independent business owner gets a 10 percent commission on all tickets booked.

"I get my commissions, and I'm very happy," says Dale Podkowa, of Chandler, Arizona, one of 110 operators on the CTSN system. Podkowa has attracted 50 clients in about six months and now makes about $300 a month. "The people at the company bend over backward to help me, making me feel like part of their family."

Podkowa works full-time for the local phone company, so Dale's Travel is a sideline business for now. He generates contacts through his job, and most of his customers come through referrals. But when he decides to take the business full-time, he will use CTSN's aggressive marketing system, which is designed to attract small-business customers who spend between $20,000 and $50,000 on travel a year.

HOTEL EXPRESS, INC., 3052 El Cajon Blvd., San Diego, CA 92104; (800)634-6526.
Franchise: No
Description: Distributors sell hotel discount memberships.
Requirements: $395 billed for ten months with no interest.
Provisions: Distributor discounts and ongoing toll-free support.
Profit Potential: Discount memberships sell for $49.95 and cost the distributor $4.95.
Comments: There are over 1,000 distributors in 9 different countries.

LEISURE GROUP, 58 River St., Milford, CT 06460; (800)999-1152.
Franchise: No
Description: Travel service.
Requirements: There is no investment or maintenance fee. Because Leisure Group members do not do domestic ticketing, costs are extremely low for both the company and the affiliates. The major requirement is a telephone to call suppliers, who all have toll-free numbers. Brochures and other reference data are provided free by the suppliers.
Provisions: The Leisure Group licenses its members to sell travel. Training is minimal. A manual is provided that tells members how to operate and newsletters are issued every two to three weeks that include numbers to call for brochures, new offerings, selling hints, etc. Optional training will cost $1,000.
Profit Potential: Each booking which takes about 1.5 hours should generate about $300 in commissions. The maximum you could earn in a year is $300,000.
Comments: The company has 158 members in 34 states and foreign countries.

TRAVEL PARTNERS, 6404 Nancy Ridge Dr., San Diego CA 92121-2248; (800)445-7333.
Franchise: No
Description: Travel service.
Provisions: The company provides training in sales and marketing, travel guides, training manuals, a travel video library, 24-hour travel information service, ticket delivery, camera-ready art package, and the 800 reservations number.
Profit Potential: Up to $100,000 per year.

TRAVEL SUCCESS MANAGEMENT, INC., 1810 Water Place, Suite 245, Atlanta, GA 30339; (404)955-7279.
Franchise: No
Description: Travel service.
Requirements: The total fee is $8,000.
Provisions: The fee provides for five days of intensive training, support, custom designed agency reporting and database software, and a travel agency internship in Atlanta.
Profit Potential: Not available.

MISCELLANEOUS

CAJUN COUNTRY CANDIES, 502 Evangeline Dr., Lafayette, LA 70501-5534; (318)232-1229.
Franchise: No
Description: Distribute homemade candy.
Requirements: Cost of total business package is $52.95. There is a 30 day unconditional refund privilege.
Provisions: You will receive a business operations manual with marketing instructions, drop ship directions (so you don't have to stock candy), a box of candy samples, 100 promotional advertising mailers, and sample ads.
Profit Potential: Your profit margin is 25%.
Comments: Personally I think 25% is too low for any mail order product to make you any money, but there have been reports of people who have made a go of this business.

FOLIAGE DESIGN SYSTEMS, 1553 S.E. Fort King Ave., Ocala, FL 32671; (904)629-7351.
Franchise: Yes
Description: Interior foliage design, sales, and or maintenance.
Requirements: The franchise fee depends on a market analysis performed by the company, but it ranges from $10,000 to $40,000 with additional costs amounting to about $5,000. The royalty is 4% of gross.
Provisions: Each franchise receives a protected territory, two weeks of training in Florida, operating manuals, operation systems, a computerized management information system to minimize adminstrative chores, leads from national advertising, and toll-free support. Plant materials can be obtained from over 200,000 sq. ft. of compnay owned greenhouses. Training covers tested and proven methods of record keeping, order writing, marketing, filing, collections, and accounting, as well as the care, design, and use of foliage in commercial and residential spaces.
Profit Potential: Not available.
Comments: This company has been in business since 1971 and has won numerous nationally recognized awards.

GLASS MECHANIX, INC., 10170 N.W. 47th St., Sunrise, FL 33351; (800)826-8523.
Franchise: No
Description: Windshield repair service.
Requirements: $1,298.
Provisions: The fee covers training, machines, and enough materials to repair 500 windshields.
Profit Potential: A windshield takes about 15 minutes to repair, and the average charge is $35. The cost is about 50 cents so it is possible to earn up to $300 a day in this business.
Comments: This company was started in a two-bedroom condominium in 1982. It now grosses over $500,000 a year.

GLAS-WELD SYSTEMS, INC., 20578 Empire Blvd,. Bend, OR 97701; (800)321-2597.

Franchise: No
Description: Glass repair service.
Requirements: $595.
Provisions: The investment includes equipment and enough materials to make 125 repairs and earn over $4,000 in revenue. A set of six training tapes are also included. Training topics include business start-up, generating sales, expansion, customer relations, advertising and promotion, and time management. Video training and field training are available options.
Profit Potential: Up to $75,000 a year.

NVS CORPORATION, 48 Springvale Ave., Lynn, MA 01904; (617)595-6224.
Franchise: No
Description: Windshield repair.
Requirements: The cost of a complete system is $1,999.
Provisions: The system includes equipment, enough materials to make 1,000 repairs, and detailed illustrated instructions.
Profit Potential: Up to $80,000 a year.

PARKER INTERIOR PLANTSCAPE, 1325 Terrill Rd., Scotch Plains, NJ 07076; (201)322-5552.
Franchise: No
Description: Your business would be delivering plants and jardeniers to offices and maintaining them as long as they're there. There is no inventory for you to keep.
Requirements: The complete cost of the training program, plus one year of advice and sales leads is $35,000.
Provisions: See above.
Profit Potential: Average profit is $2,000 per job.
Comments: This company has been in business for 45 years.

PHOTO ADVERTISING INDUSTRIES, INC., 262 S. Coconut Lane, Palm Island, Miami Beach, FL 33139; (305)673-3686.
Franchise: No
Description: Photo-keyring concessions and distribution.
Requirements: The complete start-up package is $1,800.
Provisions: The package includes equipment, one-on-one training, all necessary business forms, and ongoing support.
Profit Potential: Not available.

PROFUSIONS SYSTEMS, 2851 S. Parker Rd., Suite 650, Aurora, CO 80014; (303)337-1949.
Franchise: Yes
Description: Repair of vinyl, leather, naugahyde, and all types of plastics with perfect color matches. About 82% of the clientele served by the company are corporate accounts.
Requirements: The total investment is $20,500.
Provisions: The investment covers training, field supervision, initial equipment, and supplies. Training is held for two weeks in Denver and covers both technical and managment topics. After this initial training program, a company trainer will spend three days in your territory to help get your business started. Any client contracts from national advertising negotiated by the company are your without additional charge.
Profit Potential: Not available.

TALKING BALLOONS, Atlanta, GA; (800)328-2551.
Franchise: No
Description: A talking balloon has a 2 foot ribbon that is specially made like a record. The ribbon is pre-recorded with little grooves all the way down and when you attach it to anything that is thin or hollow like a balloon you can make it talk just by running your finger down it. It can be used for special occasions and sold through florists and balloon shops, or as an advertising specialty for any business.
Requirements: The starter package costs $346.
Provisions: The starter packasge includes enough talking balloons to gross you over $1,415. Training, particularly in marketing the product, is also included.
Profit Potential: Not available.

ULTRA BOND, 9249 Loquat Dr., Riverside, CA 92508; (800)347-2820.
Franchise: No
Description: Glass repair service.
Requirements: The combination repair kit costs $1,750. To buy exclusive rights to a protected territory, the initial total is $3,250 plus a $100 monthly supply order is required.
Provisions: Your investment covers all equipment and supplies, two days of training in California, a training viddeo, monthly newsletter, business start-up assistance, and ongoing support.
Profit Potential: Over $50 an hour.

UNITED BRONZE, INC., 181 Greenwood Ave., Rumford, RI 02916; (401)434-7312.
Franchise: No
Description: Bronzing service. Although bronzing is usually for baby shoes, it can be used for numerous other items that will become keepsakes.
Requirements: The "starter bronzing shop kit" costs $369.95.
Provisions: You will receive detailed instructions, marketing plans, and tested classified ads to run in your local newspaper.
Profit Potential: Not available.
Comments: The company claims to be able to show you how to receive at least five or six appointment cards from potential customers every day. It sounds good, if that's true.

LEARNING TO WORK AT HOME

Although there are plenty of opportunities listed in this book for people with limited skills, you have probably noticed many more that do require education or skills you don't possess. Of course, additional skills generally brings additional pay, so the incentive to learn new things is strong.

The same reasons you have for wanting to stay home to work probably affect your ability to leave home to go to classes. How do you attend classes 35 miles away after working all day? And even if you were able to find childcare during the day, can you also find it in the evening? For these reasons, home study courses have become more popular than ever before.

Home study involves enrolling in an educational institution that offers lessons specially prepared for self-directed study. The lessons are delivered, completed, and returned by mail one at a time. Each lesson is corrected, graded, and returned to the student by a qualified instructor who provides a personalized student-teacher relationship.

Generally, home study courses include only what you need to know and can be completed in much shorter time than traditional classroom instruction. With home study, you don't have to stick to somebody else's schedule. You don't have to give up your job, your time, leave home, or lose income. As in a home-based job, you work at your own pace with the school coming to you instead of you going to the school.

Listed in this section are dozens of home study schools. All of them are fully accreditied by the Naitonal Home Study Council. Although there are hundreds more such institutions, the ones presented here have been selected because they offer instruction that could help you take advantage of opportunities listed in this book.

ACCOUNTING

Citizens's High School, 5115 New Peachtree Road, Suite 300, Atlanta, GA 30341.

County Schools, Inc. 3787 Main St. Bridgeport, CT 06606.

Educational Institute of the American Hotel & Motel Assoc., Stephen S. Nisbet Bldg., 1407 So. Harrison Rd., East Lansing, MI 44826.

Hemphill Schools, 510 S. Alvarado St., Los Angeles, CA 90057-2998.

ICS Center for Degree Studies, Scranton, PA 18515.

North American Correspondence Shools, Scranton, PA 18515.

ADVERTISING

Columbia School of Broadcasting, 5858 Hollywood Blvd., 4th FLoor, PO Box 1970, Hollywood, CA 90028.

ICS Center for Degree Studies, Scranton, PA 18515.

ADVERTISING ART

Art Instruction Schools, 500 South Fourth St., Minneapolis, MN 55415.

ARTS, FINE AND COMMERCIAL

Art Instruction Schools, 500 South Fourth St., Minneapolis, MN 55415.

BOOKKEEPING

American School, 850 East 58th St., Chicago, IL 60637.

County Schools, Inc., 3787 Main St., Bridgeport, CT 06606.

Educational Institute of the American Hotel & Motel Assoc., P.O. Box 1240, East Lansing, MI 48826.

Hemphill Schools, 510 S. Alvarado St., Los Angeles, CA 90057-2998.

Home Study International, 12501 Old Columbia Pike, Silver Sprng, MD 20914.

McGraw-Hill Continuing Education Center, 4401 Connecticut Ave., N.W., Washington D.C. 20008.

North American Correspondence Schools, Scranton, PA 18515.

BUSINESS WRITING

American School, 850 East 58th St., Chicago, IL 60637.

The Hadley School for the Blind, 700 Elm St., Winnetka, IL 60093.

CARTOONING

Art Instruction Schools, 500 South Fourth St., Minneapolis, MN 55415.

CLERICAL

American School, 850 East 58th St., Chicago, IL 60637.

Citizen's High School, 5115 New Peachtree Rd., Ste. 300, Atlanta, GA 30341.

COMPUTER PROGRAMMING

Grantham College of Engineering, P.O. Box 5700, Slidell, LA 70469.

Heathkit/Zenith Educational Systems, Hilltop Road, St. Joseph, Michigan 49085.

Hemphill Schools, 510 S. Alvarado St., Los Angeles, CA 90057-2998.

ICS-International Correspondence Schools, Scranton, PA 18515.

ICS Center for Degree Studies, Scranton, PA 18515.

McGraw-Hill Continuing Education Center, 4401 Connecticut Ave., N.W., Washington, D.C. 20008.

NRI Schools, 4401 Connecticut AVe., N. W., Washington, D.C. 20008.

Peoples College of Independent Studies, 233 Academy Drive, Drawer 1768, Kisimmee, FL 32742.

COURT REPORTING

Stenotype Institute of Jacksonville, Inc., 500 9th Avenue North, P.O. Box 50009, Jacksonville Beach, FL 32250.

DATA PROCESSING

Heathkit/Zenith Educational Systems, Hilltop Road, St. Joseph, Michigan 49085.

DRAWING

Hemphill Schools, 510 S Alvarado St., Los Angeles, CA 90057-2998.

ICS-International Correspondence Schools, Scranton, PA 18515.

DRESSMAKING

Hemphill Schools, 510 S. Alvarado. Los Angeles, CA 90057-2998.

ICS-International Correspondence Schools, Scranton, PA 18515.

Lifetime Career Schools, 2251 Barry Ave., Los Angeles, CA 90064.

ELECTRONICS

Citizens' High School, 5115 New Peachtree Rd., Suite 300, Atlanta, GA 30341.

Cleveland Institute of Electronics, Inc., 1776 East 17th St., Cleveland, OH 44114.

Grantham College of Engineering, P.O. Box 5700, Slidell, LA 70469.

Heathkit/Zenith Educational Systems, Hilltop Road, St. Joseph, Michigan 49085.

Hemphill Schools, 510 S. Alvarado St., Los Angeles, CA 90057-2998.

ICS-International Correspondence Schools, Scranton, PA 18515.

ICS Center for Degree Studies, Scranton, PA 18515.

McGraw-Hill Continuing Education Center, 4401 Connecticut Ave., N.W., Washington, D.C. 20016.

NRI Schools, 4401 Connecticut Ave., N.W., Washington D.C. 20016.

Peoples College of Independent Studies, 233 Acedemy Dr., Drawer 1768, Kissimmee, FL 32742..

INCOME TAX

National Tax Training School, 4 Melnick Drive, P.O. Box 382, Monsey, NY 10952.

JEWELRY DESIGN & MARKETING

Gemological Institute of America, 1660 Stewart St., Santa Monica, CA 90404.

JOURNALISM

ICS-International Correspondence Schools, Scranton, PA 18515.

LANGUAGES, FOREIGN

American School, 850 East 58th St., Chicago, IL 60637.

Citizens' High School, 5115 New Peachtree Rd., Suite 303, Atlanta, GA 30341.

The Hadley School for the Blind, 700 Elm St., Winnetka, IL 60093.

Home Study International, P.O. Box 4437, Silver Spring, MD 20914.

LEGAL SECRETARY

Laurel School, 2538 North 8th St., Phoenix, AZ 85006.

North American Correspondence Schools, Scranton, PA 18515.

MARKETING

ICS Center for Degree Studies, Scranton, PA 18515.

MEDICAL SECRETARY

Laurel School, 2538 North 8th St., Phoenix, AZ 85006.

MEDICAL TRANSCRIPTION

American Medical Record Association, 875 North Michigan Ave., Suite 1850, Chicago, IL 60611.

At Home Professions, 12383 Lewis St., Suite 103, Garden Grove, CA 92640.

The Hadley School for the Blind, 700 Elm St., Winnetka, IL 60093.

NOTEREADING

At-Home Professions, 12383 Lewis St., Suite 103, Garden Grove, CA 92640.

Stenotype Institute of Jacksonville, Inc., 500 9th Ave., N., P.O. Box 50009, Jacksonville Beach, FL 32250.

PHOTOGRAPHY

Hemphill Schools, 510 S Alvarado St., Los Angeles, CA 90057.

ICS-International Correspondence Schools, Scanton, PA 18515.

McGraw-Hill Continuing Education Center, 4401 Connecticut Ave. N.W., Washington, D.C. 20016.

NRI Schools, 4401 Connecticut Ave., N.W. Washington, D.C. 20016.

Southern Career Institute, 164 West Royal Palm Rd., P.O. Drawer 2158, Boca Raton, FL 33427.

SALESMANSHIP

ICS International Correspondence Schools, Scranton, PA 18515.

Truck Marketing Institute, P.O. Box 5000, Carpinteria, CA 93014.

SECRETARIAL

American School, 850 East 58th St., Chicago, IL 60637.

The Boyd School, One Chatham Center, Pittsburgh, PA 15219.

Laural School, 2538 North 8th St., Phoenix, AZ 85006.

North American Correspondence Schools, Scranton, PA 18515.

SEWING

Hemphill Schools, 510 S. Alvarado St., Los Angeles, CA 90057.

ICS-International Correspondence Schools, Scranton, PA 18515.

Lifetime Career Schools, 2251 Barry Ave., Los Angeles, CA 90064.

TYPING

American Schools, 850 East 58th St., Chicago, IL 60637.

Citizens' High School, 5115 New Peachtree Rd., Suite 300, Atlanta, GA 30341.

The Hadley School for the Blind, 700 Elm St., Winnetka, IL 60093.

Home Study International, P.O.Box 4437, Silver Spring, MD 20914.

WORD PROCESSING

Columbia School of Computer Science, 5858 Hollywood Blvd., 3rd Floor, Hollywood, CA 90028.

WRITING

Art Instruction Schools, 500 So. Fourth St.., Minneapolis, MN 55415.

Columbia School of Broadcasting, 5858 Hollywood Blvd., 4th Floor, P.O. Box 1970, Hollywood, CA 90028.

Hollywood Scriptwriting Institute, 1300 North Cahuenga Blvd., Hollywood, CA 90028.

McGraw-Hill Continuing Educations Center, 4401 Connecticut AVe., N. W., Washington, D.C. 20008.

NRI, 4401 Connecticut Ave., N.W., Washington, D.C. 20008.

RESOURCE GUIDE

Periodicals

THE WHOLE WORK CATALOG.* Offers an unusually good selection of books, tapes and other materials on working from home, home businesses, alternative careers, etc. A trial subscription is $1.

NATIONAL HOME BUSINESS REPORT.* One way home-based business owners avoid feeling isolated is by plugging into networks of others in the same situation. A great deal of sharing and networking takes place in each issue of this highly personal newsletter, which is now in its sixth year of publication. Readers pass along ideas and marketing information which is often hard to find anywhere else. Subscriptions are $18/year (4 issues).

TELECOMMUTING REVIEW: THE GORDON REPORT, TeleSpan Publishing, 50A West Palm Street, Altadena, CA 91001. Organizations using or thinking about telecommuting should investigate this monthly newsletter produced by a management consultant who is a leading authority in the field.

HOME OFFICE COMPUTING, Box 2511, Boulder, CO 80302. This magazine for personal computer enthusiasts, published by Scholastic, Inc., is one of the few magazines on the newsstands directed at home workers. Contains very practical information on how to get started making money with your personal computer. A 1-year subscription is $19.95.

Books

555 WAYS TO EARN EXTRA MONEY* by J.C. Levinson. New edition. Whether you want to supplement a full-time job with extra earning projects or put together a network of part-time jobs and give up the nine-to-five altogether, Levinson's book on moonlighting and "Patchwork economics" can help. Includes steps to get started, advertising tactics, suggested company names and unique–even surprising–ways to augment your income. $16.95, postpaid.

* Items with an asterisk are available from The New Careers Center, P.O. Box 297-SB, Boulder CO 80306

CREATIVE CASH: HOW TO SELL YOUR CRAFTS, NEEDLEWORK, DESIGNS & KNOW-HOW* by Barbara Brabec. There's a good reason why over 70,000 copies of this book are in print: it is truly outstanding. Very comprehensive information with step-by-step how-to's for every aspect of a crafts business. $15.95, postpaid.

DESKTOP PUBLISHING SUCCESS* by Kramer and Lovaas. This is an outstanding guide to starting a business providing desktop publishing services to businesses, organizations, etc. Unusually comprehensive, very up-to-date information. $28.95, postpaid.

EARNING MONEY WITHOUT A JOB* by Jay Conrad Levinson. "The real answer to being your own boss is many small jobs. This book is the best guide available." –*The Next Whole Work Catalog* New edition. $11.95, postpaid.

FRANCHISES YOU CAN RUN FROM HOME* by Lynie Arden. Over 100 reputable franchises for home-based entrepreneurs are covered, including financial services, property improvement, domestic services, business services, desktop publishing, video services and employment services. Includes real-life success stories and helpful advice. $16.95, postpaid.

HOME-BASED MAIL-ORDER* by William Bond. Written by an author with 25 years of mail-order experience, this book shows how to select the right products or services, decide how to approach your market, efficiently handle orders and inquiries, and expand your business steadily while avoiding uncontrolled growth. $16.95, postpaid.

HOMEMADE MONEY: THE DEFINITIVE GUIDE TO SUCCESS IN A HOME BUSINESS* by Barbara Brabec. One of the foremost authorities on the boom in home businesses gives expert advice on getting started, selecting the right home business (and avoiding the wrong ones), planning for profits, diversifying, expanding and more. $19.95, postpaid.

HOW TO FIND YOUR TREASURE IN A GIFT BASKET* by Ron Perkins. In the early 1980's a few people found they could make a very good living putting together gift baskets for individuals and businesses (who give them to employees or clients). Over the years the popularity of these gifts–and the opportunities for gift basket services–has steadily increased. Perkins shows how to start a home-based gift basket service, starting with a minimal investment, which makes and sells beautiful baskets filled with wine, cheese, fruit, candy, soaps and other items. $18.95, postpaid.

* Items with an asterisk are available from The New Careers Center, P.O. Box 297-SB, Boulder CO 80306

HOW TO MAKE MONEY WITH YOUR MICRO* by H. Holtz. An unusually well-writen guide with ideas for money-making home ventures, worksheets and checklists that make it easier to set up your business, and all the nuts and bolts—setting fees and pricing, billing, legal and taxes, etc. $16.95 postpaid.

HOW TO QUALIFY FOR THE HOME OFFICE DEDUCTION by K. Klotzburger. Discusses what constitutes a bona fide home office, how to maximize your deductions, etc. $8.95 from Betterway Publications, Inc.

HOW TO SET UP AND OPERATE YOUR OFFICE AT HOME* by Robert Scott. Difficult-to-find information on equipment, supplies, taxes, budgeting, insurance, keeping home and business activities separate, and more. Can save you time, money, frustration and mistakes. $12.95 postpaid.

HOW TO START AND PROFIT FROM A MAILING LIST SERVICE* by Allegato and Edwards. This is an unusual two-tape audio program which covers intriguing opportunities for working at home using a personal computer and mailing list software. Explains how to create mailing lists from client-supplied data, monthly update services you can offer on a subscription basis, opportunities for compiling mailing lists on your own, etc. $21.91, postpaid.

INDEPENDENT PARALEGAL'S HANDBOOK* by Ralph Warner, attorney. Shows how to set up a legal form-typing business that can save people enormous sums of money over what they would otherwise pay to have an attorney handle routine legal matters. Very comprehensive and authoritative information, and a very solid opportunity. $21.95, postpaid.

INFORMATION FOR SALE: HOW TO START AND OPERATE YOUR OWN DATA RESEARCH SERVICE* by John Everett and Elizabeth Powell Crowe. According to this guide on becoming an information broker, you can get the training you need and lease the necessary equipment for only a few hundred dollars. Potential for growth in this field is extremely good. Includes details on marketing your service, handling copyrights and other legal issues, conducting efficient on-line searches, keeping up with changing technology and setting appropriate fees. Recommended. $18.95 postpaid.

KIDS MEAN BUSINESS: HOW TO TURN YOUR LOVE OF CHILDREN INTO A PROFITABLE AND WONDERFULLY SATISFYING BUSINESS* by Barbralu Manning. This book covers a very wide range of child-related business opportunities, including day care and other businesses that can be operated from home. $11.95 postpaid.

* Items with an asterisk are available from The New Careers Center, P.O. Box 297-SB, Boulder CO 80306

PET SITTING FOR PROFIT* by Patti Moran. Shows how you can compete with kennels by setting up a home-based pet sitting service. The author has more than 30 part-time pet sitters working for her, and this seems like a good small-scale opportunity. $11.95, postpaid.

WORD PROCESSING PROFITS AT HOME,* by Peggy Glenn. An excellent book covering personal considerations, planning, advertising, pricing, equipment, marketing and more. Highly recommended. $19.95 postpaid.

THE WORK-AT-HOME SOURCEBOOK. Additional copies of this book may be ordered directly from the publisher for $15.95 postpaid. Live Oak Publications, P.O. Box 2193, Boulder, CO 80306.

WORKING FROM HOME* by Paul and Sarah Edwards. In 488 pages the Edwards cover all aspects of home businesses including presenting a business image at home, dealing with zoning, licenses and legal obligations and setting up an efficient home office. The emphasis throughout is on computer-related businesses. $15.95 postpaid.

WORKING AT HOME: IS IT FOR YOU? by William Atkinson. This is probably the most comprehensive guide to deciding whether you will enjoy working at home. From Dow Jones-Irwin, Homewood, IL 60430.

TELECOMMUTING: HOW TO MAKE IT WORK FOR YOU AND YOUR COMPANY by Gil Gordon and Marcia Kelly. This is the definitive book on telecommuting. How your company can benefit by moving your employees out of the office and into remote locations—either the home or a satellite office—through using computer terminals linked to telephone systems. Prentice-Hall, Inc., Englewood Cliffs, New Jersey.

Organizations

Mothers' Home Business Network, P.O. Box 423, East Meadow, NY 11554. This organization offers advice to the fastest growing segment of home workers–mothers. Membership includes a quarterly newsletter with good information about how to juggle the demands of working at home and family obligations. A 1-year membership is $25.

* Items with an asterisk are available from The New Careers Center, P.O. Box 297-SB, Boulder CO 80306

Alphabetical Index

Location Index

National and/or Multi-Regional Companies

State Index

Alabama

Arkansas

Arizona

California

Opportunities for the Disabled